Bruce Nauman

Coosje van Bruggen

Bruce Nauman

RIZZOLI
NEW YORK

First published in the United States of America in 1988 by
RIZZOLI INTERNATIONAL PUBLICATIONS, INC.
597 Fifth Avenue, New York, NY 10017

Library of Congress Cataloging-in-Publication Data
Bruggen, Coosje van.
  Bruce Nauman.
  Bibliography: p. 293
  1. Nauman, Bruce, 1941–   —Criticism and
interpretation.   2. Conceptual art—United States.
I. Title.
N6537.N38B78   1987   700′.92′4   87-42686
ISBN 0-8478-0833-1

Grateful acknowledgment is made to Grove
Press, New York, for permission to quote
from Samuel Beckett's *The Lost Ones,*
Copyright © 1970 by Les Editions de Minuit,
Paris, and in English, Copyright © 1972
by Samuel Beckett. Permission is also
granted to quote from *Three Novels* by
Samuel Beckett, Copyright © 1955, 1956, and 1958

Edited by Jane Fluegel
Assisted by Rose Weil
Designed by Pierluigi Cerri
Assisted by Michela Ghigliotti and Susan O'Brian
Composition by David E. Seham Associates,
Metuchen, New Jersey
Printed by Toppan Printing Company, Japan

FRONTISPIECE:
*Copper Wallpiece with an Image of the
Shadow Projected into It.* 1966
Ink on paper
18⅞ × 24″ (48 × 60.5 cm)
Hallen für neue Kunst, Schaffhausen, Switzerland
Crex Collection

ENDPAPERS:
Small Carousel. 1988
Drypoint and aquatint
9 × 12″ (25 × 30.4 cm), plate
Published by Brooke Alexander, New York
Collection the artist

Contents

Entrance Entrapment Exit

Bruce Nauman is not interested in "adding to a collection of things that are art," as he puts it, but in "investigating the possibilities of what art may be."[1] Where his inquiry will lead next is impossible to predict, since he goes about it in a meandering way; but, like Samuel Beckett's character Molloy, he will always be "back in the saddle."[2] The route he takes may not be the "right" one, but for him the "wrong" road can be just as much of a discovery.

Nauman's education is a case in point. Born in Fort Wayne, Indiana, in 1941, he grew up in Wisconsin and went to college there, initially studying mathematics and physics. It was, he realized, the wrong thing. For a short time he performed as a jazz bass player—he had studied classical guitar and a little piano since childhood—and the next courses he took were in music theory and composition. His main interests lay in the work of such composers as Arnold Schönberg, Anton von Webern, and Alban Berg and in the late quartets of Ludwig van Beethoven. But again he decided that this was not quite right for him. Finally, Nauman signed up for art classes. "Art allowed me room for both my mind and my hands to work," he says; "I have always enjoyed making things, and I did not have any qualms about my facility to do so." He had found his field but not his path. At the University of Wisconsin, he learned how to stretch a canvas perfectly, but he considered the content of his classes stale. However, many of his teachers had participated in the art section of the Work Projects Administration in the 1930s, and while their formal ideas about art may have seemed conventional and even restricting to Nauman, they did reinforce his interest in pursuing the issue of what an artist can do in, and for, the collective society. What is a "true" artist, and what is his or her social role? These questions have occupied him ever since.

From the fall of 1964 to the spring of 1966, Nauman worked toward his M.A. at the University of California at Davis. As early as 1964 he had tried to give up painting—"my concept of being an artist was making pictures, landscapes, but intuitively I knew that that was not enough"—but since he did not yet know how to follow up this desire for something else, he returned to abstract landscapes, inspired by the Bay Area painters. His next step was to weld steel parts into organic shapes and bolt them onto his canvases; these protruding forms were integrated into the compositions by being painted over. Nauman's steel objects proved heavy and cumbersome, so he switched to fiberglass. He had already used the medium when he was a student in Wisconsin, mixing it with metal filings so it would resemble cast bronze. Now he decided not to disguise the fiberglass but to let it be obvious, a move that was straightforward and yet a rejection of the traditional media of sculpture. A breakthrough came when painting no longer seemed necessary, and he focused on the abstract, elongated fiberglass pieces alone (pp. 28–34).

Talking about painting, Nauman remembers: "I loved moving the paint and the manipulation of materials. It was very serious, but it also got in the way. I still don't trust any kind of lush solution, which painting was, and so I decided—it was a conscious decision at some point—that I was not going to be a painter. The decision was hard, but I was young enough that it wasn't *that* hard." He has never ceased to be interested in painting, however. In fact, shortly after he quit the practice himself, he saw Ed Ruscha's work for the first time and was excited by the possibilities it offered. Here were non-art-historical, distinctly contemporary American works freed of obedience to the rules that were making painting seem so pointless. Such pieces as Ruscha's *Large Trademark with Eight*

7

Spotlights, 1962, *Damage,* 1964, and *Burning Gas Station,* 1965–66, Nauman felt, were as much about thought and perception as about painting. In a like way, Willem de Kooning has always been important to Nauman:

He's a beautiful draftsman and a powerful artist—and also somebody who was struggling. Artists from that generation, and even after that, had to struggle with Picasso. Their problem was basically how to get beyond Picasso. De Kooning finally found a way, and so I trust him in his choice of how to proceed. I think where I finally ran into trouble was at Frank Stella, someone a little bit ahead of me in time. I was very interested in his early paintings because I saw incredible possibilities in the work of how to proceed as an artist, but then it became clear that he was just going to be a painter. And I was interested in what art can be, not just what painting can be. I don't think he has taken that on at all.

Around the time that Nauman was experimenting with the first fiberglass pieces, in early 1965, he went to see "A New York Collector Selects," an exhibition at the San Francisco Museum of Art, held in January of that year and chosen by Mrs. Burton Tremaine. He recalls especially two pieces by Richard Tuttle, "twiggly things stuck on the wall, about 8 feet long," their playful presence strikingly different from the contemporaneous art of, say, Donald Judd. Nauman knew already that his own working methods clashed with Judd's desire to control his materials totally.

The Tuttle pieces were closer to his own sensibilities. A hollow, linear construction called *Silver Abstract,* 1964 (p. 30), was hung horizontally, at eye level, curving down on the right. Its long, narrow side pieces are made from ¼-inch fir plywood, which is attached to the sides with hundreds of little nails. The ends of the piece are also covered with plywood, hiding the inside. At the

time, this piece was also referred to as "the silver streak," because it resembles a piece of chrome on a car. "What I liked was just being able to do a line,"[3] Tuttle told me when I asked him about the piece. "It is a sort of double joke. First it's quite something to make a line, and then something more to bend it." For his part Tuttle also felt that he and Nauman belonged to a different generation from Judd and Robert Morris: "We did not come to abstraction through reductivism. We might wake up one day and make something which was itself—whether it was abstract or figurative didn't matter."

Tuttle's quest for a balance between exerting control over materials and letting them take their own course must have struck Nauman as familiar. As he continued to work with fiberglass he had become more and more interested in the very process of making art. For an untitled piece of 1965 (p. 32), he created a long, rather flat, abstract shape out of clay, then made a plaster mold of it from which to cast the work in fiberglass. By adding pigment to the resin before casting it, he tinted the material in different colors. The finished work is in halves—two forms cast from the same mold, one pale yellow and the other pale green, leaning side by side against the wall so that each presents a different face to the viewer, making a shape at once convex and concave. The process by which the work was produced, a lasting element of the piece, is visible in the chips of plaster that stuck to the fiberglass during casting and that remain there as an integral part of the surface. A related untitled piece done in the same year (p. 33), shaped like a long, thin, pried-open hairpin, also stands against the wall. One side curves from the wall to the floor; the other, in a movement like a mirror image, lifts upward and outward into space. Other things switch in this piece: what the half toward the wall expresses as inside or back, the outer half expresses as outside or front. In part, this disturbing of back and front, inside and outside, constitutes a meditation on process. In traditional casting, what is inside the mold is considered art, but the container itself is thought to be merely functional and often destroyed. Paradoxically, in classical sculpture the emphasis lies on the shell, the exterior of the work, and the inside is ignored. Nauman has said that his interest in these issues was reinforced by Claes Oldenburg's 1966 cardboard pieces, which he had seen reproduced in magazines; Oldenburg "did a whole bathroom in cardboard. What I remember is that in all those objects, bathtub and sink and so on, the insides and outsides were the same piece of cardboard, and were given equal emphasis." The presentation of inside as well as outside is a constant throughout Nauman's work, not only in the rubber pieces of 1965–66, but also in the corridor and sealed-room installations of the 1970s (which raised questions about the priorities of public versus the private domain), and the South America chair pieces of the 1980s (which dealt with entrapment).

In his work of the mid-1960s, Nauman was involved not so much in sculpture as in matter itself, in the process of putting different materials together—doing so from an aesthetic point of view, certainly, but focusing more on the concept and on the identity of a work's material than on its status as object. One way to distance himself from conventional sculpture, he found, was to avoid giving the works a finished look:

I think in the beginning [my] things were made out of fragile materials, or materials that weren't necessarily art materials, because if I made a piece that was clearly not going to hold up, a lot of preciousness would be removed. Eventually it will fall apart, but the idea is left and could be made over again. The piece may be different but it would still carry the weight of the idea.

The roughness of Nauman's work from this period is also part of his concern with process. The art shows its making. In 1965, he expressed this concern clearly in an untitled piece (p. 34) comprising both the fiberglass product of casting and the mold in which the casting was done. One side of an oblong plywood-and-cardboard mold, with rounded ends, hangs diagonally on the wall; the textures of its materials are visible on the pink, semitransparent, hairpin-shaped fiberglass form it holds, which is slit to show the white wall behind it.

In *Shelf Sinking into the Wall with Copper-Painted Plaster Casts of the Spaces Underneath,* 1966 (p. 170), the shelf, which is made of plywood painted white, also served as a mold for the spaces underneath the shelf, which were cast in plaster and painted a copper color. "It was one of my first pieces with a complicated title, a sort of functional title," Nauman remarked. "The elaborate title enabled me to show a mold with its casts without presenting the work as such."[4]

Nauman found support for his method of reviewing the whole process of making an object (and if necessary, of backing up a step) in Ludwig Wittgenstein's *Philosophical Investigations* (posthumously published in 1953), which he read during the early 1960s: "Wittgenstein would follow an idea until he could say either that it worked or that life doesn't work this way and we have to start over. He would not throw away the failed argument, but would include it in his book."

The unfinished look of Nauman's work serves a function beyond that of art as idea (the urgent message of Conceptual art so clearly articulated by, say, Joseph Kosuth and Sol LeWitt). Originally at least in part a reaction against the clean geometries of Minimal art, the rough state of the work also serves as a way to communicate scale. For this reason Nauman prefers Robert Morris's early plywood pieces, which show their screws and edges, to his later works in smooth fiberglass, where the scale became arbitrary. When a work lacks such detail as clearly visible woodgrain, the debris from a mold, or screws, Nauman believes that not only the constructed quality of the work but also the sense of the connection between the parts and the whole disappear. He still feels that much of the communicative power of a piece is determined by the sense of scale that its texture—as well as its weight and density—establishes. This is why, when he used colors in his fiberglass pieces, he mixed them into the resin rather than painting the forms and thus concealing their surfaces.

While Nauman was studying at Davis, he had easy access to film equipment in nearby San Francisco, and he made several movies. Process is as much a part of these works as it is of his sculptures from the same period. In *Fishing for Asian Carp,* 1966, Nauman kept the camera running while his friend the artist William Allan put on boots, walked to the creek, and caught a fish. This activity, which defined the structure of the film, had a beginning and a foreseeable end, but its duration was dependent on an uncontrollable event—no one can control when a fish will bite. *Fishing for Asian Carp* is presented clearly and logically, rather like an instructional film, and, as one watches, it is difficult to tell whether it is serious or a joke. What Nauman was pursuing through Wittgenstein's *Philosophical Investigations* converged with Allan's attitude of "stupidity," of "getting the world reduced down to a rock," as Allan has put it. "It's like nondoing."[5] The duration of several other short black-and-white movies that Nauman made in 1965–66 was decided equally loosely, but from a different perspective: they run under ten minutes each, the length of a reel. In *Revolving Landscape,* the artist manipulated the camera in such a way that the landscape became abstract. This film and the following one, *Opening and Closing,* in which a door closes and window shades open, seem the product of someone who wants to explore and play with a new possibility, just as Man Ray did during the making of *Emak Bakia,* 1926, when he threw a camera in the air while it was filming.

During this same period Nauman began doing performance pieces. In an attempt to emphasize the process of making art, rather than the result, he remembers that he began to record lists of things he could do to a straight bar, such as bend it, fold it, and twist it. He used a similar list of actions in his first performance at Davis in 1965. He placed himself in various positions—standing, leaning, bending at the waist, squatting, sitting, and finally lying down—with his face turned toward, then away from the wall, now to his left and then to his right. He held each of these poses for about a minute; the whole presentation lasted for about a half hour. "In a way I was using my body as a piece of material and manipulating it," Nauman stated. "I think of it as going into the studio and being involved in some activity. Sometimes it works out that the activity involves making something, and sometimes the activity itself is the piece."[6] Sometimes both possibilities are combined in one work— as, for example, in *Cardboard Floor Piece with Foot Hole,* 1966 (destroyed; see sketch, p. 35). Another piece, *Brass Floor Piece with Foot Slot,* 1965–66 (p. 35)— which Nauman had a sheet-metal shop fabricate (in an edition of three) in order to emphasize his concept rather than its execution—also contains a foot hole, a horizontal slot with a slight slope onto which the viewer is invited to step. In both pieces the spectator becomes the performer as well, and is positioned by Nauman in a specific place in the room. They embody a kind of absurd Fluxus

Using the Foot Gasket in Hawaii. 1966
Pencil, charcoal, and colored pencil on paper
25 x 38″ (63.5 x 96.5 cm)
Private collection, New York

idea—no matter where the thing is put down, one says: "Now what?" Nauman compares the experience of this work to choreographing a dance, but first the dancer's shoe is nailed to the floor. Doing so complicates the task by limiting the dancer's movements, and at the same time, because of the precondition, simplifies it. In the drawing *Using the Foot Gasket in Hawaii,* 1966 (private collection, New York), Nauman adopts a theatrical manner to depict a similarly absurd situation, this time in an idyllic outdoor setting. In the picture someone stands on the beach looking out to sea, but he is entrapped in a gasket, an invention of man that keeps him from getting close to nature.

In a second performance in the mid-1960s, Nauman fused object and activity by using a standard fluorescent-light fixture with a lit tube, about 8 feet long, to make different shapes in combination with his own body (repeated for a videotape, called *Manipulating a Fluorescent Tube* [pp. 36–37], in 1969). The tube became almost another limb; Nauman held it in his hands, touched his feet with it, stretched out on the floor while holding it straight up in the air, laid it on the floor, and leaned over to touch it. Most of the poses formed geometric shapes, except one, in which Nauman held the tube between his legs while he sat on the floor. In carrying out the performance, he discovered that some poses just seemed to him different positions his body could take, but that others produced powerful emotional responses in him. (When he repeated the work for the videotape in 1969, he emphasized these emotionally resonant positions.) In another movie from late 1965 and early 1966, *Manipulating the T-Bar,* he again dealt with the interaction of an object and a person: laying down a set of rules for handling a *T*-shaped construction made of two 8-foot-long steel rods wrapped in black tape, like a tool of some sort, he created an ambiguous play between functional and useless human activity. The ideas in these performance and film and video works carry over to the fiberglass pieces, which shift between object and idea, and which associate themselves with the human body through Nauman's sensitive attention to scale and through the way they lean against the wall, their front or back relating to the viewer.

By 1966, Nauman felt he had exhausted the possibilities of the fiberglass works. As he puts it: "It was like de Kooning putting long handles on his brushes to fool his own painting facility, to see what he could make happen, as a way to prove himself. But once you do it on purpose, you know what's going to happen, and you would check yourself from doing it twice." As a next step Nauman started to make rubber floor pieces (pp. 38–41), all cast in the same mold, with their colors mixed into the material. Some were attached to each other and were shown dropped on the floor (p. 39), while others were hung on the wall; some, slit into segments, were fastened to the wall by one of the slices (pp. 38, 40). That same year the New York art dealer Richard Bellamy put some of these rubber pieces in his summer group show, and shortly thereafter Robert Morris, then a better-known artist than Nauman, showed some similar works in felt (p. 41). Nauman recalls that he reacted with considerable competitiveness to Morris, though he recognized Morris's ability in handling materials. But his own *Felt Formed over Sketch for Metal Floor Piece,* 1966 (p. 43), in which a sheet of felt on the floor simultaneously conceals and exposes a cardboard shape that raises the cloth but stays invisible beneath it, as if beneath a skin, was a response not so much to Morris as to Joseph Beuys, whose felt-covered fir trees (p. 43) he had heard about from a German visitor to his studio, Kasper

König. It also refers to Man Ray's *The Enigma of Isidore Ducasse,* 1920 (p. 43), in which a sewing machine is wrapped in sackcloth and tied with twine. Nauman, thinking about these various works, came to believe that art derives its power not from a surfeit of autobiographical information but from the kind of inexplicability that can occur through bringing things together out of alignment, through "giving information but at the same time withholding a part, and through trying to get underneath the surface by not stating it."

The issues of visibility and concealment raised by *Felt Formed over Sketch for Metal Floor Piece* run throughout Nauman's work. One of his ideas, from 1966, was to make a stacked piece using felt, rubber, or lead sheets with a rectangular hole through its center, and hiding a short fluorescent tube at the bottom of the hole. Nauman was not sure, though, whether to cover the hole or leave it open. He set down the concept in a sketch but never executed it in a sculpture, although he would later complete a number of pieces based on stacking or piling. He made another sketch for a "sandwich" sculpture in the same year (p. 44), again for an unrealized work; he considered stacking materials distinguished from one another by differences in texture, weight, tensility, and density. This 2-foot-thick sculpture would alternate layers of materials— from top to bottom, felt, thin plastic, lead, paper or waxed paper, rubber, cork, paper, aluminum foil, and so on— in sheets 7 feet long and 2 feet wide. Moreover, the floor beneath the work would be covered with a layer of grease. (Nauman added, pragmatically, that waxed paper could be put down before the grease was poured.) He also considered denting the stack at the center in some specific shape or impression so that the grease would squeeze out from the bottom. The proposal emphasizes the process of construction and also, again, a sense of chance: the piece, had it been made, would have looked as much like something found in the streets as a work of art.

Nauman has spoken of the need he felt for his work to make a point. "I was interested in finding out what I was doing, how I was doing it." By the end of 1966, he found himself in the midst of work that used more than one vocabulary—that of materials and that of the body. A stacked piece from this period is transitional. The work's title is an exact description of its substance: *Collection of Various Flexible Materials Separated by Layers of Grease with Holes the Size of My Waist and Wrists,* 1966 (p. 44). A related drawing (p. 44), specifying a pile of eight 18-by-90-inch sheets, each in a different material, reveals clearly an essential characteristic of Nauman's work: he sets up an ambiguity between two kinds of observation—one in which materials follow their own course and another in which the process of thinking renders to the object its lyrical form. Nauman does not anthropomorphize inanimate things, but his pieces are human signs, measured in terms of his own body—in this case, through the sheets' waist- and wrist-size holes, imprints left behind by the artist, who in his absence is still strongly present.

Where the title of *Collection of Various Flexible Materials Separated by Layers of Grease with Holes the Size of My Waist and Wrists* is utterly literal, in other works Nauman creates discrepancies between title and object, between what is known and what is seen. In *Wax Impressions of the Knees of Five Famous Artists,* 1966 (p. 45), the title and the piece are deliberately out of alignment, since the imprints in the object, a long horizontal wall piece made of fiberglass (not wax), are of Nauman's own knees. In a drawing made a year later (p. 45) for a similar but unrealized work, Nau-

man added a concern for texture to his earlier interest in weight and density. He considered using the right knees of five people, "some bare and some with pants (cloth) over them," which would produce specific textural traces in the plaster mold, like the marks left by cardboard in the mold on one of the early fiberglass pieces. After Nauman has executed a sculpture, he sometimes makes a drawing of it. Investigating and analyzing his own working process at a later moment, he can discover aspects of the work he had not noticed before. Sometimes he arrives at more or less the same conclusions but with added layers of meaning. In the 1967 drawing that recapitulates *Wax Impressions of the Knees of Five Famous Artists,* Nauman notes that he wants to "assign each knee print an identity, preferably of some (moderately) well-known artists (perhaps some historical artist, who has not been dead over 100 years?) (Do not use Marcel Duchamp.)" He scribbles in the names of William T. Wiley, Larry Bell, Lucas Samaras, and Leland Bell, all artists influential in the Bay Area, and of "W. de Kooning" (which, however, he crosses out and replaces by the word "self," a signal of his identification with this artist). Then he appears to have hesitated, writing on the drawing that "perhaps all 'knee prints' should be the same image but titled as above." The result would be the same as in the piece done in 1966, except that the five artists have been identified.

Nauman had moved to San Francisco in the summer of 1966, and his first studio was in an old grocery store with an abandoned neon beer sign in the window. "I was working very little," he remembers, "teaching a class one night a week, and I didn't know what to do with all that time. There was nothing in the studio because I didn't have much money for materials. So I was forced to examine myself and what I was doing there.

I was drinking a lot of coffee, that's what I was doing."[7] He had been reading a good deal, and it bothered him that a great part of his life was not being incorporated in his art—he wanted to include not more autobiographical details, but more of the way he thought about the world. Seeing a Man Ray retrospective at the Los Angeles County Museum of Art in 1966 freed him from the obligation of having a definite purpose and enabled him to load his work with content from all kinds of sources: "To me Man Ray seemed to avoid the idea that every piece had to take on a historical meaning. What I liked was that there appeared to be no consistency to his thinking, no one style." The fact that Man Ray had used stage settings in his photographs also encouraged Nauman to do a series of photographic works, notably *Self-Portrait as a Fountain,* 1966–67 (p. 48), in which he used theatrical lighting. In an interview with Willoughby Sharp in 1970, Nauman remarked:

I started thinking about the Fountain *and similar things. I didn't know how to present them. I suppose I might have made them as paintings if I had been able to make paintings at that time. In fact, I think I did get some canvas and paint but I had no idea of how to go about making paintings anymore. I didn't know what to do. Perhaps if I had been a good enough painter I could have made realistic paintings. I don't know, it just seemed easier to make the works as photographs."[8]

Thus, beginning at the end of 1966 and continuing into 1967, Nauman took a series of eleven color pictures, satirical narratives of daily life, that were published in 1970. In addition to *Self-Portrait as a Fountain,* these included *Bound to Fail, Coffee Thrown Away Because It Was Too Cold, Coffee Spilled Because the Cup Was Too Hot, Drill Team,* an untitled work, *Finger Touch with Mirrors* (all, p. 46), *Waxing Hot* (p. 47), and *Feet of Clay* (p. 134). "If you see yourself as an artist and you function in a studio and you're not a painter," Nauman has said, "if you don't start out with some canvas, you do all kinds of things—you sit in a chair or pace around. And then the question goes back to what is art? And art is what an artist does, just sitting around in the studio." He took events that already verged on the absurd and pushed them even further into absurdity by recording them photographically. In consequence, the events turned into serious propositions, with an ironic flavor that recalls early Pop art.

Nauman's first public assertion of the artist's role was a translucent pink-Mylar window shade from late 1966. The idea for it was inspired by the beer sign in his studio window. Words positioned around the edge of the shade read: "The true artist is an amazing luminous fountain" (sketch, p. 121). Some of the letters are scratched through the pink coating of the Mylar; others are painted in black. Nauman liked the fact that the phrase is vague, seeming to convey meaning but actually making only the most metaphorical kind of sense. Yet in *Self-Portrait as a Fountain* (p. 48), which shows Nauman from the waist up, spitting water in an arc, and in a 1967 drawing, *Myself as a Marble Fountain* (p. 49), which elaborates on it, the artist makes the idea ironically literal. The works can also be compared to Marcel Duchamp's urinal as readymade *Fountain,* 1917 (p. 48), and they refer to and subvert those art-historical traditions of the gargoyle and the Baroque fountain adorned with mythological gods and goddesses.

In 1965, Nauman had experimented with neon in *Small Neon and Plastic Floor Piece* (p. 51). By laying a thin neon tube inside a fiberglass shell, he gave the piece an orange glow. He also hooked up a short piece of neon to flash on and off, then painted it black so that the light was hidden. He was dissatisfied with the piece and eventually destroyed it, but he continued to work with the medium. Then in 1966 he conceived a work that both incorporated his concern with the figural point of reference and brilliantly posited the issue of mind-body dualism. *Neon Templates of the Left Half of My Body Taken at Ten-Inch Intervals* (p. 50) fluctuates between suggesting a dream image and describing the material reality of neon tubes, a transformer, and electrical wiring. As if projecting a drawing into space, the piece reduces Nauman's body to seven luminous contours connected by dark loops of wire, like signals with no depth; these fragile outlines, far removed from references to real body parts and loaded with high energy, float radiantly in the air. The black loops seem to be the shadows or antitheses of the glowing neon shapes.

In the 1960s, artists often employed neon. Martial Raysse, for example, had used it in such assemblages as *Spring Morning,* 1964, and *Painting at High Tension,* 1965, the latter a painted portrait of a woman, her mouth humorously outlined in Veronese-green light. Joseph Kosuth had used neon lettering in his 1965 work, *Neon,* and Jasper Johns had illuminated the word "Red" in *Passage II,* 1966. Nauman was especially interested in two works by James Rosenquist that he had seen reproduced in a magazine: *Capillary Action II,* 1963, and *Tumbleweed,* 1963–66 (p. 51). Both use evocative materials and symbolic analogies to set up ambiguous interplays between the natural and the man-made; the characteristic qualities of a tumbleweed, for instance, prickliness and lightness, are translated into barbed wire and neon, presented as intertwined lines of wire and light suspended in space and offset by pieces of wood in two *X*'s, suggesting the spools on which barbed wire is wound. The juxtaposition of media evokes a clash between rural and urban, cruelty and sensuousness, aggression and vulnerability, and so on. In *Capillary Ac-*

tion II, wedged in the cleft of a small leafless tree is a frame—Rosenquist refers to it as a "skeleton"—made of four canvas stretchers covered with clear vinyl. Several smaller frames, also covered with vinyl, are fastened to the surface of the large one; thin, dripping paint lines run across the vinyl and across one of the lanky tree branches. On another branch hangs a small neon rectangle.

Rosenquist, a master of ambiguity, here shifts overtly back and forth between the physical identities of his materials and their metaphorical and associative meanings. Nauman achieves similar effects in *The True Artist Helps the World by Revealing Mystic Truths,* 1967 (p. 51), a poetic message about the function of the artist in the form of a peach- and blue-colored neon sign. The title phrase spirals out from the center of the work, as if its meaning were expanding infinitely. Rosenquist, who had once been a sign painter and had made neon signs for Pan American airways, wanted to remain detached from commercial connotations in his work, while Nauman in this piece went for a conjunction of "high" and "low" culture, confusing signage and art, simultaneously revealing their dual natures. Both artists' works, however, elude simple interpretation by setting up multiple, opposing shades of meaning. Nauman arrived at the phrase "the true artist helps the world by revealing mystic truths" by playing with clichéd notions of what people believe an artist ought to do. He offset the mysteriousness of his personal statement by working in neon, which, in its function of public display in advertising and signs, often manifests what he calls "the straightforward fixation on doing one thing that our culture emphasizes in its slogans." As an example of these monolithic impulses, he cites a megalomaniacal neon sign in San Francisco which shows a paint company's product dripping slowly over the globe, accompanied by the phrase: "Cover the earth." Tongue in cheek, Nauman's piece allows him to preserve his willful isolation in opaqueness yet also to come up with a social statement, satisfying the standardized needs of modern society. The repetition of the idea of truth, in "true artist" and "mystic truths," both leads the sentence into tautology and gives it a sense of ambiguity and poetry. As Nauman says: "Artists are expected to live in the culture and to be part of the culture and not to be too weird. On the other hand, they are also expected to be somewhat outside of the culture and be weird— it's like you have to live other people's fantasy lives for them. It's part of the relationship that goes on between the artist and the public."

Nauman often involves his audience in his work by keeping information from them, by setting up expectations that are not fulfilled, by creating discrepancies between what the viewer knows and does not know, sees and does not see. *Dark,* 1968 (p. 53), is a square, 2,500-pound slab of steel, 4 by 48 by 48 inches, located outdoors on the grounds of Southwestern Community College in Chula Vista, California; on the bottom side, hidden from the viewer, is inscribed the word *DARK.* To Nauman, "the obvious thing [*Dark*] establishes is a place you can't get to—you have no control over it." A similar work is *John Coltrane Piece,* 1968 (p. 53), made after the death of the innovative jazz saxophonist. A flat aluminum plate, it is, like *Dark,* too heavy for a viewer to lift, yet only by lifting it would one see that the underside is polished to a mirror finish. The inaccessibility and the effacement of the reflective properties of the mirror give the work an allusive richness and suggest a wealth of metaphors; one can also find here a continuation of Nauman's concern with private and public.

That concern crystallized in a number of works on the theme of the interior of a room. In a 1970 corridor installation (p. 57) at the Nicholas Wilder Gallery, Los Angeles, Nauman sealed off a section of the space containing a camera that panned back and forth on an automated mount. From outside one could see this area on a monitor, but one could not enter it. In 1972, for *Get Out of My Mind, Get Out of This Room,* in the same gallery, Nauman installed hidden speakers wired to a tape recorder in a small room in the space. Entering the room, the visitor was surrounded by the artist's voice quietly whispering, speaking, chanting, or yelling, repeating the phrase over and over again: "Get out of my mind, get out of this room," filling the air with the artist's invisible but unavoidable presence. That same year Nauman drew a proposal for an underground chamber (p. 59) about the size of a grave; it was to be completely sealed off yet contain a television camera, be lit by a lamp, and be visible on a monitor to people outside. In 1974 *Audio-Video Underground Chamber* (p. 59) was actually built out of concrete and buried in the backyard of a house in Antwerp, Belgium. The visitor, although unable to enter the space itself, can experience the interior of the room indirectly by watching a monitor (p. 59) inside the house, owned by art dealer Anny de Decker.

The *Double Steel Cage,* 1974 (p. 58), consists of two cages made out of fence material, one inside the other. The inner one, though visible through the fencing of the outer one, is sealed off. In this installation Nauman makes one painfully aware of the separation between private and public within the gallery space. The visitor who dares to enter the narrow corridor between the two cages is at once exposed to the outside world by the see-through fence and also trapped—made to experience a sensation of imprisonment—in the claustrophobically narrow space. This theme of entrapment appears

Face Mask. 1981
Charcoal, pastel, and pencil on paper
52¾ x 70¾" (134 x 179.7 cm)
The Museum of Modern Art, New York
Gift of the Lauder Foundation and the
National Endowment for the Arts

again in Nauman's later series of South America chair pieces (pp. 80–82).

Nauman's works about enclosure have grown out of long experimentation with the effects of enclosed spaces in his own studio, whether in San Francisco in 1966, in Mill Valley, California, in 1967 and 1968, in Pasadena from the end of the 1960s until 1979, or in Pecos, New Mexico, where he has lived since 1979. "That's the thing about going into the studio to experience the quiet," he notes. "All that's there is you, and you have to deal with that. Sometimes it's pretty hard." Besides his photographs from 1966–67, works of Nauman's that deal with the experience of being in the studio include *Bouncing Two Balls between the Floor and Ceiling with Changing Rhythms* (p. 250), a film made in the artist's studio in 1968. Here he performs over and over again the simple action prescribed in the title. "When you're a painter and you take all the brushes away, how do you still function as an artist?" Nauman has asked himself. *Bouncing Two Balls* provides an absurdist answer to that question, but Nauman works with such concentration and conviction in the film that his answer is as powerful as it is silly. In all his work— performances, films, objects, installations—he tends to stick to the most unadorned actions and surfaces possible while getting his point across. This quality is reminiscent of Samuel Beckett, whose work Nauman first read while he was making his early films, in 1966–67. He found in Beckett a literary parallel to his own activities, and he explains this parallel with an anecdote from his own experience:

I knew this guy in California, an anthropologist, who had a hearing problem in one ear, and so his balance was off. Once he helped one of his sons put a roof on his house, but the son got upset because his shingles would be lined up properly, while his father's were not only laid out in a zigzag, but also the nails were bent and shingles split. When his son got upset about the mess his father had made, the anthropologist replied: "Well, it's just evidence of human activity." And that's what Beckett's stories partly deal with— for example, Molloy transferring stones from pocket to pocket.... They're all human activities; no matter how limited, strange, and pointless, they're worthy of being examined carefully.

Walk with Contrapposto, 1969 (p. 274), is a videotape in which Nauman walks in an exaggerated way, his body twisted so that hips, shoulders, and head are turned in different directions, taking up all the limited space in a corridor only 20 inches wide. The corridor form, here used as a set, became the theme of a number of Nauman's works in the 1970s and 1980s. It reflects a switch from a literal approach to the human body— exemplified by *Wax Impressions of the Knees of Five Famous Artists,* for example—to a perceptual focus. Any human activity is available to an artist for transformation into art, but to Nauman an involvement with things that are resistant, things that do not work well or are hard to figure out, seems the most interesting subject for his art. He has always been curious about the effects of physical situations on human beings, such as the uncomfortable feeling of being in too compressed or too large a space. In Nauman's work the viewer is placed in the position of the performer as soon as he or she enters a corridor or room. Behavioral patterns of life stand out in these spaces; one may start to resist their authoritarianism, obey, or look for comfortable places to rest within the stressful situation. Often one feels caught unfairly in a double bind. Nauman compares it to taking a psychology test which asks such loaded questions as "When did you stop hating your mother or your father?"

Get Out of My Mind, Get Out of This

Room, 1972, is a prime example of such a trap. The presumption was that whoever entered the room in some way violated the artist's privacy, and yet this was a gallery installation meant to be viewed by the public. Over and over in Nauman's work there is a thin line between private and public domain, between the amount of intimate information given to focus the public on the piece and Nauman's fear of exposing himself too much: "I can give only so much. If I go further, it would take away something, or do something, that would throw me off the track."[9] On the one hand the viewer participates in the installations and is exposed to the experiences of the artist, turning from observer into performer; on the other hand, while the pieces invite some viewer interpretation, the artist does not want the viewer to participate at the level where the work is invented. "I wasn't interested and I didn't want to present situations where people could have too much freedom to invent what they thought was going on," he said. "I wanted it to be my idea, and I did not want people to invent the art. The corridor was specific enough. Whatever ways you could use it were so limited that people were bound to have more or less the same experiences I had."

For the corridor installation at the Wilder Gallery in 1970 (p. 57), Nauman made six corridors (see drawing, p. 56) that were open at the top, running the length of one arm of the *L*-shaped space and finishing in dead ends at the wall. Some corridors the viewer could enter easily; the others were too narrow, and those, only 2 or 3 inches wide, one could hardly see into. Mounted high up near the entrance of the broadest corridor was a camera connected to a monitor at the far end, so that as one walked down the corridor, one saw oneself from above and behind, paradoxically getting smaller and smaller as one drew nearer the screen. A second, adjacent monitor played a tape of the corridor when empty. The issues raised here—of concealment, dislocation, enclosure—resonate throughout Nauman's corridor pieces. As with his objects, Nauman often leaves the materials of his corridors bare; when he paints them he uses a neutral color. When he does invoke color, he works with light, as in *Green-Light Corridor,* 1970–71 (p. 54), for example; this work also conveys a strong sense of paradox. The green light is quite beautiful but at the same time proves very fatiguing to the eyes. In an unrealized proposal for a corridor from 1971 (p. 55), he explored disorientation by proposing a *U*-shaped structure, the section in the middle lit with blue light and the two arms with yellow. When one walked in the blue corridor, one would see on a monitor an image of a yellow corridor and vice versa. The only time one would be able to see oneself would be as one turned the corner—but always within the other corridor's color.

Beginning in 1972, and in tandem with his various corridor installations, Nauman also worked on tunnel pieces. The first (p. 63, top), unrealized, was an underground passage, reachable by a stairway in a shaft through which one could look up at the sky; farther along the tunnel, which culminated in a dead end, was another shaft that, because it was angled, had no view. In these and later tunnels Nauman pursued the idea of either isolation or its opposite—a space claustrophobically jammed with people. The corridor pieces juxtapose the physical confinement imposed by their narrow walkways with a mental exit (whether through the television images that frequently open up the space again or through the passage from one place to another that the corridors sometimes afford); the tunnel pieces, on the other hand, are terminal, usually literal dead ends. The *Model for Tunnels: Half*

Three Tunnels Interlocking, Not Connected. 1981
Charcoal, powdered charcoal, and chalk on
paper
60 x 60" (152.4 x 165.1 cm)
Texas Gallery, Houston

Square, Half Triangle, and Half Circle with Double False Perspective, 1981 (p. 74), consists of tunnels in three different shapes and media, but the parts remain separated by walls. Sometimes Nauman creates installations that are large maquettes for tunnels he envisions underground but may never build. These installations are usually larger than the corridor pieces, and their space is darker, more intimidating (unlike the corridors, they are always roofed), and more confusing to the viewer. One such work was *Room with My Soul Left Out, Room That Does Not Care,* 1984 (pp. 76–77), an installation at the Leo Castelli Gallery, New York, consisting of three intersecting black-Celotex tunnels, two horizontal and one vertical. Where the three tunnels intersected, the floor was covered with a grating through which one could see the vertical shaft continuing down into the basement. Inside the passageways a yellow light glowed dimly, absorbed immediately by the black walls. One had the insecure feeling that at any moment it might flicker and go out. The opening paragraph of Beckett's *The Lost Ones* (1970), a book Nauman read after he started his tunnel projects, provides the perfect description: "Abode where lost bodies roam each searching for its lost one. Vast enough for search to be in vain. Narrow enough for flight to be in vain. Inside a flattened cylinder fifty metres round and sixteen high for the sake of harmony. The light. Its dimness. Its yellowness."[10]

There was no sense of the passage of time, no event to relate to, no traffic flow through the tunnels of *Room with My Soul Left Out, Room That Does Not Care.* The air inside was nearly dead, and one felt lost. There was little to do except wait or listen to the footsteps that came and went in the silence, or look down through the grating and up into space above it, into areas out of reach. Standing where the three passageways came

together, one felt conspicuously exposed; people could look in from different directions. Nauman, who had become conscious of the influence of crowds on human behavior by reading Elias Canetti's *Crowds and Power* (published in English in 1962), compared the experience with what he calls the "telephone-booth syndrome": In order to make a private telephone call, Nauman pointed out, "one has to step into a booth, which makes one stand out uncomfortably, because of the separation from the crowd of people outside."

Meanwhile, in 1981, out of a desire to work in "real scale" after making maquettes for tunnels, Nauman had returned to making sculptural pieces, but now he added political references to the bleak Beckett-like quality of his previous work. His South America series of that year can be seen against the backdrop of V. S. Naipaul's writings (for example, *The Return of Eva Perón: Bound with the Killings in Trinidad,* 1980), with which he feels strongly connected. Furthermore, in that year Nauman read *Prisoner without a Name, Cell without a Number* (1981), the account of the Argentine newspaper-publisher Jacobo Timerman of his imprisonment and torture by the Argentine government. Timerman wrote:

They sit me down, clothed, and tie my arms behind me. The application of electric shocks begins, penetrating my clothing to the skin.... I keep bouncing in the chair and moaning as the electric shocks penetrate my clothes. During one of these tremors, I fall to the ground, dragging the chair.[11]

Nauman began to work with a chair hanging by a cable from the ceiling, at first with no structure around it. Next, he made drawings of the chair, but they seemed too literal (p. 80). Then he thought, "because it hangs, it swings, and if it swings it can crash into something else; I should make that part of the piece. And then, if it makes noise, I can also adjust the noise, I can tune it." (Turning a chair into a musical instrument reflects an attitude of the Fluxus artists—for example, Walter De Maria and La Monte Young in *Instrument for La Monte Young,* 1966.) The *Mock-Up for South America Triangle,* ca. 1981 (p. 81), consisted of three 14-foot lengths of board linked to form a triangle, which was suspended from the ceiling by cables that converged at a central point, allowing the form to rotate. Hanging from the same point was an upside-down, slightly abstract wooden chair, which swung gently to and fro like a Foucault pendulum demonstrating the rotation of the earth. The triangle and chair had a forceful, aggressive effect, in part because they were approximately at eye level.[12] Nauman had to give up the idea of letting the chair crash into the girders; it would have had to hang very low to have a swing that would reach them. The suggestion of a crash remained, however, in the dangling juxtaposed objects. The final *South America Triangle,* 1981 (The Saatchi Collection, London), composed of a steel triangle with 14-foot sides and a cast-iron chair, not only forces the viewer to take care not to run into the bare metal so as to protect one's eyes, but also suggests entrapment, through the enclosure of the symbolically charged chair.

Nauman made two variations on the South America theme, both in 1981, one with a circle as the surrounding form (pp. 80, 82) and the other with a square (see study, p. 80); in each case he hung the chair differently—first sideways, then on edge. In another chair piece from the same year, *Diamond Africa with Chair Tuned D E A D* (p. 83), he expressed his opposition to apartheid by tuning the sound that the chair legs made, when struck, to the notes *D, E, A,* and *D*— "dead." (In 1968 he had made the film *Playing a Note on the Violin While I Walk around the Studio* [p. 253], a performance in which he played the notes *D, E, A,* and *D* repeatedly.) In 1983 he returned to the chair image in the *Dream Passage,* based on a powerful dream in which he had come down a corridor and entered a room at the end; in the room, around the corner to the left, stood a figure. At first, Nauman did not know how to transform this image into art. He made an attempt in an installation at the Museum of Fine Arts in Santa Fe, where he built a corridor and a small room, lit by yellow and red fluorescent lights, containing a welded-steel chair and table instead of the dream figure. A video camera at the entrance to the corridor was hooked up to a monitor on the table, so that each visitor was filmed walking through the passage but could never see him- or herself on the screen. This piece did not satisfy Nauman, and in a second version of the work (p. 78), also in 1983, he created a mirror image by extending the corridor on the other side of the room, and by duplicating the table and chair with an identical set suspended upside down from the room's ceiling. The mirroring was an indication of Nauman's idea that the figure in the dream was himself, or a reflection of himself. Another chair piece is *White Anger, Red Danger, Yellow Peril, Black Death,* 1984 (pp. 86–87), in which Nauman suspended a pair of steel girders in an *X* shape. A white chair whose shape resembles a swastika hangs near the edge of the *X,* and slid over the girders in different places are a black, a yellow, and a red chair, made respectively of aluminum, square steel tubing, and cast iron. The work combines the hallucinatory quality of the balanced and dangling chairs with colors whose connotations are racial, political, and emotional. Moreover, the loaded catch phrases of the title point in complex directions, all threatening: totalitarianism, racism, plague.

Nauman's willingness to let simple materials do the work allows him to avoid "monumental seriousness" and prevents him from becoming consumed in sophisticated techniques. When the execution of a work becomes more complicated, he realizes that he can, as he puts it, "have an idea and just sort of sketch it out, then give it to somebody else." This attitude underlies the series of neon works about sex and power that were made to Nauman's designs in 1985 (pp. 91–100). Shown both individually and in groups, these alluring signs, in garish primary colors and softer secondaries, flash on and off, moving in and out of phase with one another in both the actions they depict and the rate at which they flash. The signs shift between composing images of sex and violence and breaking down into abstract body parts: in mechanical repetition, an arm moves up and down, a leg kicks forward and back, a penis stands and falls, and a tongue flicks in and out. Vaudeville seems to be the operative genre here, offering such attractions as *Sex and Death by Murder and Suicide* (pp. 94–95), *Sex and Death: Double 69* (p. 96), *Mean Clown Welcome* (p. 100), and *Punch and Judy: Kick in the Groin, Slap in the Face* (p. 188). These satirical comedies of social comment are like contemporary versions of Bertolt Brecht and Kurt Weill's *Threepenny Opera* or *Rise and Fall of the City of Mahagonny* combined with Eugène Ionesco-like elements of follow-the-leader herd instinct pushed to and past the limits of the bizarre.

Nauman's concerns in these neon pieces are prefigured in his earlier works, but there they tended to appear more obliquely. For example, in *From Hand to Mouth,* 1967 (p. 90), a wax cast of a section of a woman's body (hand and arm, shoulder, neck, and chin and mouth), the expression "living from hand to mouth" is both objectified and made intensely literal. The piece can be compared to Duchamp's *With My Tongue in My Cheek,* 1959, a drawing combined with a cast of the artist's cheek pushed out by his tongue. However, when he made *From Hand to Mouth,* Nauman did not know of this work. The influence of Duchamp on Nauman was channeled through his understanding of the work of Jasper Johns. As Nauman puts it: "It's sort of like my understanding of Freudian philosophy, which is probably a very American version of it coming through [William] Faulkner. It's no longer from Freud, but digested and rearranged." Johns had a significant impact on Nauman: "I loved de Kooning's work, but Johns was the first artist to put some intellectual distance between himself and his physical activity of making paintings." Nauman cites especially the inclusion of a cut-open, upside-down chair with a cut-open cast of a human leg sitting on it in Johns's painting *According to What,* 1964. In this work the interior of the cast and the inside of the chair face the viewer. According to Johns, "if the chair were in the position with which we usually associate it, what would be absent would be too important in the fragment of the figure."[13] The act of making that kind of displacement in order to focus one's attention differently, as well as Johns's idea that "through thought or through accumulation of other thoughts, something that's very charged can lose its charge, or vice versa," confirmed for Nauman his use of the tension between what is told and what is deliberately withheld, as well as his own attempts to objectify his experiences rather than to leave autobiographical traces in the work. In Nauman's videotapes of 1968–69, the camera is usually set up above or behind him so that his face does not show or is cropped. The mouths, genitals, and other intimate body parts in his various casts and photographs are often reproduced very realistically, yet they are shown so abstractly and in such a distanced way that they seem not to belong to a particular person. These are recognizable parts of actual bodies, yet they are used as objects. In the same way, the neon signs of 1985 have impact because their tough imagery is stylized into abstraction.

Nauman decided to show these signs in large groups because he hoped to exert pressure on the viewers by creating a no-exit situation for them. The connotations that neon has acquired through its use in popular culture—whether in glamorous nightclubs in 1930s movies or more recently outside sleazy bars—are offset in these works by blatantly corny, even nasty imagery. On entering an exhibition of Nauman's neon pieces, one is at first seduced by their glowing color, then immediately staggered by their raucousness. Gradually one begins to distinguish the different components in each sign and the ways they change. Over time, the constant blinking makes the figures disintegrate into images of separate limbs; meanwhile, the repetition abstracts the sequences even further, until what seemed at first to be the content has vanished. All one is left with are powerful afterimages—for example, of the two hands that seem continually about to come together in greeting, but in the end always miss one another (p. 99).

A quirky streak in the artist? The Clown Torture installations (pp. 102–04) continue the subject of nonalignment. Of the *Clown Taking a Shit* (p. 102), Nauman wrote:

I have thought of times when work was difficult as mental constipation, so that when the image of a clown taking a shit occurred, I immediately considered producing a film or videotape (not just of the person of the clown but the location of the toilet, a public restroom—a gas station, an airport—places where privacy is qualified or compromised).

If you think of times when work is dif- *ficult as mental constipation, then the image of a clown taking a shit (not in a household bathroom but in a public restroom—a gas station, an airport—places where privacy is qualified or compromised) can show a useful parallel.*

You are given two pieces of information: you are having difficulty in working and [you see] the image of a clown as a threatening disguise. Can you provide a connecting riddle?[14]

The clown, the artist's alter ego, another protective yet provocative disguise, shows both his funny, laughing side and his nasty side—on the one hand a compromising fool without any privacy, used by society, and on the other, a resister. After all, perhaps only a fool may tell the truth.

Notes

An earlier version of this chapter was published in *Artforum* 24:10 (Summer 1986): 88–98.

1. *Unless otherwise noted, all quotations from Bruce Nauman come from a series of interviews with the author between June 1985 and April 1986.*

2. *Quoted from* Three Novels by Samuel Beckett: Molloy, Malone Dies, The Unnamable *(New York: Grove Press, 1955), p. 30.*

3. *Richard Tuttle, in conversation with the author, 1986.*

4. *Quoted in Willoughby Sharp, "Nauman Interview,"* Arts Magazine, *March 1970: 27.*

5. *Quoted in Joe Raffaele and Elizabeth Baker, "The Way-Out West: Interviews with 4 San Francisco Artists,"* Artnews, *Summer 1967: 40.*

6. *Quoted in Sharp, "Nauman Interview": 26.*

7. *Quoted in Sharp, "Nauman Interview": 24.*

8. *Quoted in Sharp, "Nauman Interview": 25.*

9. *Quoted in Jan Butterfield, "Bruce Nauman: The Center of Yourself,"* Arts Magazine, *February 1975: 55.*

10. *Samuel Beckett,* The Lost Ones *(New York: Grove Press, 1972), p. 7.*

11. *Jacobo Timerman,* Prisoner without a Name, Cell without a Number *(New York: Vintage Books, 1982), pp. 60–61. Originally published in the United States in 1981.*

12. *Earlier Nauman had used this kind of device in a much less confrontational manner in* Untitled (Eye Level Piece), *1966, a work that hangs on the wall.*

13. *Jasper Johns in conversation with the author, February 1986.*

14. *Nauman to the author, dated September 6, 1986.*

OVERLEAF:
Having Fun, Good Life, Symptoms. 1985
Neon tubing with clear-glass tubing
suspension frame
69″ × 10′11¼″ × 16″ (175.3 × 333.4 ×
40.6 cm)
The Carnegie Museum of Art, Pittsburgh
Museum Purchase: Gift of the Partners of
Reed Smith Shaw & McClay and
Carnegie International Acquisition Fund

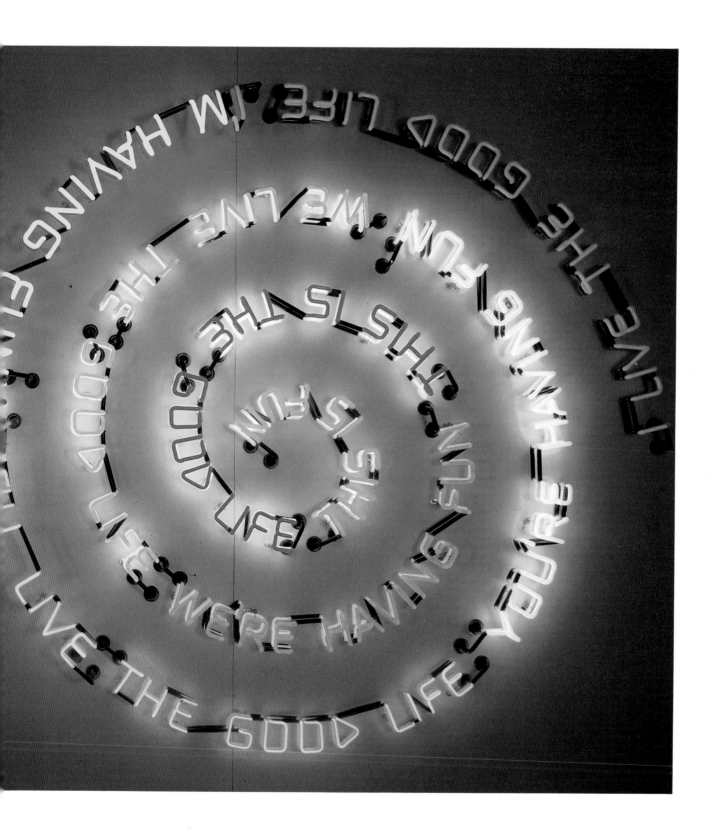

Untitled. 1965
Fiberglass
24″ × 11′ × 5″ (61 × 335.3 × 12.7 cm)
The Saatchi Collection, London

Untitled. 1965
Fiberglass
8′ × 28″ × 18″ (243.8 × 71.1 ×
45.7 cm)
Hallen für neue Kunst,
Schaffhausen, Switzerland
Crex Collection

Untitled. 1965
Fiberglass
6′11″ × 6′11″ × 8″ (210.8 × 210.8 ×
20.3 cm)
Collection Gerald S. Elliott, Chicago

Untitled. 1965
Fiberglass
Ca. 48 × 16″ (121.9 × 40.6 cm)
The Oliver-Hoffmann Family
Collection, Chicago

Untitled. 1965
Fiberglass
6'11" × 48" (210.8 × 121.9 cm)
Private collection, San Francisco

Untitled. 1965
Fiberglass
6′3″ × 6′3″ × 10″ (190.5 × 190.5 ×
25.5 cm)
Kaiser Wilhelm Museum, Krefeld,
West Germany
Lauffs Collection

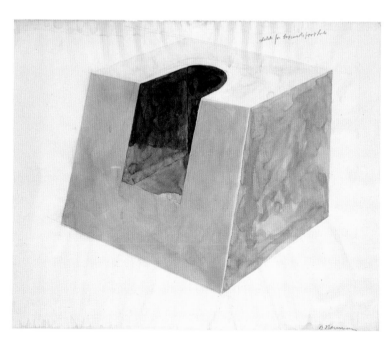

Stills from *Manipulating a Fluorescent*
Tube. 1969
Videotape, black and white, sound, 60 min.

Untitled. 1965–66
Latex rubber with cloth backing
8′ × 50″ × 3½″ (243.8 × 127 × 8.9 cm)
The Panza Collection, Milan

Untitled. 1965–66
Latex rubber with cloth backing
14″ (35.6 cm) high
Private collection, Greenwich, Connecticut

BELOW, FROM LEFT TO RIGHT:
Untitled. 1965
Fiberglass
Destroyed

Untitled. 1965
Fiberglass
Destroyed

Untitled. 1965–66
Latex rubber with cloth backing
7'4" × 6" × 2" (223.5 × 15.2 × 5 cm)
Oeffentliche Kunstsammlung, Basel

BELOW:
Untitled. 1965–66
Latex rubber with cloth backing
8' × 15" × 2" (243.8 × 38.1 × 5 cm)
Private collection

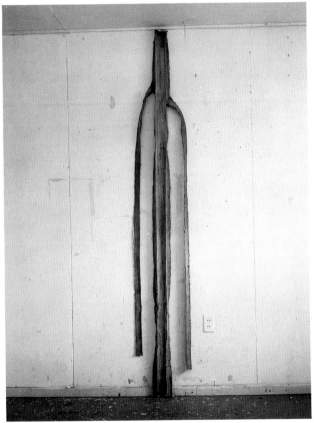

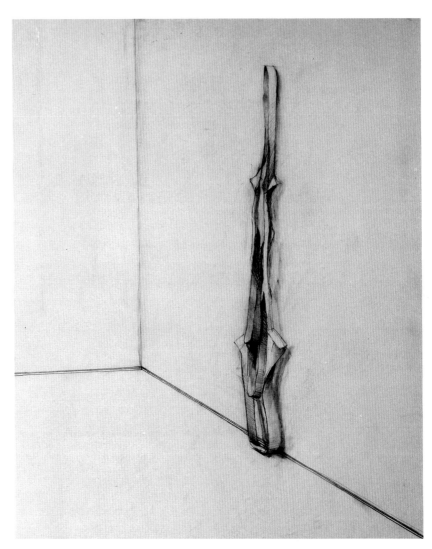

Untitled (Model for Room in Perspective)
1966
Fiberglass
29 × 24¾ × 7½″ (73.7 × 61.9 × 19 cm)
Oeffentliche Kunstsammlung, Basel
Depositum Emanuel Hoffmann Foundation

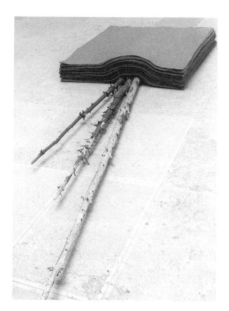

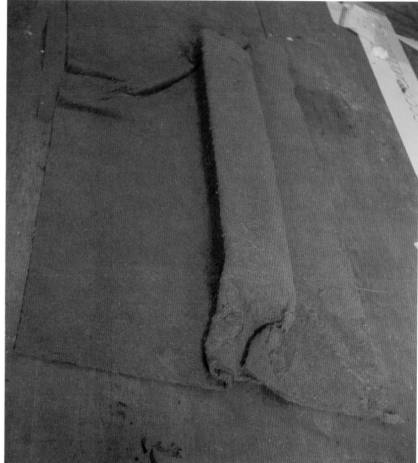

*Collection of Various Flexible Materials
Separated by Layers of Grease with Holes
the Size of My Waist and Wrists.* 1966
Aluminum foil, plastic sheet, foam rubber,
felt, and grease
1½″ × 7′6″ × 18″ (3.8 × 228.6 ×
45.7 cm)
The Saatchi Collection, London

*Collection of Eight Kinds of Flexible
Materials, 18″ × 7′6″, Separated by Layers
of Grease and Pierced by Holes the Size of
My Waist and Wrists.* 1966
Ink on paper
19 × 24″ (48.3 × 60.9 cm)
Collection Sonnabend, New York

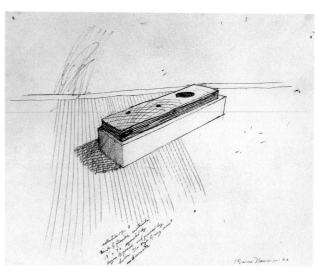

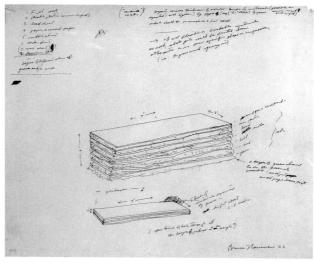

BOTTOM RIGHT:
Untitled (Study for Sandwich Sculpture)
1966
Inscribed: "1. Felt pad/ 2. flexible plastic
(semi-rigid)/ 3. lead sheet/ 4. paper or
waxed paper/ 5. rubber sheet/ 6. cork
sheet/ 7. (wax sheet)?/ 8. aluminum foil./
or/ layers of different colors of/ greases
and/or waxes/ ('sandwich' / sculpture)./
Layers of various thicknesses of various
kinds of materials (flexible or/ semi-rigid/ and rigid)/ separated (held together) by
layers (say ½″ or 1″ thick) of grease./ Whole
should be as much as 2 feet thick./ If all
flexible or breakable materials/ are used,
whole pile could be dented down/ at the
center or in some specific shape or
impression/ (i.e., the grease would squeeze
out)./ 2′/ 7′/ 2′ paper or cardboard/ thin
plastic/ lead/ rubber/ felt/ lead/ glass/ etc./
A layer of grease should/ be on the floor if/ possible (could put/ waxed paper down
first)./ Or perhaps 7″ × 7′ × 1′/ 5 kinds
of/ materials separated/ by grease/ height
about 6–8 inches/ some kind of hole
through all/ the layers,/ perhaps at an
angle?)."
Ink on paper
18¾ × 24″ (48 × 61 cm)
Oeffentliche Kunstsammlung, Basel
Depositum Emanuel Hoffmann Foundation

TOP:
Wax Impressions of the Knees of Five Famous Artists. 1966
Fiberglass
2¾″ × 15⅝″ × 7′1¼″ (7 × 39.7 × 216.5 cm)
The Saatchi Collection, London

BOTTOM:
Untitled (After *Wax Impressions of the Knees of Five Famous Artists*). 1967
Inscribed: "Make plaster molds of the right knees/ of 5 people—some bare and some with pants (cloth)/ over them./ Make a plaster positive and incorporate/ the positive into a mold for a slab of 3 or 4″/ thickness./ Pour and paint or splash wax to/ a sufficient thickness to prevent warpage/ (to appear as a solid slab)./ Or— try to make a thick slab and see/ if the impression of a knee can be made in the slab just from body heat—pressure./ — assign each knee print an identity— preferably of some (moderately) well known contemporary artists—(perhaps some/ historical artist who has not been dead over 100 years?)/ (Do not use Marcel Duchamp/ W. DeKooning/ self?/ William T. Wiley/ Larry Bell/ Lucas Samaras/ Leland Bell/ Or/ perhaps all 'knee prints'/ should be the same/ image but titled as above."
Ink on paper
19 × 24″ (48.3 × 61 cm)
Oeffentliche Kunstsammlung, Basel
Depositum Emanuel Hoffmann Foundation

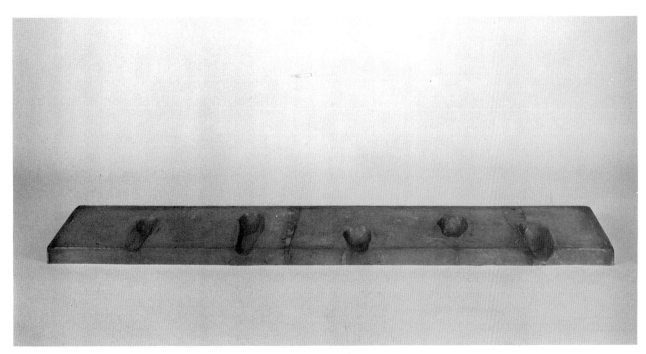

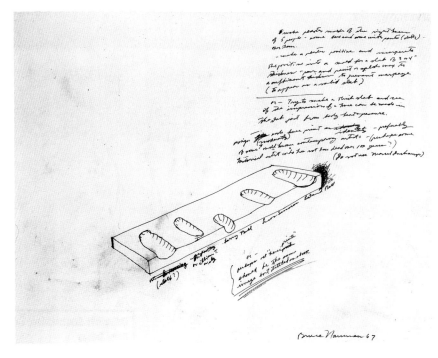

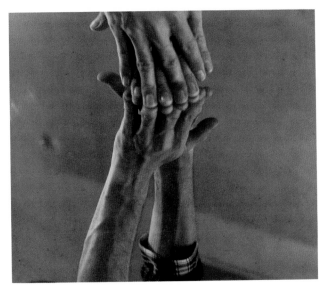

Eleven Color Photographs. 1966–67
Portfolio, edition of eight
Sizes vary
Published Leo Castelli: Gallery, New York,
1970

OPPOSITE LEFT, TOP TO BOTTOM:
Bound to Fail
*Coffee Spilled Because the Cup Was Too
Hot*
Untitled

OPPOSITE RIGHT, TOP TO BOTTOM:
*Coffee Thrown Away Because It Was Too
Cold*
Drill Team
Finger Touch with Mirrors

BELOW:
Waxing Hot

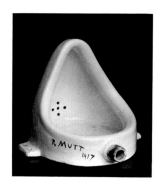

TOP:
The Artist as a Fountain. 1966–67
Black-and-white photograph
8 × 10″ (20.3 × 24.5 cm)
Collection the artist

BOTTOM:
Myself as a Marble Fountain. 1967
Ink and wash on paper
19 × 24″ (48.3 × 61 cm)
Oeffentliche Kunstsammlung, Basel
Depositum Emanuel Hoffmann Foundation

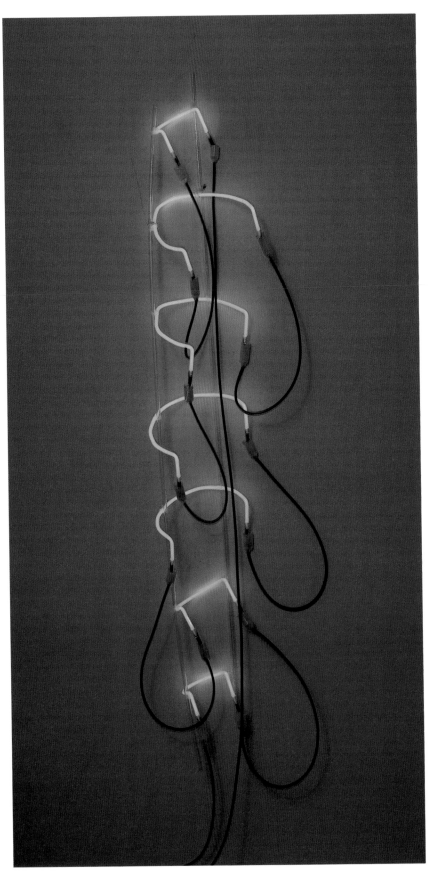

LEFT:
Neon Templates of the Left Half of My Body Taken at Ten-Inch Intervals. 1966
Neon tubing on clear-glass tubing suspension frame
70 × 9 × 6″ (177.8 × 22.9 × 15.2 cm)
Collection Philip Johnson,
New Canaan, Connecticut

OPPOSITE LEFT, TOP:
Small Neon and Plastic Floor Piece. 1965
Fiberglass and neon tubing
Ca. 48″ (121.9 cm) long
Destroyed

OPPOSITE RIGHT:
The True Artist Helps the World by Revealing Mystic Truths (Window or Wall Sign). 1967
From an edition of three plus artist's proof
Neon tubing with clear-glass tubing suspension frame
59 × 55 × 2″ (149.9 × 139.7 × 5 cm)

OPPOSITE LEFT, BOTTOM:
JAMES ROSENQUIST
Tumbleweed. 1963–66
Oil on wood with chrome-plated barbed wire and neon tubing
54 × 60 × 60″ (137.2 × 152.4 × 152.4 cm)
Collection Mr. and Mrs. Bagley Wright, Seattle

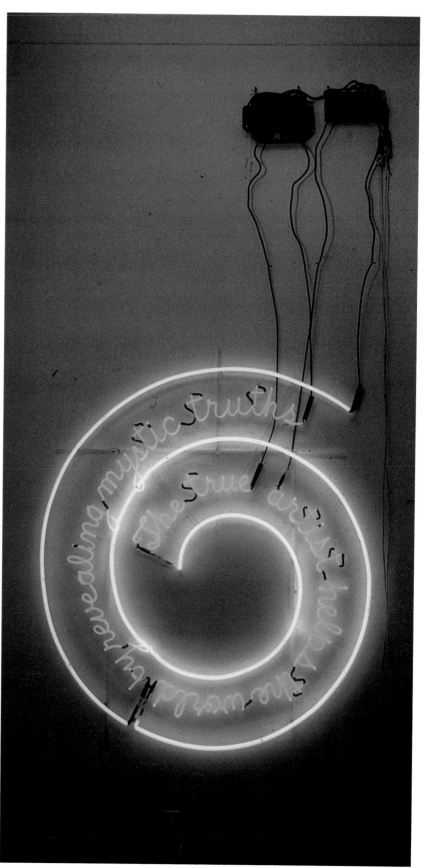

TOP:
Dark. 1968
Steel
4 × 48 × 48″ (10.2 × 121.9 × 121.9 cm)
Southwestern Community College,
Chula Vista, California

BOTTOM:
John Coltrane Piece. 1968
Aluminum with mirror-finish
bottom face
3 × 36 × 36″ (7.6 × 91.4 × 91.4 cm)
Neue Galerie—Sammlung Ludwig,
Aachen, West Germany

Green-Light Corridor. 1970–71
Two parallel plasterboard walls and four
green fluorescent tubes
Walls 10′ (304.8 cm) high; tubes
8′ (243.8 cm) long
The Panza Collection, Milan

TOP:
Untitled (Blue and Yellow Corridor). 1971
Pencil and pastel on paper
18 × 24″ (45.1 × 61 cm)
Collection Sonnabend, New York

BOTTOM:
Untitled (Blue and Yellow Corridor). 1971
Pencil and pastel on paper
18 × 24″ (45.1 × 61 cm)
Collection Sonnabend, New York

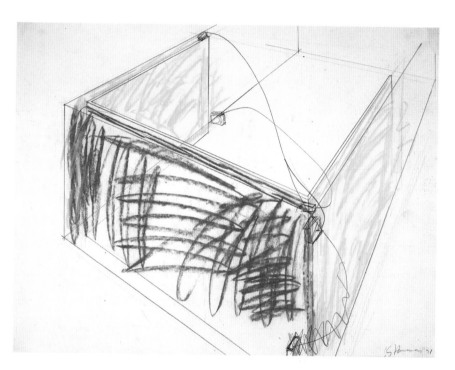

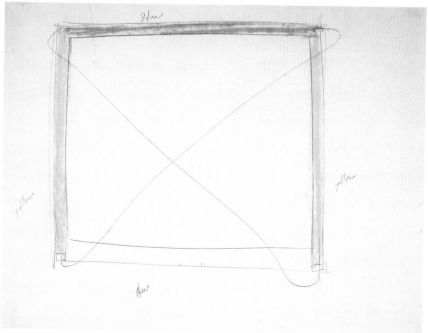

Study for *Corridor Installation*. 1969
Inscribed: "5 walls/ 6 corridors/ 3
passable, 3 impassable/ live video (3)/
videotape (1)."
Graphite and ink on paper
23 × 24⅝" (58.4 × 62.5 cm)
Hallen für neue Kunst,
Schaffhausen, Switzerland
Private collection

Corridor Installation (detail). 1970
Installed Nicholas Wilder Gallery,
Los Angeles, January–February 1970
Panels, video camera, monitors, and
videotape
Overall, ca. 11 × 30 × 40' (335.3 ×
914.4 × 1,219.2 cm)
The Panza Collection, Milan

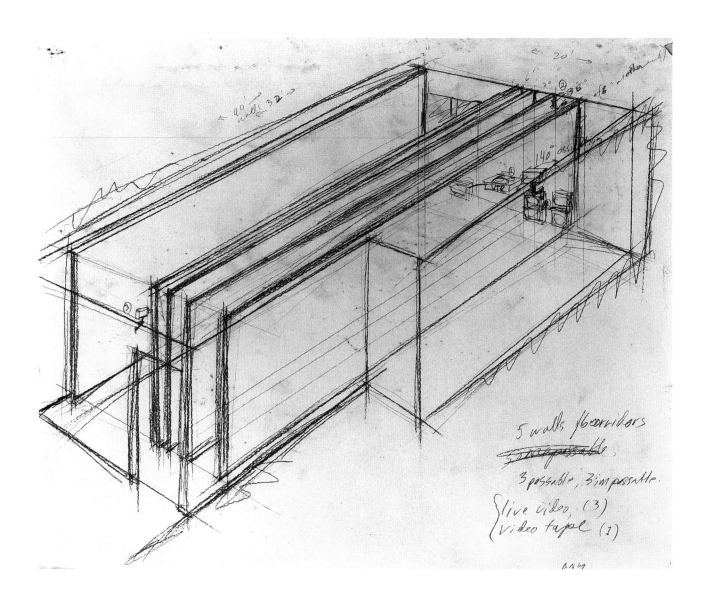

Double Steel Cage. 1974
Steel
7′ × 13′6″ × 16′6″ (213.4 × 411.5 ×
502.9 cm)
Museum Boymans–van Beuningen,
Rotterdam

Audio-Video Underground Chamber.
1972–74
TOP: Concrete chamber (containing video camera and microphone), rubber gasket, steel plate, bolts, and cord
27½ × 35½″ × 7′2½″
(70 × 90 × 220 cm),
buried 8′2½″ (250 cm) deep
BOTTOM: Monitor
Collection Lohaus–De Decker,
Antwerp, Belgium

Study for *Audio-Video Underground Chamber.* 1972
Inscribed: "(Some kind of hole for/ microphone at this end.)/ Walls are 7 to 10 cm thick/ smooth inside./ Whole chamber/ may be cast in place in/ order: part 1, part 2, and part 3/ so that it is 1 piece/ (not sections joined)./ About 50 cm by 70 cm inside dimensions./ About 2 meters long—

2.5 m long is possible./ Buried about 1.5 meters deep./ rubber gasket/ seal/ steel plate/ 1.5 cm thick/ gasket around cord and hole./ Bolts cast in place./ Hole large enough to admit camera."
Ink and pencil on paper
16¾ × 24″ (42.5 × 61 cm)
Collection Lohaus–De Decker,
Antwerp, Belgium

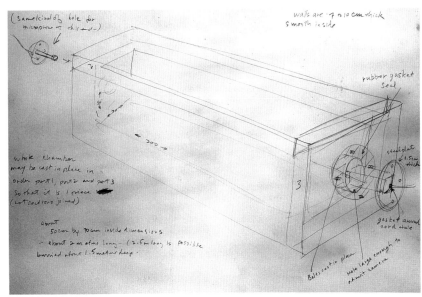

Model for Trench and Four Buried Passages
1977
Plaster and fiberglass
65″ (165.1 cm) high; outer circle, 30′
(914.4 cm) diameter; inner circle, 16′
(487.7 cm) diameter
The Saatchi Collection, London

TOP:
Model for Underground Passages (Spoke Piece). 1977
Cast iron and wood
$7\frac{1}{2}''$ (19 cm) high; $16'4\frac{7}{8}''$ (500 cm) diameter
Hallen für neue Kunst,
Schaffhausen, Switzerland
Crex Collection

BOTTOM:
Two views of *Ramp.* 1977
Wood, plaster, and iron
Ca. $13\frac{3}{4}'' \times 13'9\frac{3}{8}'' \times 43\frac{3}{8}''$
($35 \times 420 \times 110$ cm)
Hallen für neue Kunst,
Schaffhausen, Switzerland
Private collection

BELOW:
Model for Underground Space: Saucer. 1976
Plaster and plywood
19 × 57½ × 38″ (48.3 × 146 × 96.5 cm)
Collection Sonnabend, New York

Model for Outdoor Piece: Depression. 1976
Plaster and plywood
9¾″ × 6′9″ × 6′9″ (24.8 × 205.7 × 205.7 cm)
Leo Castelli Gallery, New York

RIGHT:
Untitled (Study for *Underground Space: Saucer*). 1973
Inscribed: "(Underground)/ entrance shaft at the edge—square./ (1″ = 1′)/ 50′ diameter/ 10′ deep."
Pencil, pastel, and watercolor on paper
41½ × 53⅜″ (105.3 × 135.7 cm)
Hallen für neue Kunst, Schaffhausen, Switzerland
Crex Collection

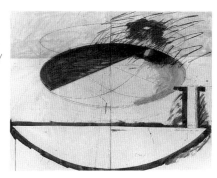

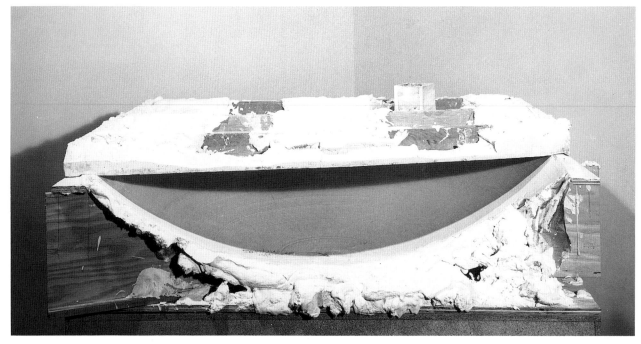

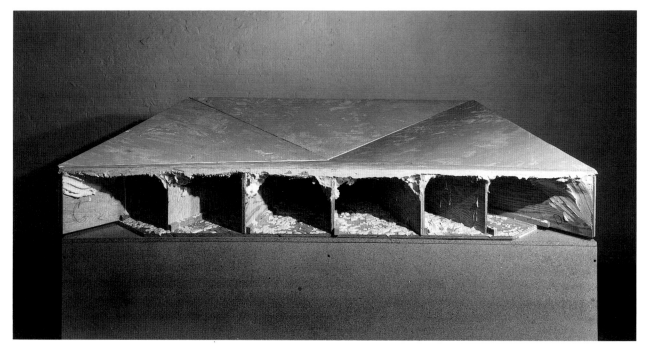

RIGHT:
Concrete Shaft, Two-Thirds Underground
(Study for First Tunnel Piece). 1972
Pencil and charcoal on paper
20⅞ × 30¾″ (53 × 78 cm)
Private collection, Krefeld, West Germany

TOP:
*Model for Underground Tunnel Made from
Half Circle, Half Square, and Half Triangle.*
1981
Cardboard, string, wire, paint, styrofoam,
and wood
13 × 68 × 55″ (33 × 172.7 × 139.7 cm)
Collection William J. Hokin, Chicago

BOTTOM:
Studio Piece. 1978–79
Photographed artist's studio, Pasadena,
California
Plaster reinforced with steel, wood, and
wire
44″ × 14′ × 14′ (111.8 × 426.8
× 426.8 cm)
Museum Boymans–van Beuningen,
Rotterdam

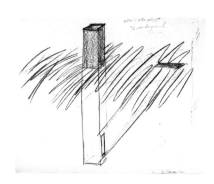

Model for Tunnel. 1978
Fiberglass with wood supports
$27\frac{5}{8}'' \times 13'5\frac{7}{8}'' \times 13'5\frac{7}{8}''$ (70 × 411.3 ×
411.3 cm)
Hallen für neue Kunst,
Schaffhausen, Switzerland
Private collection

*Model for Tunnel Made Up of Leftover
Parts of Other Projects.* 1979–80
Fiberglass, plaster, and wood
22″ × 22′11½″ × 21′3⅞″
(56 × 700 × 650 cm)
Hallen für neue Kunst,
Schaffhausen, Switzerland
Private collection

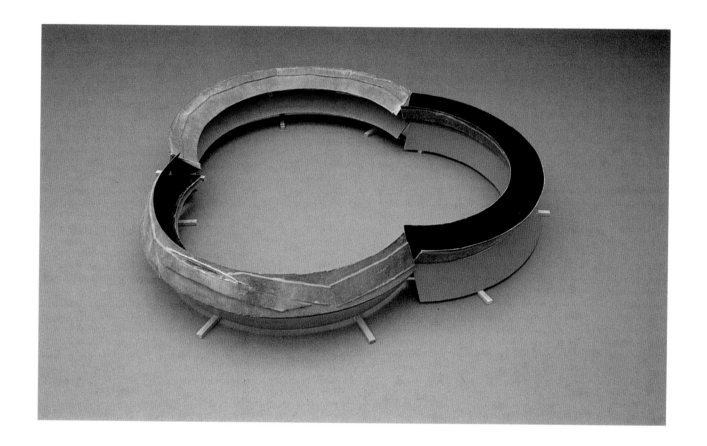

TOP:
Smoke Rings: Two Concentric Tunnels, Skewed and Noncommunicating. 1980
Plaster and wood
21″ (53.4 cm) high × 15′2″ (462.3 cm) diameter
Leo Castelli Gallery, New York

BOTTOM LEFT:
Untitled (Study for Tunnel: Triangle to Circle to Square). 1977
Pencil and charcoal on three sheets of paper taped together
$40\frac{1}{4}$ × $7′6\frac{1}{2}″$ (102.2 × 229.9 cm)
Museum of Fine Arts, Dallas

BOTTOM RIGHT:
Untitled (Study for Cast-Iron Model of Underground Chamber). 1977
Pencil on two sheets of paper taped together
$30\frac{1}{4}″$ × $6′8\frac{1}{2}″$
Daniel Weinberg Gallery, Los Angeles

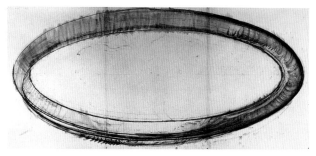

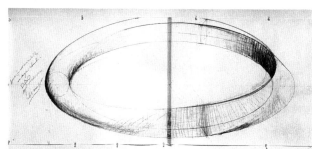

Model for Tunnel: Square to Triangle. 1981
Plaster and wood
28½″ (72.4 cm) high × 21′ (640 cm)
diameter
Leo Castelli Gallery, New York

Three Dead-End Adjacent Tunnels,
Not Connected. 1979
Plaster and wood
21″ × 9′7″ × 8′8″ (53.3 × 292 ×
264.1 cm)
Leo Castelli Gallery, New York

Three Dead-End Adjacent Tunnels,
Not Connected. 1981
Cast iron
25″ × 9′7″ × 8′8″ (53.3 × 292.1 ×
264.2 cm)
The Saatchi Collection, London

Untitled (Study for Underground Tunnel
Made from Half Circle, Half Square, and
Half Triangle). 1981
Charcoal, powdered charcoal, and pastel
on two sheets of paper taped together
40 × 50⅛″ (101.6 × 127.3 cm)
Private collection, Chicago
See *Model,* p. 63

Untitled (Study for Underground Tunnels
and Passages). 1980
Inscribed: "(Parallel)/ 60°/ 120° on axis/
on edge?/ 90°/ 120° on axis/ 120° on axis/
72° on axis."
Pencil and charcoal on paper
36¼ × 45″ (92 × 114.3 cm)
Oeffentliche Kunstsammlung,
Küpferstichkabinett, Basel

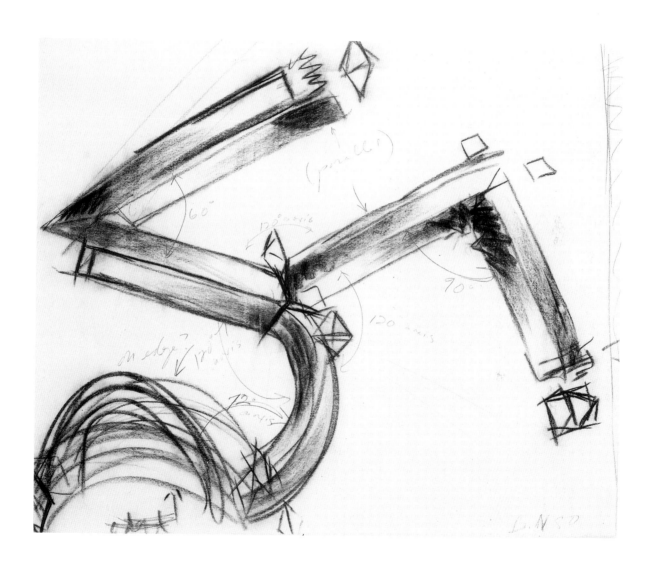

Untitled (After *Model for Tunnels, Butted and Adjacent: Triangle to Square, Square to Triangle*). 1981
Charcoal, powdered charcoal, chalk, and tape on paper
60 × 63¾" (152.4 × 162.6 cm)
Private collection, New York

Model for Tunnels, Butted and Adjacent: Triangle to Square, Square to Triangle. 1981
Plaster and wood
16′ (487.7 cm) long × 16′ (487.7 cm) wide
Collection the artist

Model for Tunnels: Half Square, Half Triangle, and Half Circle with Double False Perspective. 1981
Plaster reinforced with steel, wood, and wire
35″ × 15′7″ × 14′8″ (88.9 × 475 × 447 cm)
Leo Castelli Gallery, New York

Square, Triangle, and Circle. 1984
Plaster reinforced with steel, wood, and
wire
45″ × 20′2″ × 20′2″ (114.3 × 614.7 ×
614.7 cm)
Oeffentliche Kunstsammlung, Basel

Three views of *Room with My Soul Left Out, Room That Does Not Care*. 1984
Installed Leo Castelli Gallery, New York, October–November 1984
Celotex and other mediums
34′ × 48′ × 30′6″ (1,036.3 × 1,463 × 929.2 cm)
Destroyed

OPPOSITE:
Model for Room with My Soul Left Out, Room That Does Not Care. 1984
Wood, foam core, wire, and pencil
60 × 60 × 60″ (152.4 × 152.4 × 152.4 cm)
Full scale: 48 × 48 × 48′ (1,463 × 1,463 × 1,463 cm)
Leo Castelli Gallery, New York

Dream Passage. 1983
Wood panels, two steel tables, two steel
chairs, and fluorescent tubes
Corridor, 39'4½" long × 42" wide (1,200
× 106.5 cm); at widest part, 9'4¾" (286.5
cm) long × 8'1¼" (247 cm) wide; height
variable
Hallen für neue Kunst,
Schaffhausen, Switzerland
Crex Collection

TOP:
Dream Passage, Truncated. 1984
Charcoal and pastel on paper
$53\frac{1}{4}''$ × $6'2\frac{3}{4}''$ (135.6 × 189.9 cm)
U.S. Equities Realty, Inc., Chicago

BOTTOM:
Dream Passage. 1984
Charcoal and pastel on paper
62″ x $6'7\frac{1}{2}''$ (157.5 x 201.9 cm)
Sperone Westwater, New York

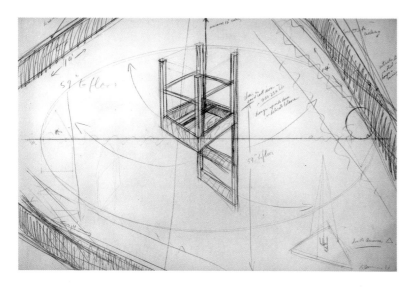

Untitled (Study for *South America Triangle*). 1981
Inscribed: "To ceiling/ minimum 12'
ceiling/ to ceiling ←14'→/ 59" to floor/
open—no/ seat bottom/ chair in/ sand cast
iron/ 200–250 lb./ hangs upside down/ in
delicate balance/ outside △ in steel/ hangs
and/ swings/ 59" to floor/ South America
△."
Pencil and colored pencil on paper
59⅞" × 7'6" (152 × 228.5 cm)
Kunsthaus Zürich, Graphische Sammlung

Untitled (Study for *South America Square*)
1981
Inscribed: "32" from floor./ Back of the
chair is/ in the plane of/ the top edge of/
the steel square—/ hangs from/ just above/
center of/ gravity./ 14' steel sq./ 20" to
floor./ South America □."
Pencil on paper
60" × 7'1⅝" (152.4 × 217.5 cm)
Private collection, Tiburon, California

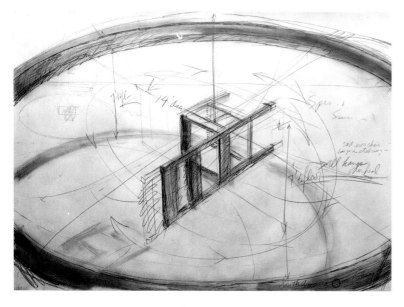

Untitled (Study for *South America Circle*)
1981
Inscribed: "7' to floor/ 14' dia/ Spins and
swings/ cast iron chair/ hangs in steel ring/
all hang overhead./ 7' to floor./ South
America ○."
Pencil on paper
60" × 6'11⅝" (152.4 × 212.4 cm)
Oeffentliche Kunstsammlung, Basel
Depositum Emanuel Hoffmann Foundation

Mock-Up for South America Triangle
Ca. 1981
Wood
Destroyed

South America Circle. 1981
Steel and cast iron
14′ (426.7 cm) diameter
Collection Jay Chiat, New York

*Diamond Africa with Chair Tuned
D E A D.* 1981
Steel and cast iron
60″ × 23′9″ × 11′6¼″ (152.4 × 723.9 ×
351.2 cm)
The Art Institute of Chicago
Mr. and Mrs. Frank G. Logan Prize

Musical Chair. 1983
Two steel I-beams and cold-rolled-steel chair
34" × 16' × 16'9" (86.4 × 487.7 × 510.5 cm)
Collection J. W. Froehlich, Stuttgart, West Germany

OPPOSITE LEFT:
Untitled (Study for *Musical Chairs).* 1983
Inscribed: "Abstracted chair for Musical Chair II/ Welded cold rolled steel./ To ceiling/ 1¾" square/ Make 2/ #1 hang/ as shown/ #2 hang from edge,/ on side./ same cut to/ length./ Ground flush/ after welding/ all outside corners./ To ceiling./ Drill hole in the bottom/ to bring to balance/ (seat must be horizontal)/ (do not pull through seat)./ 3" × 6"/ Steel I-beams/ 24' × 6"/ I-beams stacked and bolted, ¾" section."
Pencil and watercolor on paper
40 × 30" (101.6 × 76.2 cm)
Konrad Fischer, Düsseldorf, West Germany

TOP RIGHT:
Untitled (Study for *Musical Chair*). 1983
Inscribed: "Center beam meets center of/
abstract chair./ Center of chair hangs
down/ from center/ of circle so that/
(upper) beams swinging will/ sometimes
hit—sometimes not./ (Center beam will/
always hit seat of chair)."
Ink on paper
11 × 14″ (28 × 35.6 cm)
Collection Annick and Anton Herbert,
Ghent, Belgium

BOTTOM RIGHT:
Musical Chairs. 1983
Installed Museum Haus Esters, Krefeld,
West Germany, November–December
1983
Two steel I-beams and two cold-rolled-
steel chairs
14′ long × 14′ wide (426.7 × 426.7 cm)
Collection Annick and Anton Herbert,
Ghent, Belgium

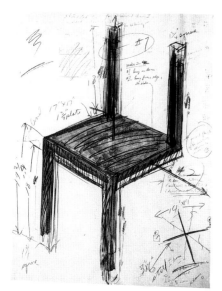

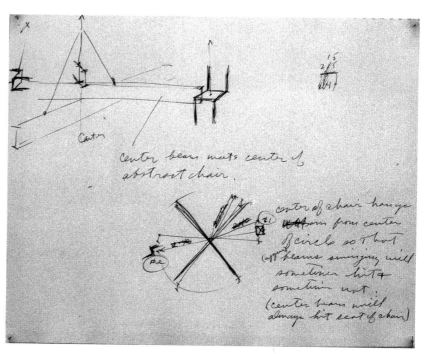

White Anger, Red Danger, Yellow Peril,
Black Death. 1984
Two steel I-beams, four spray-painted
chairs in steel, aluminum, steel tubing, and
cast iron
Ca. 14' (426.7 cm) diameter
Private collection, New York

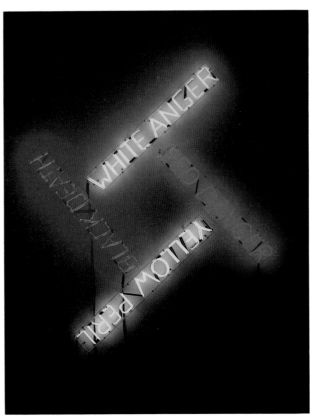

White Anger, Red Danger, Yellow Peril,
Black Death. 1985
Neon tubing with clear-glass tubing
suspension frame
6'8" × 7'2½" (203.2 × 219.7 cm)
The Rivendell Collection

Untitled (Musical Chair Suspended as Foucault Pendulum). 1981
Inscribed: "Musical chair suspended as Foucault pendulum/ D E A D/ Cast stainless steel chair—legs tuned D E A D,/ allowed to 'swing'/ as Foucault pendulum?/ Steel/ pins to/ barely touch/ legs,/ Line of daily rotation."

Pencil on paper
53 × 59¼" (134.6 × 150.5 cm)
Private collection, New York

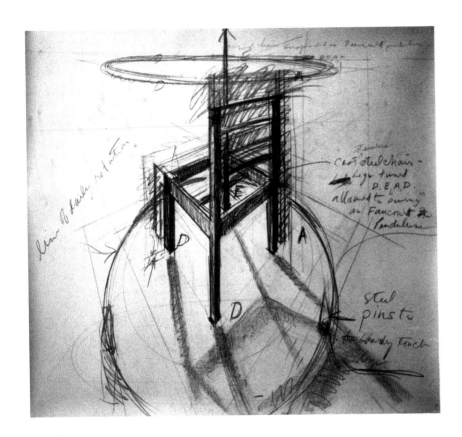

From Hand to Mouth. 1967
Wax over cloth
30 × 10 × 4″ (76.2 × 25.4 × 10.2 cm)
Collection Joseph A. Helman, New York

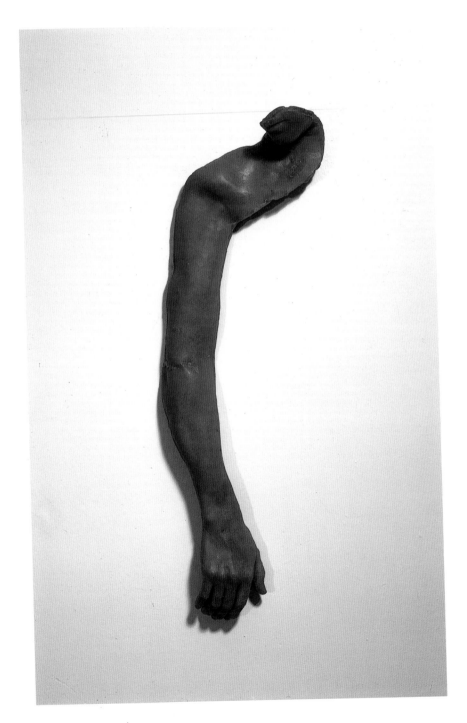

TOP:
Welcome. 1985
Pencil and watercolor on paper
22½ × 30″ (57.2 × 76.2 cm)
Galerie Yvon Lambert, Paris

BOTTOM:
Study for *Big Welcome.* 1985
Inscribed: "Welcome/ Full scale/ hand/
(2 × life size)/ Building/
welcome/ Welcome."

Pencil and watercolor on two sheets of
paper taped together
42¼ × 55″ (107.3 × 139.7 cm)
Oeffentliche Kunstsammlung, Basel
Depositum Emanuel Hoffmann Foundation

BELOW AND OPPOSITE:
Big Welcome. 1985
Neon tubing with clear-glass tubing
suspension frame, mounted on two
aluminum panels
Panels, 38 × 60 × 16″ (96.5 × 152.4 ×
40.6 cm) each
Leo Castelli Gallery, New York

BELOW AND OPPOSITE:
Two phases of *Sex and Death by Murder and Suicide.* 1985
Neon tubing with clear-glass tubing suspension frame, mounted on aluminum panel
6′ × 8′ × 12″ (182.9 × 243.8 × 30.5 cm)
Oeffentliche Kunstsammlung, Basel
Depositum Emanuel Hoffmann Foundation

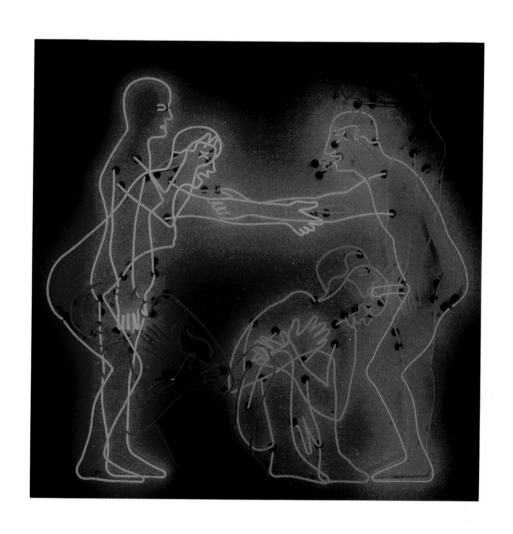

TOP:
Three phases of *Sex and Death: Double 69*
1985
Neon tubing with clear-glass tubing
suspension frame, mounted on aluminum
panel
7'1" × 53" × 12" (215.9 × 134.6 ×
30.5 cm)
Leo Castelli Gallery, New York

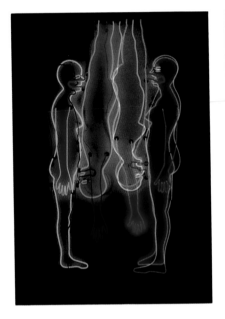
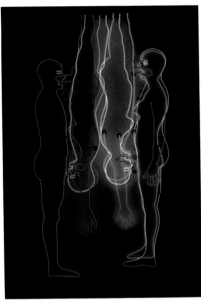
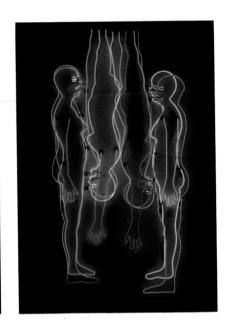

Untitled (Study for *Five Marching Men*)
1985
Pencil and watercolor on two sheets of
paper taped together
6'6½" × 10'8¼" (199.4 × 325.8 cm)
Leo Castelli Gallery, New York

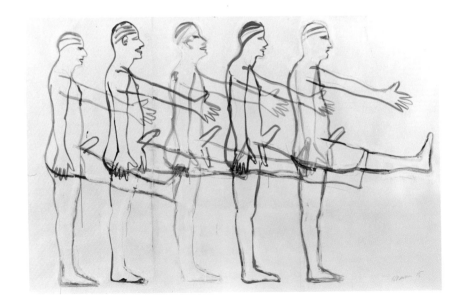

Four phases of *Five Marching Men.* 1985
Neon tubing with clear-glass tubing
suspension frame, mounted on aluminum
panel
6'7¼" × 10'9⅛" × 11½" (201.3 × 328 ×
29.2 cm)
Leo Castelli Gallery, New York

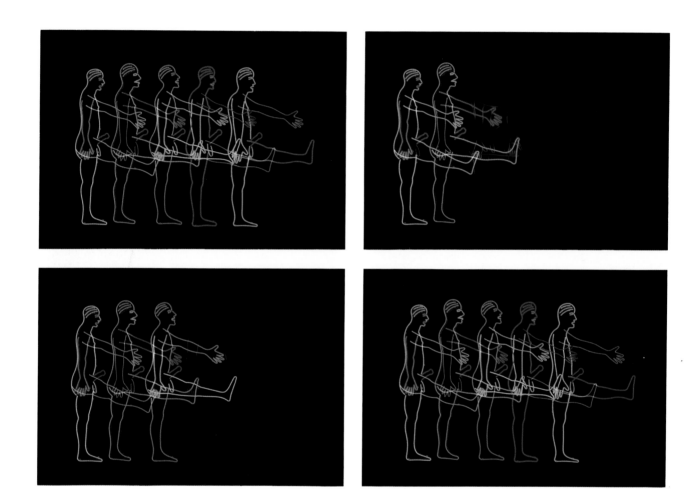

TOP:
Untitled (Study for *Double Poke in the Eye*). 1985
Inscribed: "Eye ear nose & mouth/ tongues flash 1/ 2/ 3/ 4/ 1/ 2/ 1/ 1/ Then/ all flash together—repeat./ Heads A + B always lit./ A. Blue head/ 1. yellow to eye 2. green to nose/ 3. purple to ear/ 4. red to mouth/ B. Orange head/ 1. green to eye/ 2. red to nose/ 3. yellow-green to ear/ 4. coral to mouth."
Pencil and watercolor on paper
17 × 28½″ (43.2 × 72.4 cm)
Galerie Yvon Lambert, Paris

BOTTOM:
Untitled (Study for *Double Poke in the Eye*). 1985
Inscribed: "Double Poke in the Eye I/ 1 + 2 flash back + forth/ 3 + 4 flash back + forth/ slightly different rate/ so in and out of sync./ (4 hands) #1. purple hand/ #2. red hand/ #3. orange/ #4. green./ A. Blue head green eye/ B. Yellow head orange eye."
Pencil and watercolor on paper
30 × 22½″ (76.2 × 57.2 cm)
Collection Claude Berri, Paris

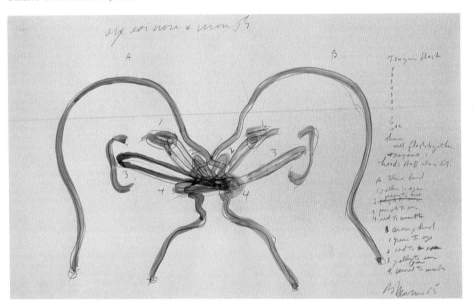

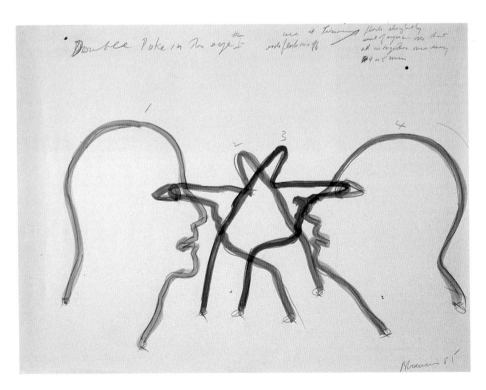

Untitled (Study for *Mean Clown Welcome*).
1985
Inscribed: "Move figures together/ so that/
hands overlap/ 6 [inches]."
Pencil and watercolor on paper
6′ × 6′10½″ (182.9 × 209.5 cm)
Leo Castelli Gallery, New York

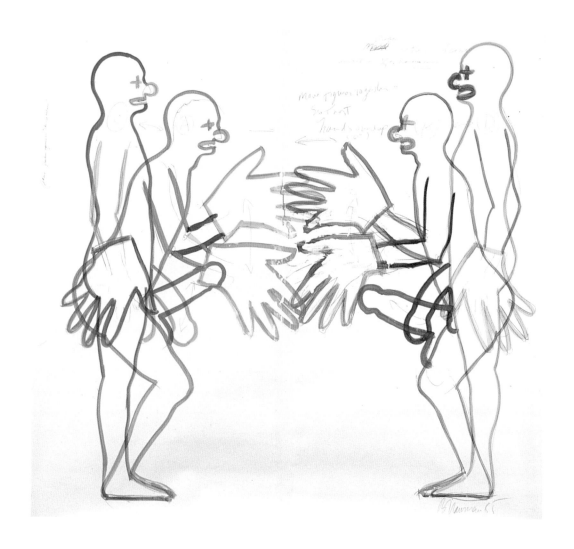

Six phases of *Mean Clown Welcome.* 1985
Neon tubing with clear-glass tubing
suspension frame, mounted on
aluminum panel
6' × 6'10" × 11½" (182.9 × 208.3 ×
29.2 cm)
Leo Castelli Gallery, New York

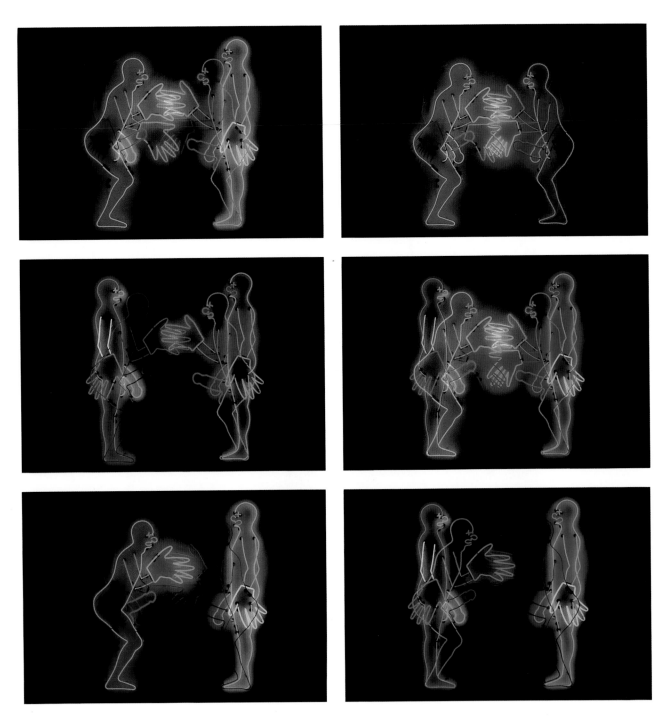

Run from Fear, Fun from Rear. 1972
From an edition of six
Neon tubing with clear-glass tubing
suspension frame
Two parts, $7\frac{1}{2} \times 46 \times 1\frac{1}{4}''$ ($19 \times 116.8 \times$
2.8 cm) and $4\frac{1}{4} \times 44\frac{1}{2} \times 1\frac{1}{4}''$ (10.8×113
$\times$ 2.8 cm)

Clown Torture: Clown Taking a Shit. 1987
Still from videotape surprinted with text
written by the artist in 1986; tape from
video installation with four monitors and
two projectors
Leo Castelli Gallery, New York

Clown with Video Surveillance. 1986
Watercolor, pencil, and collage on paper
42¾ × 37¾" (108.6 × 95.9 cm)
Collection Louisa Stude Sarofim, Houston

The True Artist Is an Amazing Luminous Fountain

For Bruce Nauman, drawing is equivalent to thinking. From 1966, when he left the University of California at Davis, until about 1968—when he alternated between traveling in Europe and working in his studio in Mill Valley, California—he drew mostly small, quick sketches that served as notes for sculptures or diagrams for films, videotapes, and performances. Nauman drew these in pencil while sitting at his desk, much as if he were writing. At the same time he made larger drawings in which he tried to solve problems in the execution of a sculpture or imagine how it would work out; these include *Shoulder,* 1966 (p. 132), done in charcoal, and *From Hand to Mouth,* 1967, done in pencil and wash. Occasionally, Nauman would make a representational drawing of a work after it had been executed, as in his sketch after *Neon Templates of the Left Half of My Body Taken at Ten-Inch Intervals,* 1967 (p. 122), reasoning that "when I take distance I can see aspects of the work that did not appear before, but which now seem the most important."[1]

Nauman approaches his projects systematically, even if he often pushes their inner logic to absurdity. But his move from one series of works to the next is usually a leap. In the interview with Willoughby Sharp in 1970 he stated:

I was reading Dark as the Grave Wherein My Friend Is Laid, *Malcolm Lowry's last book. . . . It's a complicated situation. The main character, an alcoholic writer, has problems finishing his books and with his publishers. He is sure that other writers know when their books are finished, and how to deal with publishers and with their own lives. I suppose it's the normal artist's paranoia and that was more or less the way I felt at the time, kind of cut off, just not knowing how to proceed at being an artist.[2]*

Because Nauman has never been able to stick to one thing, he has had to test himself over and over, putting himself in the position of an "amateur" starting from scratch—with the exception that he brings to each new task his experience of having taken similar risks before. "I can never give up wanting to do what I don't usually do," he has remarked. Add to that his restless attitude of "hitting the road like Kerouac" in search of the unknown. Moving on sometimes solves the problem of not knowing how to proceed. The different conditions of a new studio, for example, may stimulate work in another direction. This happened when Nauman moved to Pasadena, where from 1969 through the first half of the 1970s he had a large studio on the second floor of an industrial building. A disadvantage of the location was that it was hard to get materials—heavy steel bars, buckets of plaster, and lumber—up to the studio. As a result he made few large sculptures in that space and limited himself to building demountable, full-scale maquettes for corridor installations out of small pieces of plasterboard and wood. In this situation, drawing helped to fulfill his need to be involved in the physical activity of working. Nauman would pin large sheets of paper to the walls of his studio and draw on the paper while he was standing in front of it; from time to time he would stop and walk around, then come back to the drawings. At this time the planning and mapping out of three-dimensional installations for rooms became his substitute for making sculpture.

Earlier Nauman had made most of his pieces himself and only sporadically wrote notes on his sketches; now, because the work had to be executed by other people, he added to the drawings practical instructions about how to build the pieces, their dimensions, and other information. He would still start by sketching and composing freely on the page. After he felt he had made his point clear, he would straighten everything out by using a triangle or T-square, which would give the drawing an architectural character. Written notes were not put just anyplace; instead, readability—clarity of information—became part of his approach, as in his study for *Parallax Room,* 1971 (p. 123), a project to have been constructed in the Sonnabend gallery in Paris. He not only draws the piece in perspective, but also provides a ground plan with written notes that state: "any distance over 2 or 3 meters to end wall. These ends must be fairly clean and sharp. Partition walls are smooth surface wall board painted white. Spacing must be carefully followed. Walls don't necessarily have to extend to ceiling but should be 2½ or 3 meters high." The *Parallax Room* was never executed in Paris, but it was eventually built in the Hayward Gallery in London in 1971. The parallax effect (because of the way partitions were placed in the space) did not allow the visitor to focus both eyes on the end wall, which became almost invisible. The result was that images of lines seemed to float in space, which the viewer was unable to place in a fixed location.

In a 1971 untitled work composed of a white bar (p. 124), the light behind it is brighter than the bar itself, so that one has difficulty in focusing on it, in a way relating to the *Parallax Room.* But there Nauman relies more on illusion while White Bar vacillates between being an object dividing the room and a seeming illusion, a thing hard to locate and perceive.

Not every project Nauman drew was executed. After trying out an idea on paper, he sometimes rejected the project but preserved the drawing, such as the sketch for *Parallax Room with Three Horizontal Bars,* 1971 (p. 123). In this piece the three bars, planned to have been painted either all white or all black, were to have been suspended in a room at different angles to each other. Because the viewer had to look into the room by means of a very small vertical slot, he would have no way to decipher the scale, attachment, or relationship of the bars to one another. It was natural for Nauman to keep his drawing, even when he decided the concept was not interesting enough to be executed, because he drew primarily to record his ideas and to clear his mind. This is still the case. As he puts it: "When I start thinking about just formal things, like, dark over here, light over there, that's when there's no point to the drawing. That's when I throw it away. If a drawing works it explains the idea somehow. Sometimes I'm still drawing, and I'm still excited about drawing, but there is no idea left. That's when I get into trouble."

Nauman not only avoids adopting a standard technique that would force him to work in a consistent manner, he also resists having many tools around because they make one do things in certain ways, blocking new inventions. To avoid routine procedures Nauman occasionally designs his own devices. For example, in the summer of 1966 he completed the *Brown Crayon Box,* containing a crayon on a string. Intended to keep his drawing utensil close at hand, the piece nevertheless was destroyed in the fall of that same year. However, in 1967 he made a sketch of it (p. 125) to preserve the idea. The *Brown Crayon Box* prevented one from making a drawing of anything in particular because the box would always get in the way and one's movements were limited by the length of the string the crayon was attached to. Nauman was interested in thinking up conditions that would simplify his art but also make it more complex. By using unconventional tools, by turning over or cutting up sheets of paper and later taping them together again, by leaving his mistakes as part of the drawing—much as Wittgenstein left his errors in his *Philosophical Investigations*—Nauman totally de-

stroys the pure, classical surface. These departures from established procedures give many of the drawings, especially those of the 1980s, their radical physical presence.

In 1979 Nauman left the urban surroundings of Pasadena and moved to the mountains of Pecos, New Mexico, far from any major city—another leap into the unknown. In Pecos he found that the question of the artist's role in society became crucial again. He got an uncluttered view of "what affects people's lives, what pressures they feel," but realized that the kind of art he made was irrelevant to most of his neighbors:

A lot of people I know in New Mexico have been brought up in the mountains. Their life is about being in the mountains: they're guides, hunters, packers, and cowboys. They live a very different life than I do. I enjoy living like that for a week or two at a time, but at a certain point I recognize that I couldn't possibly continue to live that way. There's another part of me, the part of me that's an artist, that is more important, that needs to be taken care of.

Through living in a place where art is more or less irrelevant, Nauman avoids the art establishment and the deadly recognition it can impose; alone, he can concentrate on his art. "I am sympathetic to the frontier spirit," he remarked, "because as an artist you feel that you're on your own, you function by yourself. And that's a sort of glorified version of the frontier—you're the first one there, and if you can't figure it out, there is no one to help you. I think that most artists, poets, and composers function in a similar, solitary kind of way."

In Pecos, Nauman built himself a hangarlike studio, where he executed several large plaster tunnels (pp. 72–73), as well as a number of chair pieces, including *Diamond Africa with Chair Tuned D E A D* (p. 83) and the South America series (pp. 80–82). Working in the large

open space of his new studio, Nauman pinned up huge sheets of paper—some as long as 12 feet, assembled from smaller sheets taped together—in order to draw on a scale closer to that of the sculptures themselves. His large studies for tunnels include two from 1981—on one of which he jotted down: "3 tunnels interlocking not connected" (p. 20), done in charcoal, powdered charcoal, and chalk, and another on which he wrote: "vertical horizontal 23½° 1:100 scale drawing for cast iron for tunnel" (p. 126). He used tape not only to enlarge the size of the drawing but also to add a tactile element to its surface, so as to indicate the contrast between the actual and the illusory scale of the thing depicted. *Diamond Africa with Tuned Steel Chair,* 1981 (p. 127), done in pencil, pastel, charcoal, and collage, and the heavy charcoal and conté crayon *Musical Chairs,* 1983 (p. 127), both studies for sculptures (pp. 83, 84), are examples of drawings that are no longer purely conceptual; in making them Nauman was concerned not so much with representation as with "catching the energy" of his ideas. He built up tactility by using materials such as chalk and conté crayon, which emphasize both the surface of the paper and the gesture of the artist's hand. As in *Diamond Africa with Tuned Steel Chair* he disrupted the surface of several drawings by pasting or taping something onto them, thereby bringing them closer to sculpture and emphasizing their physical presence in the room. An extreme example of this is *American Violence,* 1983 (p. 128), a drawing for a neon piece. Originally cut up for use in another collage, the drawing was eventually reassembled—but in the process nearly all the letters of the two words were covered up with a translucent tape.

From the start Nauman has considered a drawing completed when it has made its point; for that reason most of his drawings have a raw, unfinished look.

"I do a lot of drawings where I indicate the major course of the drawing and finish only certain parts in detail," he remarked. "The more unfinished, schematic parts ought to be read as though they were done the same way. I remember even in school when I was making the first fiberglass pieces, my instructor would say: 'Well, you didn't clear all the plaster off.' It would never occur to me to do that as I wasn't trying to make a perfect object, I was just trying to make a point. It seemed to me that when the point was made clear you could just quit, you didn't need to belabor it." Nauman leaves signs of his mental process visible on the drawings—corrections, erasures, parts that have been labored over until they make sense.

But sometimes, while the artist keeps struggling to complete a drawing, working through all the possibilities, the surface becomes so dense that it is indecipherably black—the idea has been used up, nothing is left, nothing can be reworked anymore. In these situations there is only one solution: to go back to where he started. The reason for making the drawing may have been clear, but perhaps an incorrect assumption led him to the wrong outcome. It is Nauman's conviction that it is necessary to go through this cycle of building up and then starting over; he thinks it is the only way he can arrive at something else. This attitude is present in all of his work—the casts of body parts, the corridor and video installations, the films and holograms, and the models for tunnels; it appears very prominently in his conceptual drawings as well. What the main character says in Beckett's *Molloy* may apply to the diversity of Nauman's thought as set down in his drawings: "The mind cannot always brood on the same cares, but needs fresh cares from time to time, so as to revert with renewed vigor, when the time comes, to ancient cares."[3]

THE ORIGINAL SLANT STEP, 1965–66

In the autumn of 1965, in Mill Valley, California, William T. Wiley and William Allan discovered a wooden object covered with linoleum in the Mount Carmel Salvage Shop, a junk store they explored now and then, looking for curiosities they could integrate into their work. Shortly thereafter Wiley, one of the teachers at the University of California at Davis who encouraged Nauman in his work, took him to the shop to look at this rare specimen they dubbed "The Slant Step" (p. 129). Nauman recalls that he later made a pencil drawing of the object (p. 129) from memory: "It is kind of interesting, because I was wrong on various details." He continued to think about the Slant Step, and asked Wiley to purchase it—which he did, for 50 cents. "At first the shopkeepers, some women, didn't want to sell it," Nauman remembers, "because they said they needed it to get things from higher shelves. But then they realized they couldn't really use it for that purpose because the object was slanted, so they agreed to sell it." Wiley took the Slant Step to Nauman's studio at Davis and left it there. Early in 1966 Nauman produced a more accurate representation of the step in watercolor; on it he wrote: "The original slant-step / wood and linoleum" (p. 130).

In September 1966 Wiley organized "The Slant Step Show," at the Berkeley Gallery in San Francisco. He included twenty-one artists, among them William Allan, William Geis, Robert Nelson, Robert Hudson, Louise Pryor, and William Witherup. Wiley himself showed his *Slant Step Becomes Rhino, Rhino Becomes Slant Step*, 1966 (p. 130). Nauman had built his "modernized version" of the Slant Step, made of wood covered with plaster; he had rounded off the corners while preserving its basic profile and proportions. Then he cut away the wood and kept the rough plaster mold in two parts (see p. 131); it was this that he submitted to "The Slant Step Show" and included in his first solo exhibition: *What I was trying to do was find a way to make objects . . . that appear to have a function. [Making objects was] apparently an excuse for the formal invention that was going on, but . . . they didn't have an actual function and, in fact, the design of the pieces was arbitrary or invented. The Slant Step was an example of that because it was something everybody thought had a function until you really tried to use it . . . and so it was sort of like when you are thinking about something and then you read about it . . . [It] reinforces ideas you have or validates them.*[4]

In this work Nauman's vision paralleled Wiley's idea of "seeing with the dumb eye: looking at things innocently and unlearnedly so you can see them for what they are instead of what they are named for."[5]

Nauman's last involvement with the Slant Step came in the spring of 1966, when he worked with William Allan on a short movie they titled *Building a New Slant Step*. They collaborated on a wooden model of the step for this project (p. 129), but the film was never finished. "At first we were going to do a film called 'Watercolor Landscapes for Shut-ins,'" Nauman recalls.

We were going to set up the camera and just film some landscapes for people who couldn't get out of the house but could make watercolors. Then I remembered that when I still was an undergraduate in Wisconsin, I had seen an industrial film, a kind of documentary. It was a picture of an elevator going up and down . . . and a hand came on, pushed a button, and the door opened; somebody got in, and the door closed. There were beautiful shots of the cables and all the way down to the machinery, gears, electricity, and the box, then of all the things running. Finally, the elevator stops and the door opens. *I had no idea whether it was serious or a joke because it was so corny. It was extremely straightforward, and yet such a beautiful film. I was very intrigued by the idea that you didn't know what was intended, and yet it was so beautiful. It's like something you find on the street, but you don't know what its function is—you can just look at it and be entertained. So we did a film basically in that spirit, about making an object. You could show it to a crafts class in high school. Everything was well made and well documented, and the instructions were very clear, and when we had finished, no one knew what it was that we had made. I made copies of the Slant Step, and this and that, but making a film about it was most interesting, because it's about how to make a film as well as how to make an object, without even knowing what it is. It gets very tongue in cheek.*

Nauman's tongue-in-cheek attitude toward art was shared by Wiley, whose work has a Pop and Neo-Dadaist streak and whose puns and wordplay are well known. Wiley recalls that Nauman came up to him around that time with a little cardboard portfolio containing cutout magazine images of lips, mostly women's, in various sizes—an early indication of his later obsession with casting body parts. After Nauman had left Davis and moved into his first studio in San Francisco during the summer of 1966, he and Wiley became friends. The next year, when Nauman moved to Mill Valley, the two collaborated on a piece of true process art: Wiley had seen Nauman's first word images done in neon and conceived an idea for a piece in which a neon form would be drenched in motor oil. He had a box fabricated in heavy, transparent plastic; then both artists met at Wiley's studio and randomly dropped pieces of string on the floor. According to Nauman, the snarl almost spelled something; according to Wiley, it formed the letters *V E L*. The artists traced the string and had its form duplicated in neon. Then tl ey poured ten gallons of motor oil into a box, put the neon in it, and turned it on. The yellow tube looked bluish green through the oil. The result, however, was not exactly what the artists had pictured beforehand, so the piece sat around the studio. Eventually the box began to leak, and Wiley wrapped it in a piece of plastic. The last time Nauman saw it, the piece was lying in Wiley's backyard covered over by a heap of leaves. By then all the oil had leaked out.

SHOULDER, 1966

In his first studio in San Francisco, during the summer of 1966, Nauman was an artist without much money. The primary thing he had to figure out was what kind of work he could afford to do. Alone in his studio, with only himself as a reference, he began to measure his surroundings in terms of his own body; he grew increasingly interested in its reifications and applied its functions of sitting, standing, pacing, and the like in his performances. This attitude of detachment, which had begun as a way to make sculpture, would remain an essential characteristic of his work; it was reinforced by reading Beckett, particularly *Molloy,* where the central character is able to forget about his hands, his arms, even his legs, and can observe his own limbs as if from a distance: "And when I see my hands, on the sheet, which they love to floccillate already, they are not mine, less than ever mine, I have no arms, they are a couple, they play with the sheet."[6]

In the drawing *Shoulder,* 1966 (p. 132), Nauman uses part of his own anatomy, shown in different positions, as a purely formal element in a proposed sculpture. The objectified body fragments, drawn in a thick, heavily, textured charcoal line, derive plasticity from their being truncated and from strong contrasts of light and shadow, which bring out their concave and convex shapes. It is as if cast shoulder fragments were assembled, then attached to the end of a post. In his sketch Nauman seems to have been more concerned with clarifying his original idea than in completing the drawing itself. Impatient with filling in the square background that frames the piece, he finished the right bottom corner with a few smears. Nauman said that at the time he found it "difficult to leave things alone." Transforming an idea into art required intervening visibly rather than simply "letting things stand by themselves." By using the post he tried to introduce an extraneous element into the work: "One way I worked was by using the tension of two kinds of information that don't quite line up—it's not just the object that you contemplate and experience; it's the object in connection with some other piece of information that you have to deal with." Nauman made a plaster piece of three shoulders stuck together that did not work out, so he left it lying around the studio. Then in 1967 he made a drawing of a shoulder part in three positions (p. 135)—with the arm forward, upward, and to the side—on which he based *Device for a Left Armpit,* 1967 (p. 133), a plaster piece with a rough, sketchy outside and smooth, hollow inside. In its echoes of Futurism, this drawing relates to an early piece from 1965, in which a styrofoam cup cast in plaster is shown in stages of falling over. The idea returned in a photographic work of 1966–67 entitled *Coffee Spilled Because the Cup Was Too Hot* (p. 46), in which images of the different positions of the falling cup and spilled coffee are superimposed. In *Three Positions of My Shoulder to Make a Three-Legged Stool,* 1967 (p. 134), a drawing done in charcoal and pencil, Nauman used the same shoulder positions as in the earlier drawing, but the sense of movement of the forms is arrested because the shoulders are stuck together

108

in a cross shape and turned into a static stool.

In *From Hand to Mouth,* 1967 (p. 90), Nauman again tried to add an extraneous element to the work; however, the idea remains unresolved in a representational drawing. Both hand and mouth are rendered stiffly, as if they had already been cast in plaster; the section of the piece that links those two elements seems to be of a different substance altogether. It was to have been another kind of structure antithetical to flesh and bones; Nauman had thought of using a rod or some other linear element, but he eventually abandoned the idea. Instead he literalized the expression "living from hand to mouth" by making a wax mold of a body fragment in which a hand and a mouth are connected by an arm. He took a similar approach in *Feet of Clay,* 1966–67 (p. 134), a photograph of his own feet covered with clay. He not only pushes the saying upon which it is based into absurdity, but he has found a clever way to make the feet more general by hiding their individuality, thus preventing the work from taking on the autobiographical aspect Nauman was trying to avoid. He has commented that "if you can manipulate clay and end up with art, you can manipulate yourself in it as well. It has to do with using the body as a tool, an object to manipulate. That's what the photographs and the drawings for making faces are about."

In these works Nauman not only removes such body parts as mouth, teeth, testicles, and kneecaps from their usual context, transforming them into self-contained objects, but he also distorts or physically stretches them, as in the two drawings called *Six Inches of My Knee Extended to Six Feet,* both 1967 (p. 136). These drawings were based on an earlier work, *My Last Name Extended Vertically Fourteen Times,* also 1967, which was later translated into neon (pp. 137, 138). Knees have little definition to

begin with; when extended as they are in the drawings, they become very abstract. In the drawings *Tree Standing on Three Shoulder Joints* and *Three Positions of My Shoulder to Make a Three-Legged Stool,* both 1967 (pp. 139, 134), the idea of "linking two kinds of information that don't quite line up" returns, this time in proposals in which Nauman establishes formal analogies between the three shoulder joints and the roots of a tree and between the three shoulder parts and a stool. In the latter drawing another layer of confusion is added by the fact that a stool's legs are already named after a body fragment.

Nauman recalls that he had long been fascinated by *The Siren of the Sea* (p. 134), a carving by Auguste Rodin in the M. H. De Young Memorial Museum in San Francisco, in which a head protrudes from the remnant of what must have been a much larger block of stone. He was surprised by the equal importance given to figuration and geometrical volume in the piece, as well as by the connection between the head and the stone block, which, besides serving as a neck, seemed to be a third element with its own identity. He also noticed that Rodin would cast plaster figurines and join them together in a great variety of arrangements, often in an abstract way. Rodin appeared to treat each cast as just "a piece of stuff, a formal thing you could cut and change around," Nauman remarks. "I think I was aware of Rodin's method when I was working on these. His sticking parts together gave me permission to try out all those things." Later Nauman tried to translate the drawings of *Tree Standing on Three Shoulder Joints* into a sculpture; he used the plaster piece of the three shoulders stuck together— the one he had found unsatisfactory earlier—as a base for a leafless trunk with one branch (p. 139). But in the end he destroyed the entire piece.

LARGE KNOT BECOMING AN EAR (KNOT HEARING WELL), 1967

During the 1966 Man Ray exhibition at the Los Angeles County Museum of Art, William Wiley was looking through catalogues of the artist's work in the University of California at Davis library. He noticed that two titles, *The Riddle* and *The Enigma of Isidore Ducasse,* were given for the same piece (p. 43), a sewing machine wrapped in coarse cloth with twine around it. The second title, he discovered, was an allusion to le comte de Lautréamont, who, in a well-known passage of his poem *Les Chants de Maldoror,* proposed the most improbable juxtapositions, including "the chance encounter of a sewing machine and an umbrella on a dissecting table," which became one of the key phrases of Surrealism. This sort of disjunction between two pieces of information, or the concealment of information in order to rupture the expected unity of the story, became the distinguishing characteristic of several pieces Nauman made around that time—for example, *Platform Made Up of the Space between Two Rectilinear Boxes on the Floor* (p. 170), and *Felt Formed over Sketch for Metal Floor Piece* (p. 43), both 1966.

In discussing the internal contradictions of Man Ray's titles, Wiley and Nauman, then still Wiley's student at Davis, came up with the idea of sending a note to the artist H. C. Westermann. Nauman knew of Westermann's work from a piece he had seen at The Art Institute of Chicago. He remembers that in the stairwell of the museum he came upon "a kind of lighthouse tower with prominent windows," *The Mysteriously Abandoned New Home,* 1958 (p. 145), which Nauman found "strangely out of character with all the rest of the stuff in the museum." Over the years, the piece, built of pine and more than 50 inches high, had stayed in his mind. Wiley discovered that Westermann had lived in

San Francisco for two years, but left before Wiley had a chance to look him up. Now he and Nauman found a reason to start a correspondence with him. "We put the letter together with a piece of carbon paper, folded them up, and sent them to him," Nauman recalls. "The letter would pick up scratches, fingerprints, folds, and so on while it was handled in the mail. We thought it would be funny. We didn't make any marks ourselves, but it would arrive with whatever marks had appeared during the trip."

That kind of joke, derived from a Fluxus attitude, also seems to be a pun on automatic writing. Wiley remembers that Westermann's answer was an enigma in itself, something like: "You may think I am a mean thing but slow down what's your hurry." Wiley pursued the correspondence further, but Nauman did not; nevertheless, later in 1966 he began a group of drawings in response to Westermann's work and, through it, to Man Ray's as well. In these drawings, art about art done in a tongue-in-cheek manner, Nauman used both artists as a springboard to his own vision. Three drawings of 1967—*Large Knot Becoming an Ear (Knot Hearing Well)* (p. 140); an untitled charcoal-and-watercolor drawing (p. 142) that compares a double loop of rope to the crossing of two arms; and a variation of this, *The Square Knot (H. C. Westermann)* (p. 142)—are sketches for two other pieces, an untitled plaster (p. 143) and *Westermann's Ear* (p. 144), both 1967. The critic Max Kozloff wrote that Westermann's art "represents all the materials and the memories that a lonely seafarer might cherish."[7] Examples of Westermann's use of ship imagery are *The Big Change,* 1963–64 (p. 140), the huge, smooth wooden knot, 56 inches high, made out of laminated plywood, and *A Rope Tree,* 1963, 30¼ inches high, in which, according to Kozloff, an analogy is drawn

"between the strength from the braiding of hemp and the laminating of wood, their fibers equally ratcheting together." Nauman in his turn draws an analogy between an ear and a knot based both on their physical resemblance and their flexibility. He remembers another experience that contributed to this series of works as well. Just off the highway near Santa Cruz he noticed a park in which the branches of the trees had been trained to grow in various shapes: a ladder, a knot, and a heart, for example. In making this series, Nauman, like Westermann, deliberately drew on popular sources—here, a curious form of American folk art—but in a more distant manner. His drawing comparing crossed arms to a square knot goes beyond being art about art and becomes instead a type of pun in which two kinds of information are mixed, resulting in a moment of bewilderment followed by illumination. Sense appears from nonsense in a completely visual way, without the need for verbal explanation.

Another of Nauman's art-about-art series, referring to the work of sculptor Henry Moore, includes the drawings *Seated Storage Capsule (for H.M.)* and *Seated Storage Capsule for H.M. Made of Metallic Plastic,* both 1966 (pp. 145, 146); the two studies for *Henry Moore Trap,* 1966 and 1966–67 (pp. 146, 145); the drawing *Bound to Fail,* 1966 (p. 147), its bright-yellow wax model, and the cast-iron version, *Henry Moore Bound to Fail,* 1967 (p. 147); and two large photographic works—*Light Trap for Henry Moore No. 1* and *No. 2,* both 1967 (p. 148). Nauman's concern with Moore began around 1966, when he read in art magazines about the negative reactions to Moore of younger British sculptors. Nauman responded with his own idea: "Moore had been the dominant presence in British art for years; he was pretty powerful. I figured the younger sculptors would need him some day, so I came up

with the idea for a storage capsule."

Although the Seated Storage Capsule in Nauman's two drawings resembles the seated coffin figure in René Magritte's *Perspective II: Le Balcon de Manet*, 1950, Nauman's idea did not so much emphasize the passage of time as deal with the issue of the preservation of life in a science-fiction way. His storage capsule anticipated Stanley Kubrick's futuristic motion picture *2001: A Space Odyssey*, 1968, in which members of the crew of a spaceship were placed into capsules in a state of suspended animation in order to be transported to the far reaches of outer space. In Nauman's drawings the storage capsule looks something like a mummy or an Iron Maiden; it also suggests the sculptural process through its resemblance to a casting mold, where simple contour and surface conceal complex details inside. In a profile of Henry Moore by Donald Hall entitled "The Experience of Forms," Nauman recalls reading about the sculptor's plaster castings decaying outdoors. According to Nauman, in one passage Hall described Moore walking with his wife in a pasture near his home at Much Hadham, where crumbling old plaster castings and leftover molds loomed through the fog. In fact Hall wrote: "In a corner of land, five hundred yards from the house, where her husband leaves old plasters of large sculptures to break into unpredictable shapes, Mrs. Moore has planted bluebells. In the spring, the fragmented white forms hover over bluebells."[8]

In his creative misreading or misremembering of Hall's passage, Nauman's imagination is fused with the ghostly mood evoked by Moore's Shelter Drawings, in which bodies blend into the darkness, as in a fog, and figures are built up through rounded, scratchy lines, as if they had been carved out of stone. Moore made these drawings of people seeking shelter in the subway tunnels

110

from the night bombing raids by the Germans during World War II. He saw "rows and rows of reclining figures," most of them asleep, and would go into "different shelters and make mental notes, just observing."[9] The next day he would transform his memories into drawings. Nauman knew about the Shelter Drawings and liked them "because they are so heavy-handed."

Moore didn't have a light touch in any of them, neither the ones in crayon and wash nor the ones in pen and ink. All of them were very heavily worked; it seems as though he didn't have much facility in his drawing—at that time, anyway. I didn't know if he achieved more facility later. But I liked that about those drawings, that he had to struggle to get them right. My drawings have always been like that—I've always had to beat them into shape as much as anything else.

Nauman's crayon-and-acrylic study for *Henry Moore Trap,* 1966–67 (p. 145), is a play on Moore's Shelter Drawings in its modeling with rotating scratchy lines. Moore's spirit seems to have rubbed off on Nauman even more in *Henry Moore Bound to Fail* (p. 147), Nauman's only figurative, modeled-clay sculpture. This is a distorted version of a photographic work—entitled simply *Bound to Fail* (p. 46; see variations, p. 141)—which shows Nauman from the back, his arms tied with ropes. The effect of cloth over a form tied with rope recalls Moore's drawing *Crowd Looking at a Tied-Up Object,* 1942 (p. 145), which curiously enough Nauman had never seen, and is similar to Man Ray's *The Enigma of Isidore Ducasse,* as well.

The photographs *Light Trap for Henry Moore, No. 1* and *No. 2* (p. 148), address the mystical idea of capturing the artist's spirit. Nauman set up a camera for a time exposure, and in a dark room recorded a drawing he made in the air with a flashlight, in the same way Gjon Mili recorded Picasso at work in 1949. Nau-

man's photographs show intangible spiraling lines, which might have been spirit writing in a ghostly seance. In an anticipatory work about extraterrestrial activity, *Failing to Levitate in the Studio* (p. 149), done in 1966 but never shown, Nauman made a double exposure of himself falling off a chair to the floor. The idea of trapping a person's spirit is continued in another photographic work, the *William T. Wiley or Ray Johnson Trap,* 1967 (p. 149); in this case, though, Nauman used objects instead of lines. As he explains: "It had to do with the primitive idea of being encapsulated by artifacts and gaining psychic control over them."

In Westermann's work Nauman found a quality of mystery combined with a high degree of craftsmanship and a truth to materials—sophisticated, yet rooted in folk art. In some ways Moore represented the art-historical tradition he opposed, but in the face of Moore's rejection by a younger generation, Nauman felt it important to recognize the older sculptor as a major artist. In his final work of this group he attempted to capture the spirit of his teacher and friend, William T. Wiley. Nauman set himself free from all three artists, while acknowledging his artistic debt to them. Art about art of this kind is unusual for him. He prefers to pace his own studio rather than follow in the footsteps of other artists.

LOVE ME TENDER, MOVE TE LENDER, 1966

In 1966 Nauman felt that his work was not based strongly enough on his thinking. He started to play with language games in connection with objects and to invent ways to put them together. Taking as a model Wittgenstein's method, in his *Philosophical Investigations,* of including contradictory and nonsensical arguments, Nauman rejected a purely abstract, logical way of thinking and began

to load his objects with meanings from many sources. Seeing Man Ray's work in the Los Angeles County Museum of Art exhibition that same year convinced him that it was not always necessary to have a clear reason to work and reinforced him in his desire to introduce humor, poetry, and irony into his art and to present his work without explanations.

"Freedom produces jokes and jokes produce freedom," wrote the novelist Jean-Paul, and, "Joking is merely playing with ideas."[10] This is precisely what Nauman does in the drawing *Love Me Tender, Move Te Lender,* 1966 (p. 150). In this work he lightheartedly pushes against the limits of the way one thinks about things. *Love Me Tender* is, of course, the title of a song by Elvis Presley, which begins with the refrain, "Love me tender, love me true." By switching the first character of each word in the song title, Nauman shows something familiar in a new and surprising light; sense becomes nonsense. Though the rearrangement of the letters is slight, the result seems to suggest an entirely new meaning. At the same time, one is unsure whether Nauman intends specific meanings or if the changed phrase is simply a poetic enigma. Another way in which Nauman disrupts our normal process of understanding is by first showing the whole sentence, then separating the words in it into syllables. Arrows show how the first letter of the words could be rearranged, and the layout on the page indicates the various combinations that can be made of the divided words. Nauman's treatment is ambiguous: we do not know whether the work is a drawing or a handwritten note. In making *Love Me Tender, Move Te Lender,* Nauman just scribbled the sentence down. To him it had no particular meaning; his point was to make a drawing out of an arbitrary rearrangement of the words. He did not feel the need to defend this sort of method, given the long tradition in art of turning puns into physical objects, extending from Marcel Duchamp, who made it very clear that words are not merely a means of communication, to the Fluxus movement, and, closer to home, to such West Coast artists as William Allan and William T. Wiley.

Besides notes and drawings, another way Nauman found to substantiate his plays on words, and charge them with meanings they do not usually have, was to turn them into neon signs. In doing this he found visual equivalents for verbal ideas to which he was attached. For example, he was able to work with simple anagrams, such as *None Sing Neon Sign* (p. 153); with palindromes, as in a found saying based on an absurd University of Wisconsin football cheer, *Sugar Ragus* (see studies, p. 151); and with homonyms, as in *Suite Substitute* (p. 154), a pun on the title of the popular song "Sweet Substitute." In the fabrication drawing for this work, done in graphite and color pencil, a transformer is placed above the word *Substitute,* in which the *S, U, I, T,* and *E* are doubled to indicate the superimposition. On the drawing, Nauman wrote: "Design for wall hanging neon sign alternately lighting suite and substitute for multiple edition (art to replace your favorite furniture)." The neon piece is programmed so that first the word *Suite* lights up for five seconds in pink, then *Substitute* flashes on for five seconds in green; next both *Suite* and *Substitute* light up together for ten seconds. Finally the whole sign goes off for three seconds, after which the program is repeated. Nauman made a drawing based on this same idea, to which he applied a cutout from a Sears, Roebuck and Co. catalogue of a set of furniture in which he had replaced the cushions with Hershey bars.

Later, though, Nauman decided to destroy it. Instead he made another neon sign, *Sweet Suite Substitute* (p. 155), in which both the original phrase and the variation are present, due to the superimposition of three layers of signs: first *Sweet* appears in red, then *Suite,* in yellow, and finally *Substitute,* in blue; all flash at the same rate as the parts of the earlier *Suite Substitute.* Again Nauman wrote on the fabrication drawing for this piece, "Art to replace your favorite furniture." In such witty flashes of the mind Nauman transforms straightforward, everyday information into poetic wordplay. His ideas are embodied in neon signs, objects that, because they flash on and off, seem to have little material substance and instead turn into pure surface—writing in space, which is repeatedly erased and rewritten. The message, which gets broken down by being flashed on and off, holds the viewer's attention by its seductive visual display and by its seemingly nonsensical quality. In a watercolor in this series (p. 152), Nauman has replaced some letters in the word "substitute" with asterisks. This is the only case in which he refers to neon signs in which letters aren't working. In making this drawing he was inspired by Alain Robbe-Grillet's novel *Jealousy,* and particularly by Roland Barthes's introduction to it. Barthes mentions a huge sign on the Gare Montparnasse in Paris "that would read *Bon-kilomètres* if several of its letters were not regularly out of commission. For Alain Robbe-Grillet," Barthes continues, "this sign would be an object par excellence, especially appealing for the various dilapidations that mysteriously change place with each other from one day to the next."[11]

In his 1968 study for *Raw War* (p. 156), Nauman employs neon signage for a serious statement. On this drawing he wrote "sign to hang where there is a war on." Here Nauman makes no pretense at literary analogies or art, but conveys an unadorned statement. At first he planned to make a sign that would flash the letters *a, R, e, A, War.* Instead he made *Raw War,* 1970 (p. 157), in which the words *Raw,* in red, and *War,* in orange, flash in alternation. In another piece, *Violins Violence Silence,* 1981–82 (p. 160), Nauman combines poetic conceit with a serious statement, merging phonetic play in the sounds of the three words with political overtones. As Nauman puts it: "Those words load each other more through their combination. The work expresses generalized fear and anger about the way people mistreat other people." *Violins Violence Silence* parallels Jacobo Timerman's writing about the political situation in Argentina in *Prisoner without a Name, Cell without a Number:* "What there was, from the start, was the great silence, which appears in every civilized country that passively accepts the inevitability of violence, and then the fear that suddenly befalls it. That silence, which can transform any nation into an accomplice."[12] Commissioned to create a piece for the Music Department building at the California State University in Long Beach, Nauman proposed one version of *Violins Violence Silence* in which the words, 2 feet high, would be repeated, superimposed upon each other forward and backward in mirror-image letters; however, this idea was turned down. Instead, the sign was presented in 1982 along the front and side elevations of a new wing at The Baltimore Museum of Art (p. 160). Brenda Richardson, curator of the museum's concurrent exhibition of Nauman's neon works, described this piece as "friezelike, with the superimposed words VIOLINS SILENCE, and VIOLENCE VIOLENCE on one plane, and the words SILENCE VIOLINS around a corner on an adjoining plane."[13] The message of *Violins Violence Silence* is again subdued, because of the confusing overlay of the words. But at the same time its cryptic ambiguity distinguishes it from other street signs and keeps it in the viewer's mind.

112

In the impressive interior neon piece *One Hundred Live and Die,* 1984 (p. 161)—for which he made a fabrication drawing in pencil, pastel, charcoal, and watercolor, on different pieces of paper glued together—Nauman represents the ongoing flow of human life through a mixture of found sayings, arbitrary phrases, and personal statements, each of which is idiosyncratic and yet general enough to become art—*Suck and Die Suck and Live; Fear and Die Fear and Live; Red and Die Red and Live.* The piece is programmed so that at times the phrases flash on and off in order, by columns, giving an effect of continuity, while at other times the phrases appear in random sequence, as if disruptive jumps of thought are being made. Here, as in all his works based on words, Nauman is trying not so much to make a grand statement about life and death, or the transcience of human existence, as to put power back into clichés. By rearranging or decomposing these phrases, and presenting them in brightly colored, blinking signs, he attempts to recapture some of their original mystery and truth.

A ROSE HAS NO TEETH, 1966

A Rose Has No Teeth (p. 162) is a representational drawing for, according to Nauman's inscription, "a lead or bronze plaque to be attached to a tree in the woods so that it will be grown over." It is the inscription that arouses one's curiosity; due to the three-dimensional rendering of the plaque, the first letter of each of the nouns, "rose" and "teeth," is hidden. This would seem to put more emphasis on the plaque itself than on the phrase or the objects it refers to. Nevertheless, the phrase "a rose has no teeth" has an allusive richness that leaves one puzzled as to its possible meaning. Does the word "teeth" allude to the prickliness of the rose? Or is "a rose has no teeth" a play on the sounds of the words, suggesting something like "teeth have

rows but a rose has no teeth"? Or is it a response to Marcel Duchamp's female alter ego, which he ironically named "Rrose Sélavy," Rose being the most banal name he could think of, and the whole phrase being a phonetic play on the phrase "Eros, c'est la vie," as well. Nauman's phrase also recalls Gertrude Stein's "Rose is a rose is a rose." But none of the above explanations fully unravels the enigma. It turns out that Nauman selected the cryptic inscription for his plaque from a passage in Wittgenstein's *Philosophical Investigations:* " ' A newborn child has no teeth'—'A goose has no teeth'—'A rose has no teeth'—This last at any rate—one would like to say it—is obviously true! It is even surer than that a goose has none—And yet it is none so clear. For where should a rose's teeth have been?"[14]

What interests Nauman most about Wittgenstein's method, here and elsewhere in his writing, is the way he logically develops arguments, taking them further and further until, through absurdity, they are shown to be incorrect. For Nauman creative freedom lies in what cannot be figured out, and that is one reason that he uses the philosopher's phrase here. However, Nauman's method of making the unacceptable phrase acceptable is not done by pursuing the argument logically but by embodying the enigmatic phrase in a plaque (p. 162)—an object with a defined role in society, normally used to identify a building or site or to commemorate a person or event. A plaque is a manufactured object that has unquestionable authority. Nauman decided to place his plaque outdoors because he felt that Wittgenstein's phrase "a rose has no teeth" had "as much to do with nature as anything else." He also considers the piece, in part, a comment on outdoor sculpture: "I thought that outdoor sculpture was usually big and durable," he stated in an interview in 1967, "but that seemed very

dumb, because it's already nice outside, with trees and fields, and I didn't want to put something there and change it all. So I thought I'd make something which fell apart after a while—which would return to nature. Like dirt, or paper, that would disintegrate. Then I made this piece. . . . After a few years, the tree would grow over it, and finally cover it up, and it would be gone."[15] The concept of nature taking over in *A Rose Has No Teeth* returns in a drawing of 1966–67 called *The Negative Shape of the Right Half of My Body Carved into a Living Tree* (p. 163), on which Nauman further noted: "The cut should be sealed so the tree will not die. In some years the tree will grow at least partly closed. (If I were to stand in the spot for several years, my body would be partly closed in by the tree and I could not get away.)"

In September 1969 Nauman conceived two other outdoor pieces that he presented in the "Art in the Mind" show, held from April 17 to May 12, 1970, in the Allen Memorial Art Museum, Oberlin, Ohio. Again he revealed his desire to clearly separate nature from the artificial and man-made. One piece was simply to "drill a hole into the heart of a large tree and insert a microphone. Mount the amplifier and speaker in an empty room and adjust the volume to make audible any sounds that might come from the tree." The other: "Drill a hole about a mile into the earth and drop a microphone to within a few feet of the bottom. Mount the amplifier and speaker in a very large room and adjust the volume to make audible any sounds that might come from the cavity."

The idea of things gradually disappearing, as if going out of sight in slow motion, returns in *First Poem Piece,* 1968 (p. 164), and *Second Poem Piece,* 1969 (p. 165). Four studies exist for *First Poem Piece,* all done in 1968; on each drawing the sentence "you may not want to be here" is arranged over a grid pattern. The first line at the top of the paper shows the whole phrase; the succeeding lines present all the possible variations of the phrase that can be constructed by leaving out different words. Some of these modifications even reverse the meaning of the original sentence—for instance, "you may be here"—while others simply distort it to "you hear" or "you want." On one drawing Nauman noted, "tape loop—1 word each second—80-second loop," but this work was never executed.

While the drawings are relatively abstract and comparable to writing, in 1968 Nauman realized the *First Poem Piece* on a 500-pound steel slab, approximately 60 inches square and a half-inch thick, giving the "page" a strong physical presence in terms of weight and density. The words are engraved over the intersections of the grid, in accordance with notes Nauman had scribbled on some of the drawings. In the *Second Poem Piece,* for which no study exists, the phrase "you may not want to screw here" is deconstructed in the same way as in the first one, and is also engraved on a heavy steel slab over the intersecting lines of a grid.

The juxtaposition of deconstructed information with durable materials occurs again in a series of granite pieces from 1984, for which Nauman made several fabrication drawings (p. 166). In 1983, he received a commission from the Stuart Foundation for a work to be placed outside the theater on the campus of the University of California at San Diego. He proposed doing a piece on which the names of playwrights of his choice would be inscribed. However, he could not find enough writers whose work he liked, and so he changed the idea to a listing of virtues and vices. In general, Nauman prefers to use commonplace words and phrases whose origins are often unknown but which happen to be familiar in the culture. It

turned out that the campus theater was built of stucco, not stone, however, and was unsuited to a carved inscription; therefore neon seemed more appropriate as a material for the piece. Although execution of Nauman's proposal has been held up pending the outcome of an environmental-impact study, the seven virtues executed in vertical neon lettering and the seven vices in italic, superimposed on one another, have been temporarily placed around the top of the Powell Structures Laboratory, a building specifically designed to withstand the effects of earthquakes; each character is 7 feet high.

In 1983, while Nauman's proposal for the theater was under discussion, the idea of inscribing the virtues and vices in stone still preoccupied him, and a year later he executed the work independently. The seven carved granite stones of this piece, with virtues and vices superimposed, were shown leaning against the wall or lying flat on the floor like tombstones (pp. 167–69)—although they still had the potential to be installed on the façade of a building or embedded in a floor, in the architectural configuration they had been intended for. These granite pieces may be seen as literalizations of what Nauman had done illusionistically in lithographs. In 1972, while printmaking at Gemini G.E.L. in Los Angeles, he had drawn words on the litho stone as though they had been chiseled—for example, in *Clear Vision,* 1972–73. To the seven virtues and vices that were carved in English in 1984, the artist added an extra piece in German, *Hoffnung Neid* (Hope Envy), as a sample for possible editions in various languages.

Like the bronze plaque in *A Rose Has No Teeth,* the granite stones provide a solid foundation for Nauman's list of virtues and vices. One would expect the four cardinal virtues, prudence, justice, temperance, and fortitude, combined

with the three theological virtues of faith, hope, and charity, to be lined up with the seven deadly sins as perfect opposites, like good and evil. However, as Nauman discovered, the members of the two groups—with the exception of gluttony and temperance—have more of a glancing than a diametrical relationship. Because of this, some of the correspondences Nauman made seem arbitrary, or simply the result of a process of elimination, as in his pairing of prudence and pride. This nonalignment of virtues and vices is further emphasized by the fact that the words are superimposed and blend together, which is even more disorienting when they share the same letters. By combining these seeming (but not actual) opposites in this way, Nauman makes their juxtaposition as erratic and irritating to conventional logic as Wittgenstein's rose with no teeth.

A CAST OF THE SPACE UNDER MY CHAIR, 1966–68

The drawing for *A Cast of the Space under My Chair* (p. 171) was inspired by a remark Nauman attributed to Willem de Kooning: "If you want to paint a chair, don't paint the thing, but paint the spaces between the rungs of the chair." The resulting object, *A Cast of the Space under My Chair,* 1966–68 (p. 171), for which the drawing serves as a sketch and plan, is a concrete block with indentations on each corner, like the imprints of the legs of an absent chair; from the side the impressions of phantom crossbars can be seen. In a way this piece derives from *Shelf Sinking into the Wall with Copper-Painted Plaster Casts of the Spaces Underneath,* 1966 (p. 170), only in this case the matrix itself—the chair—is absent.

In its reversal of expectations the *Cast of the Space under My Chair* is related to Jasper Johns's well-known *Painted Bronze,* 1960 (p. 171), in which the artist presented two sculpted-bronze cans of

Ballantine Ale on a low base. This work was also made in response to a remark attributed to de Kooning—in this case, a comment supposedly made about the art dealer Leo Castelli: "You could give the son of a bitch two beer cans and he could sell them."[16] In his sculpture Johns made one ale can hollow and the other solid; he has said that in deciding to make the piece this way he was affected by Marcel Duchamp's *Why Not Sneeze Rose Sélavy?*, 1921 (p. 171), a small sculpture consisting of a cage filled with what appear to be sugar cubes. When the cage is lifted, however, it proves to be surprisingly heavy—the cubes are actually made of marble.

Johns's use of the tension between what is revealed and what is deliberately withheld reinforced Nauman in following his own direction. In fact Nauman's interest in Duchamp was channeled through his awareness of Johns's work. As Nauman puts it: "For years mathematicians tried to 'square the circle'—to turn a square into a circle with the same amount of space. Finally, though, someone proved it impossible, and wiped the problem out. I equate that with the way Duchamp or Johns make problems irrelevant, so it's no longer necessary to attempt even to solve them."

FILM WITH SOUND: 1. STAMPING, 2. BECKETT WALK?, 1968

In describing this diagram (p. 172) for the videotape *Slow Angle Walk*, 1968, which the artist may originally have intended to film, Nauman wrote:

In the diagrams the squares indicate the length of a step. These steps are made by raising the leg, without bending the knee, until it is at a right angle to the body, then swinging 90 degrees in the direction indicated in the diagram (follow the larger scale diagram or the very small diagram on the first sheet). The body then falls forward onto the raised foot and the other leg is lifted to again make a straight line with the body (which now forms a T over the support leg). The body swings upright with the non-support leg swinging through the vertical and into the 90-degree position, as at the start, and proceeds into the next 90-degree position, as at the beginning. Three step-turns to the right and then three step-turns to the left will advance you two paces—each three steps advances you one step.

A second diagram (p. 173) has written on it, in the upper-left-hand corner: "Right leg swings and steps. Left leg pivot and step. First swing to r. 3 times then l. 3 times. Repeat." Working alone in the studio, Nauman was able to alienate himself in a Beckettian manner from his arms and legs, so they seemed to have lives of their own, detached and objectified. *Slow Angle Walk* (pp. 174–75), the videotape for which the two diagram drawings were made, represents an action that takes place over the course of an hour. The distance of the artist is strongly felt; he is not behind the camera making decisions—a single, fixed camera position is used—but in front of it: an anonymous figure dressed in a white T-shirt, blue jeans, and boots, following a rigid, meanderlike path that took him in and out of the frame on his way from here to there, with his hands clasped behind his back. During the action not only are his head and other parts of his body frequently cropped out by the frame, but at times he is not in the image at all and is present only through the sounds of his footsteps. As a result the tape loses its immediacy as a record of a live performance. We are allowed to look into Nauman's studio; however, the artist's public and private domains are kept distinctly separate. The artist is always trapped in his isolation, while the public does not partake in the action but is kept in the position of voyeur.

The *Slow Angle Walk* does not consist of random wandering. The patterns described by the body are geometrically correlated, and as the artist moves from one end of the studio to the other, he occupies its space lavishly. As Nauman has put it: "It's like a woman I saw once in a restaurant. She sat down in a chair, sprawled out in it, dropped a cigarette lighter at one spot on the table, threw her handbag down in another—she, with all her belongings, took up a huge amount of space." In making *Slow Angle Walk* Nauman ran obsessively through all the possible variations on the program. In the finished tape he repeats the movements over and over, his actions punctuated by the sound of his feet hitting the floor. This is varied by the scraping sound caused when he makes the turn from one end of the studio to go back to the other. Nauman, who never stopped to rest during the hour, allowed chance circumstances to play an important role in the performance. For example, a kind of muffled tension is produced when he nearly loses his balance from time to time, and once even falls over. As in *A Rose Has No Teeth, First Poem Piece,* and *Second Poem Piece,* the process of slow decay in time is part of it all.

At the time of this videotape, Nauman was reading John Cage on Merce Cunningham, in which Cage talked about how difficult it is to perform a simple activity and how much practice and skill is required to present it as a dance. Convinced of the truth of this, Nauman practiced the actions in the piece in a highly concentrated way for a long time before he finally executed the tape:

If you really believe in what you're doing and do it as well as you can, then there will be a certain amount of tension—if you are honestly getting tired, or if you are honestly trying to balance on one foot for a long time, there has to be a certain sympathetic response in someone who is watching you. It is a kind of body response, and the viewer feels that foot and that tension. But many things that you could do would be really boring, so it depends a lot on what you choose, how you set up the problem in the first place. Somehow you have to program it to be interesting.[17]

The *Slow Angle Walk* is based on a set of rules whose rationale cannot be figured out, no more than one can determine why Beckett's Molloy transfers pebbles from pocket to pocket:

Taking a stone from the right pocket of my greatcoat, and putting it in my mouth, I replaced it in the right pocket of my greatcoat by a stone from the right pocket of my trousers, which I replaced by a stone from the left pocket of my trousers, which I replaced by a stone from the left pocket of my greatcoat, which I replaced by the stone which was in my mouth, as soon as I had finished sucking it.[18]

For Nauman, the idea of running through all the possible variations of an action as a means of timing the tape was also suggested by the composer Arnold Schönberg's method of composition, based on an original row of twelve tones with three variations: retrograde, inversion, and retrograde inversion. Each of these variations can be applied to each of the twelve notes, so that in the end there are forty-eight different rows to work with. All the rows are structurally related to and integrated with each other in specific ways. To avoid "privileged" notes, no note can be repeated until the other eleven in the row have been sounded.

Like Andy Warhol's *Sleep*, filmed in July 1963, *Slow Angle Walk* is not an exposition of a narrative but an apparently real-time record of a human activity. This gives it a documentary's authority that is not questioned by the audience. But Warhol's 16-millimeter silent, black-and-white movie, which lasts for six hours, was actually filmed over a period of several weeks and consists of six different shots repeated twice.

Each 100-foot reel records the sleeper in a different position, but the audience rarely stays long enough to observe the changes; it tends to drop in and out. Therefore the positions seem not to change. The film is shot in the usual 24 frames per second but projected at 16 frames per second, accentuating the stillness of the sleeper. This stillness is accentuated even further by the use of barely noticeable slow motion. Each of the six sections is extended by loop printing, and the film even ends by freezing a still image of the sleeper's head. Who the sleeper is—actually, the poet John Giorno—does not matter; he is treated as a confined, nearly abstract object within the frame. The movie is carefully calculated to advertise Warhol's aesthetic posture of indifference. "It started with somebody sleeping," Warhol remarked in a tape recording of 1965, "and it just got longer and longer and longer. Actually, I did shoot all the hours of the movie, but I faked the final film to get a better design."[19]

Executing simple activities, as in *Slow Angle Walk* and most of his other videotapes—as well as in such films as *Playing a Note on the Violin While I Walk around the Studio,* 1968 (p. 173)—Nauman traps himself within the frame in the way that Warhol trapped his "stars"; like Warhol, Nauman never emphasizes his own personality, whether behind or in front of the camera, but unlike Warhol, he is not interested in a minimum of cautiously calculated manipulations for the sake of "a better design." In fact, in *Slow Angle Walk* Nauman, who attempts to avoid autobiographical elements in the reification of his own body, employs video as a device of limited observation—a frame cropping off his head, his limbs, or showing his back only—in order to turn himself into an anonymous performer and to direct the attention of the audience to the activity itself. The grainy

quality of his early films and tapes, the lack of editing, proper lighting, or changes of camera angle, cause everything to become somewhat generalized. In *Slow Angle Walk,* the audience is never given any of the comforting illusionary tricks of conventional film, but instead is forced to confront directly the sense of distance and alienation experienced while watching the artist within the double confinement of his studio and the frame.

A CUBIC FOOT OF STEEL PRESSED BETWEEN MY PALMS, 1968

In 1968 while working in San Francisco, Nauman made a drawing designed to manipulate the viewer's knowledge and perception in order to unsettle fixed habits of observation and to set up discrepancies in the apparent meaning of the work. Based on this drawing, Nauman created a 4-foot-square floor piece out of a 3½-inch-thick, heavy steel plate and inscribed the word "silent" on the bottom, emphasizing the work's hidden face. Nauman proposed a related piece in a drawing for an "unfinished sculpture" (p. 176), which called for "a cubic foot of steel pressed between my palms." In fact, the completed work (p. 176) was 24 inches square by 3 inches thick, implying that the artist's handling had indeed compressed the steel from a cubic shape.

On his first trip to Europe in 1968, while staying in the attic of Konrad and Dorothee Fischer's apartment in Düsseldorf, Nauman drew a proposal for a piece (p. 177) in which steel plates 23⅝ inches square by 1¼ inches thick, weighing 269 pounds each, were stacked up, and memorabilia from his life were sandwiched between them. This piece can be seen as his recognition of Carl Andre, whose work first made Nauman aware of the effect that the sheer weight of a sculpture can have, and of Joseph Beuys's work as well. In the drawing

Nauman revealed what would be hidden between the steel plates, labeling the various elements from top to bottom: first, "plain steel plate," then "steel plate squeezed between my palms," then an inventory of personal belongings and props used in performances: "Some (soft) things from my pocket, photo of two balls, photo of my violin, photo of my face."

In the 1970s, Nauman's concern with questions of concealment and the psychological manipulation of perception was extended from single pieces to public spaces and to hidden private domains within such spaces. Most often, these were either corridors or specially constructed rooms. In his corridor installations, Nauman often used a video monitor as a kind of electronic mirror, allowing the visitor to shift from performer to observer and from public to private experience. In so doing Nauman dealt with two different kinds of information: "There's the real space and there's the picture of the space," he notes. In the V-shaped *Corridor Installation with Mirror* (pp. 178–79), a piece he made at San Jose State College, California, in May 1970, Nauman used a mirror instead of a monitor for the same purpose. In this piece the converging corridors were 2 feet wide at the entrances, but narrowed down to 16 inches wide at the end. Nauman described the effect of the piece:

Going into it is easy, because there is enough space around you for you not to be very aware of the walls until you start to walk down the corridor. Then the walls get closer, and force you to be aware of your body. It can be a very self-conscious kind of experience . . . and still the interest—since you are looking into the mirror and seeing out of the other corridor—the visual interest is pretty strong and it's centered somewhere else; it's either in the mirror or looking beyond the mirror into the end of the V.[20]

In a 1986 interview, Nauman looked back on this piece:

I was thinking a lot about the connection between public and private experiences. I think it came from working in the studio. You work alone in the studio, and then the work goes out in a public situation. How do people deal with that? It's different when someone comes to my studio and sees my work. I mean, you have those experiences by yourself as opposed to coming to a museum, where there are going to be a lot of people around. So you tend to try an experience with art but protect yourself in some way. You have to learn to shut yourself away from the rest of the public. So in those corridor pieces, which were about the connection between public and private experience, the video helps the private part, even though it's a public situation. The way you watch television is a private kind of experience.[21]
For an installation at "Documenta 5," in Kassel, West Germany, in 1972, Nauman built in a different kind of self-protection. He proposed a piece that would consist of two walls, each 15 feet high, in the form of two elliptical arcs. The visitor would enter the narrow space between these curving walls through a door in the center of one of them; this door was normally to be locked, to ensure privacy. Viewers were to be given instructions on how to get a key. Only one visitor at a time could be in the space, and could stay for no longer than an hour.

In 1986, this work was reconstructed at the Museum of Contemporary Art in Los Angeles, where it is called *Kassel Corridor: Elliptical Space* (p. 180). The walls of the work converge as one walks either to the right or to the left. At either end of the corridor one can see openings—but cannot reach them, because they are only 4 inches wide. People on the outside can look through these gaps into the chamber, but there is one area in the center near the door that, because

of the curvature of the walls, is hidden from sight. Someone inside could step into that space and be alone, separated from the thousands of viewers visiting the exhibition. The visitor entering this space goes through the same experiences as the artist, who in his work publicly exposes his most profound feelings and at the same time offsets his disclosures by withholding one part, thus preserving his privacy. During the 1970s, Nauman continued to deal with the relationship of public to private space in his series of tunnel pieces. In 1979 he stated in the magazine *Vanguard*: "When you are alone, you accept the space by filling it with your presence; as soon as someone else comes into view, you withdraw and protect yourself. The other poses a threat, you don't want to deal with it. . . . What I want to do is use the investigative polarity that exists in the tension between the public and the private space and use it to create an edge."[22]

A prime example is *House Divided* (p. 181), Nauman's first permanent outdoor project, realized in 1983 in the Nathan Manilow Sculpture Park at Governors State University in Illinois. The site is one of the few parcels of land near Chicago that is still unfarmed, virgin prairie, with native grasses and brush. When Nauman visited it, a phrase from Abraham Lincoln's Gettysburg Address came to mind: "A house divided against itself cannot stand." Seen from a distance, *House Divided* could be just another blocklike building stuck onto the land. But the house, cast in concrete, differs from any suburban home in its simplified, abstract form and its three oversized doorless openings, 5 feet wide by 9 feet high, which quite confuse its scale. The interior is divided diagonally into two triangular spaces. One is private because it is completely sealed off, and the other, no more than a shell, protects one from rain and gusts of wind but offers no place to hide because of the openings at its three corners. In Nauman's mind, the interaction between inside and outside remotely echoes Frank Lloyd Wright's concept of the Prairie house. The public, exposed space is illuminated from above by a parking-lot style yellow light. This uncomfortable exposure guarantees the visitor to the room safety, a concern of any artist doing public sculpture.

STUDIES FOR THREE INTERSECTING
CIRCULAR TUNNELS, 1977

In three studies from 1977 (pp. 182–83) for a work to consist of three ring-shaped underground tunnels, Nauman paradoxically juxtaposes the pull of gravity with levitation and function with sculptural qualities. These drawings, studies for maquettes (pp. 184–85) of a proposed tunnel project, show three circular, hollow spaces, triangular in cross section, which are tangential to one another underground. Their highest point appears at the surface as an outcropping and is thought of as an entrance to the tunnels. These tunnels, of course, must be strong enough to withstand the mass of dirt surrounding them. However, the maquettes double as sculptures—works in which three lightweight rings, made of fiberglass, seem to float in space. The three intersecting rings are decoratively colored in yellow, green, and red. The third side of each ring is omitted, stressing the triangular form and revealing the unpainted fiberglass interior.

In these pieces Nauman has produced a manneristic takeoff on his own use of the tunnel concept in other work, playing with the dual nature of a maquette—it is a model but also a sculpture in its own right. On the one hand, these pieces are sculptures of an average size; on the other, they provide a reduced representation of a three-part tunnel project that probably will never be built. While the decoratively colored fiberglass tunnel pieces have lost their original function—

as is evidenced by the fact that they have been shown in museum exhibitions as untitled formal sculptures—the drawings preserve the artist's original intention, through the notes written on them indicating tunnel entrances and ramps.

In most of his models for tunnel pieces, Nauman emphasizes their temporary nature by using such rough materials as plaster, wood, and fiberglass (see pp. 64, 68), evoking the appearance of a mold. In doing so he stresses the process of construction by showing the final piece in progress rather than in its finished form. By using wooden supports to hold the passageways off the ground, he also indicates that these are studio pieces rather than completed sculptures. Nauman's aim is to give the tunnel maquettes a powerful sculptural presence through their weight, density, and tactility, and thus to avoid turning them into precious objects.

STUDIO PIECES, PECOS, 1983–84

Another example of Nauman's approach to sculpture can be found in his studio pieces, such as the one he put together in Pecos in 1983 out of leftover parts of earlier projects. He thought of including a chair from *Dream Passage* and a cast-iron chair from the South America series. This studio piece was destroyed, but a working drawing has been preserved (p. 186). It shows a complex setting of a triangle and an *X* shape within a circle, all hanging at eye level, suspended from the ceiling by cables that converge at a central point. Two abstract chairs are arranged near the edge and one at the center of the circle.

Before making a more durable version of the work, called *White Anger, Red Danger, Yellow Peril, Black Death*, 1984 (pp. 86–87), with steel girders and four aluminum, steel, and cast-iron chairs painted in the colors indicated by the title, Nauman made the improvisatory piece out of wood to try out his idea.

Later a version of the studio piece, called *Musical Chairs* (p. 187), was made for an exhibition at the Konrad Fischer gallery in Düsseldorf, held in November 1983. About two days before the show's opening Nauman learned that a fiberglass sculpture being cast in Düsseldorf had not worked out. He decided instead to complete the chair piece, which he had been constructing in his studio in Pecos. He had brought a photograph of the unfinished work. "Konrad and I spent the whole day driving around finding junk to nail together," Nauman recalls. But the process of making the piece was not as casual as this may sound. Nauman, in fact, is very particular about the materials he uses. On another occasion he explained: "It's easy here [in Pecos] to go and get some large lumpy scrap of lumber, and nail something together. In Europe lumber has a different value. It's not stuff to use and throw away, as it is here. Not knowing those values sometimes throws me off."

In Düsseldorf Nauman built the piece out of carefully assembled materials—a rough wooden *X* shape painted white, an unpainted wooden triangle, and a bright aluminum circle. He added an office chair with blue upholstery and black frame, which was hung sideways; a natural-finish wooden chair, which he suspended from the ceiling by cables in the center in a normal upright position; and a chair reduced to its seat and supports (which were elongated by taping on pieces of wood) and hung at the periphery of the aluminum circle. The embodiment of the idea of a piece is more important to Nauman than its embellishment. Having the freedom to take that idea anywhere, without the availability of special tools, gave him the confidence he needed to make the chair piece within two days. But he also recognized that if he were to follow that approach too often, he would lose his sense of himself: "It was too risky to just show up and try to invent something. It was important to begin with a good idea, and then lots of materials could start to work for it." Over and over again, it is the central need to make his point clear that gives Nauman a reason for producing a drawing, sculpture, performance, or installation, and determines which medium or materials he will use.

CRIME AND PUNISHMENT (STUDY FOR PUNCH AND JUDY), 1985

The fabrication drawing *Crime and Punishment,* 1985 (p. 189), is a study in pencil, charcoal, and watercolor for the neon piece *Punch and Judy: Kick in the Groin, Slap in the Face,* 1985 (p. 188), and they are part of a series of drawings and neon pieces Nauman has made on the themes of sex and power. For the figures in this work, Nauman traced cardboard templates he had made of his own body parts and those of Harriet Lindenberg. The double contours of the drawing, executed in different colors, indicate where neon would be used, and the layered figures indicate in one plane the ways in which the figures might appear to move forward or lean backward as the neon flashes on and off. In the finished piece the male figures appear in the primary colors red, yellow, and blue, and the female figures in softer colors— pink, green, and orange. A simple sequence of movements is set up. Nauman's instructions state: "The standing female figure flashes back and forth with the female figure which leans back and kicks. The standing male figure with arm outstretched (slapping) and penis erect, flashes back and forth with the crouched figure (penis limp)." At first the female figures flash on and off very slowly; gradually, over a period of five minutes, the flashing accelerates to the point where it becomes a blur. Then the program is repeated. The male figures flash more rapidly than the female figures because of a one-minute difference in their

cycles; the figures move in and out of phase—hitting and missing, kicking and being kicked, fast and slow. At times they seem to disintegrate into unrelated parts, constantly changing places.

Because Nauman did not want to present a specific moral in the work, he changed the title for the neon version, emphasizing the reference to the popular puppet theater of Punch and Judy rather than the classic, somewhat elitist literature of Feodor Dostoevski's *Crime and Punishment.* In the puppet theater the amoral Punch yields to his violent impulses and acts brutally toward those around him, knocking them over the head, or worse; moreover, in contrast to man in real life, he always gets away with this violence. Nauman's Punch slaps Judy in the face—but here, instead of scolding, Judy responds in kind, kicking Punch in the groin. Nauman's piece is not about retaliation for a crime nor about inequality between men and women, but rather about the escalation of violence. He compares the relationship of the figures in this piece to a situation he found himself in as a child: "I used to walk to school with this guy, a friend of mine. In the winter, if I threw a snowball and hit him with it, instead of him making one and throwing it back at me he would take my hat, throw it in a mud puddle, and step on it. It was always confusing to deal with him, because I didn't know what he was going to do. But one thing I did know was that it was going to be way beyond whatever I had done."

Punch and Judy: Kick in the Groin, Slap in the Face has more of a story line than other pieces of 1985 such as *Five Marching Men* (p. 96) and *Mean Clown Welcome* (p. 100). To Nauman the theme of violence between men and women lends itself to translation into other media, such as film and videotape. *I made a list of incidents and actions that would be violent—a slap in the face, for*

example—and then had the idea of connecting them all, rather than having them be separate. It would start with something like pulling a chair out from under somebody, which is a bad joke to start out with, and then it could escalate in a Laurel and Hardy way, only without humor. I've thought about first presenting the male and female roles in the traditional way, and then reversing them, so that it confuses the meaning of a lot of the actions. I want to set up an emotionally loaded situation that runs through all the possible variations on these incidents, and thus confuses our expectations of them. Some of these actions would seem very abstract, and others would be very real and powerful.

For a 1986 video, *Violent Incident* (p. 192), Nauman wrote the following proposal:

The scene includes a table set for two with chairs in place and cocktails on the table.

The scene is shot in one take starting with a tightly framed low angle shot that will spiral up and away and clockwise until the finish of the action with the camera at a fairly high angle (looking down on the scene from above head level) and having made one revolution of the scene.

Both part one and part two are shot with the same directions.

I would see the action taking place on the left side of the table.

Shot in accurate color.

1.1. The man holds a chair for the woman as she starts to sit down. The man pulls the chair out from under her and she falls to the floor. Man is amused but woman is angry.

2. Man turns and bends over to retrieve the chair and as she gets up she gooses him.

3. Man stands up and turns and faces her now very angry also and calls her a name (shit-asshole-bitch-whatever).

4. The woman reaches back to the table and takes a cocktail and throws it in the man's face.

5. *Man slaps woman in the face.*
6. *Woman knees or kicks man in the groin.*
7. *Man is hurt and bends over, takes gun from belt or shoulder holster, they struggle and she is shot, is thrown to the floor, realizes she now has the gun, and*
8. *Shoots the man.*

II. *All instructions are the same except the roles are reversed—Woman holds chair for man, pulls it away, man falls, gooses woman, she calls him a name, he throws drink, she slaps, he kicks, she shoots (need work out where she gets gun—concealed on her person, out of purse, takes it from him?) and he shoots her.*

III *and* IV. *The scene is played out with two women and then with two men.*

Nauman goes through a wide range of variations in this work: reversing the roles of the man and woman; repeating the actions with two men or with two women; carrying out the actions in slow motion; and finally changing the color scheme. In this way he sets up a nearly ritualistic, highly formalized pattern of action that is gradually deconstructed and analyzed. By including rehearsal takes in the finished piece Nauman stresses this process even more: "One part of the tape is just rehearsals," Nauman said recently. "The man who was helping do the direction is talking to the woman carrying the camera. They're walking through it and he says, 'Now the chair!' He's breaking the action apart even more: 'Chair!—Goose!—Yell!—Throw the cocktail!—Slap!—Take the knife!—Stab!—Fall down!—Finish!' It takes 18 seconds to carry out the action correctly, and then 45 seconds when you take it apart and talk about it. I liked all this—I wanted to keep taking it apart, taking it apart."[23]

By using neon as a vehicle for his ideas on sex and power Nauman made the pieces particularly complex. Because of the difference in timing cycles, not only between the male and female figures in *Punch and Judy* but also between the pieces themselves when shown together, they evoked a sort of "neon wilderness." In the video *Violent Incident* the effect of a confusing overlay of images, similar to that of the earlier neon piece *Violins Violence Silence* (p. 160), is arrived at by the use of numerous monitors. The possibilities of simultaneous timing enable Nauman to make disjunctive leaps from one action to another—confused even

further by the inclusion of rehearsal takes—in order to avoid a banal, realistic narrative, and to create powerful, poetic images. In their masked presence the awesome traces of violence take on an even stronger significance.

The theme of violence and the use of multiple figures recurred in Nauman's elaborate, densely layered videotapes and films of 1986. In *Circle of Death?*, 1986 (p. 191), an unexecuted proposal fixed in a drawing which is in part inspired by the engraving *Battle of Ten Naked Men* (p. 191) by the fifteenth-century artist Antonio Pollaiuolo, Nauman depicts a kind of gruesome, choreographed dance in which six men beat a victim to death with baseball bats. In this proposal a sense of the ridiculous and the absurd reappears, with baseball bats. In this proposal a sense of the absurd reappears, but completely without humor. The performers are caught in a no-exit situation. Nauman combines a slapstick technique with acts of cruelty that become ritualized into geometric patterns of circle, square, and triangle—a direct reference to his 1981 South America series (pp. 80–82).

Notes

1. *Unless otherwise noted all the quotations from Bruce Nauman in this chapter come from a series of interviews with the author between June 1985 and April 1986.*

2. *Quoted in Willoughby Sharp, "Nauman Interview,"* Arts Magazine, *March 1970: 25.*

3. *Quoted from* Three Novels by Samuel Beckett: Molloy, Malone Dies, The Unnamable *(New York: Grove Press, 1955), p. 64.*

4. *Quoted in "The Slant Step Revisited,"* Richard L. Nelson Gallery, University of California, Davis, January 13–February 13, 1983.

5. *William T. Wiley in conversation with the author, Feburary 1986.*

6. *Quoted from* Three Novels by Samuel Beckett, *p. 66.*

7. *Quoted in* H. C. Westermann, *Los Angeles County Museum of Art, November 26, 1968–January 12, 1969, pp. 7 and 9.*

8. *Quoted in Donald Hall, "The Experience of Forms,"* The New Yorker, *December 11, 1965: 68.*

9. *Ibid., December 18, 1965: 80.*

10. *Quoted in Sigmund Freud,* Jokes and Their Relation to the Unconscious *(New York, London: W. W. Norton, 1963), p. 11.*

11. *Quoted in Roland Barthes, Introductory Essay to Alain Robbe-Grillet,* Jealousy *(New York: Grove Press, 1978), p. 13.*

12. *Quoted from Jacobo Timerman,* Prisoner without a Name, Cell without a Number *(New York: Vintage Books, 1982), p. 51.*

13. *Quoted in Brenda Richardson,* Bruce Nauman: Neons, *The Baltimore Museum of Art, December 19, 1982–February 13, 1983, p. 92.*

14. *Quoted from Ludwig Wittgenstein,* Philosophical Investigations *(New York: Macmillan, 1953), p. 221.*

15. *Quoted in Joe Raffaele and Elizabeth Baker, "The Way-Out West: Interviews with 4 San Francisco Artists,"* Artnews, *Summer 1967: 75–76.*

16. *Quoted in Calvin Tomkins,* Off the Wall *(Garden City, New York: Doubleday & Company, 1980), p. 184.*

17. *Quoted in Willoughby Sharp, "Bruce Nauman,"* Avalanche *2 (Winter 1971): 29.*

18. *Quoted from* Three Novels by Samuel Beckett, *p. 69.*

19. *Quoted in Stephen Koch,* Stargazer *(New York: Praeger Publishers, Inc., 1973), p. 37.*

20. *Quoted in Sharp, "Bruce Nauman": 24.*

21. *Quoted in Chris Dercon, "Keep Taking it Apart: A Conversation with Bruce Nauman,"* Parkett *10 (1986): 56.*

22. *Quoted in Ian Wallace and Russell Keziere, "Bruce Nauman Interviewed,"* Vanguard *8, no. 1 (Feburary 1, 1979): 16.*

23. *Quoted in Dercon: 61.*

The True Artist Is an Amazing Luminous
Fountain. 1966
Inscribed: "Design for around the edge of/
a window or wall of/ these proportions."
Pencil and ink on paper
24 × 19″ (61 × 48.2 cm)
Collection Sonnabend, New York

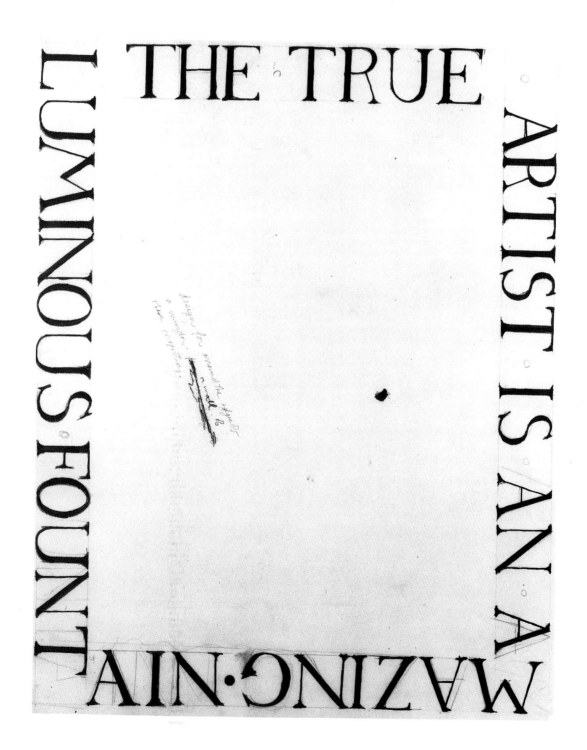

Untitled (After *Neon Templates of the Left*
Half of My Body Taken at Ten-Inch
Intervals). 1967
Pencil on paper
18 × 24″ (45.7 × 61 cm)
Collection the artist

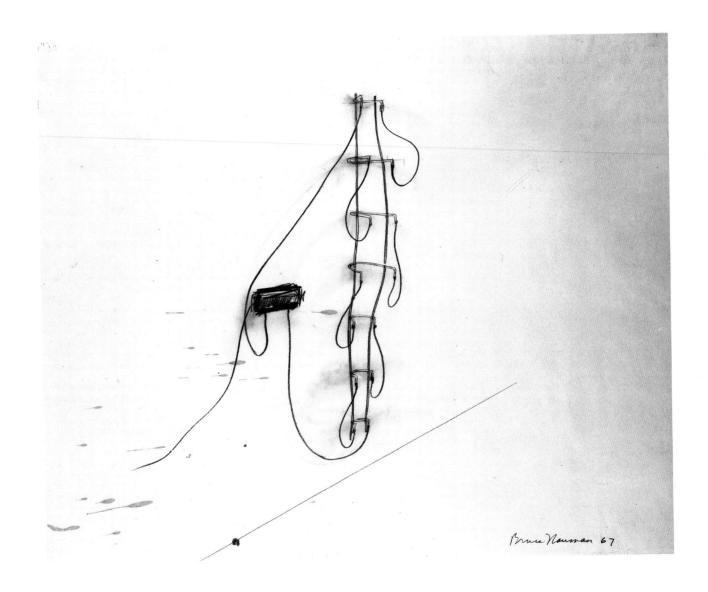

TOP:
Untitled (Study for *Parallax Room*). 1971
Inscribed: "Any distance over 2 or 3
meters to/ end wall./ These ends must be/
fairly clean and/ sharp,/ partition walls are
smooth, surface wall/ board painted white.
Spacing must be/ carefully followed./
Walls don't necessarily have to extend to/
ceiling but should be 2½ or 3 meters high."
Pencil on paper
19¾ × 26" (49.4 × 66 cm)
Collection Sonnabend, New York

BOTTOM:
Untitled (Study for *Parallax Room with
Three Horizontal Bars*). 1971
Inscribed: "Angle of visibility/ All white or
all black/ Eye level."
Pencil on paper
20 × 31¼" (50.5 × 79 cm)
The Panza Collection, Milan

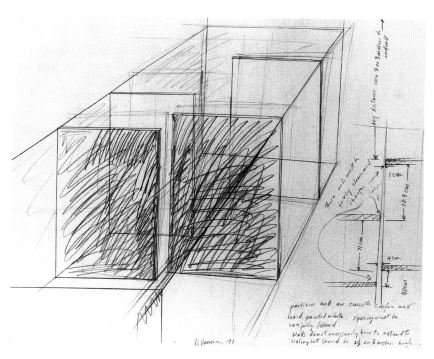

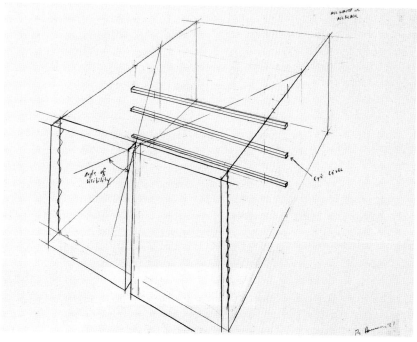

Untitled (White Bar). 1971
Wood
$5\frac{1}{2}'' \times 14'10'' \times 2\frac{3}{4}''$ (14 × 452 × 7 cm),
size variable
Collection Dorothee and Konrad Fischer,
Düsseldorf, West Germany

Untitled. 1967
Inscribed: "Drawing of the Brown Crayon
Box/ completed Summer 1966/ destroyed
Fall 1966."
Pencil on paper
19 × 24″ (48.3 × 61 cm)
Oeffentliche Kunstsammlung, Basel
Depositum Emanuel Hoffmann Foundation

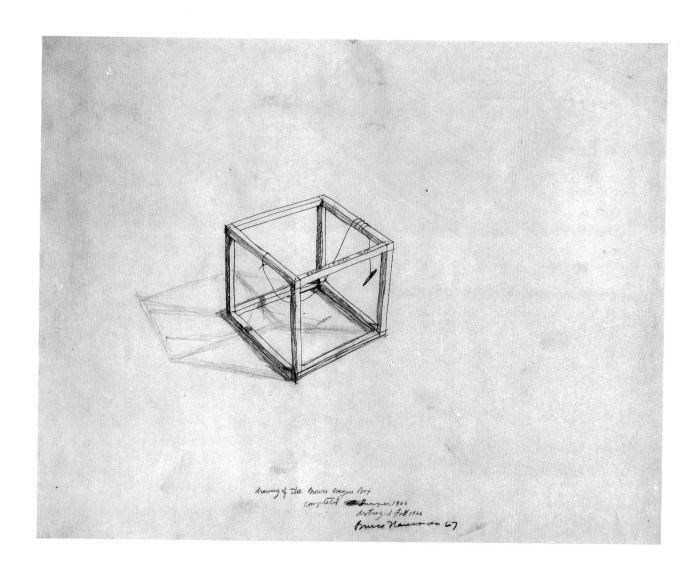

Untitled (Study for Cast-Iron Model of
a Large Buried Chamber: Triangle to
Circle to Square). 1981
Inscribed: "Vertical/ horizontal/ $23\frac{1}{2}°$ 1:100
scale drwng for cast iron/ for tunnel."
Charcoal, powdered charcoal, and chalk
on taped paper
$37\frac{3}{8}'' \times 11'9\frac{3}{4}''$ (95 × 365 cm)
Rijksmuseum Kröller-Müller,
Otterlo, the Netherlands

TOP:
*Diamond Africa with Tuned
Steel Chair.* 1981
Pencil, pastel, charcoal, and collage
on paper
52″ × 6′3½″ (132 × 191.8 cm)
Private collection, Krefeld, West Germany

BOTTOM:
Musical Chairs. 1983
Charcoal and conté crayon on paper
68″ × 6′8″ (175 × 203 cm)
Collection Frits Becht, Naarden,
the Netherlands

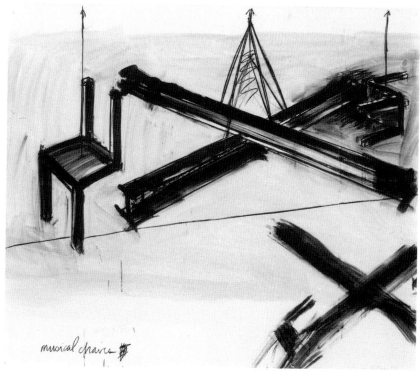

American Violence. 1983
Pencil on taped paper
30 × 39″ (76.2 × 99 cm)
Collection J. W. Froehlich,
Stuttgart, West Germany

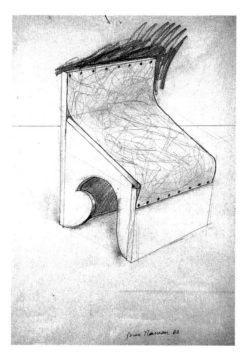

TOP LEFT:
WILLIAM T. WILEY
Slant Step Becomes Rhino,
Rhino Becomes Slant Step. 1966
Plaster, acrylic paint, and metal chain
22 × 12 × 12″ (55.9 × 30.5 × 30.5 cm)
Collection Ron Wagner
Extended Loan to Richard L. Nelson
Gallery and The Fine Arts Collection,
University of California at Davis

TOP RIGHT:
The Original Slant Step: Wood and
Linoleum. 1966
Ink, wash, and pencil on paper
22 × 18¼″ (56 × 46.5 cm)
Oeffentliche Kunstsammlung, Basel
Depositum Emanuel Hoffmann Foundation

BOTTOM:
Mount Carmel Salvage Shop, Lovell Street,
Mill Valley, California, where William T.
Wiley found the Slant Step in 1965

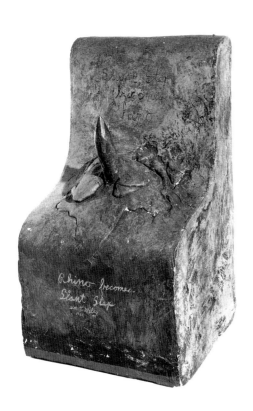

Mold for a Modernized Slant Step
(foreground). 1966
Installed Nicholas Wilder Gallery, Los
Angeles, May–June 1966
Plaster
22 × 17 × 12″ (56 × 43 × 30.4 cm)
Collection Gerald S. Elliott, Chicago

Shoulder. 1966
Charcoal on paper
35¾ × 30½″ (90.7 × 77.4 cm)
Collection Mr. and Mrs. Joseph Pulitzer, Jr.,
St. Louis

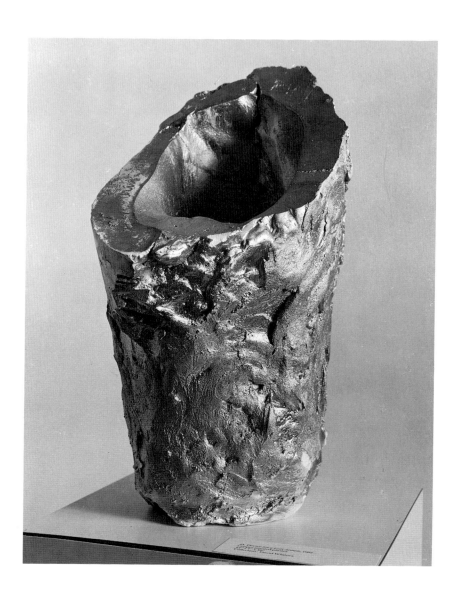

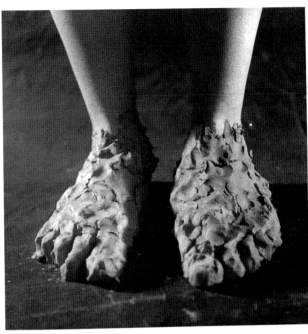

Untitled (Shoulder Sketches) 1967
Pen, ink, colored pencil, and
ballpoint pen on paper
16¾ × 24¼″ (42.5 × 61.6 cm)
Collection the artist

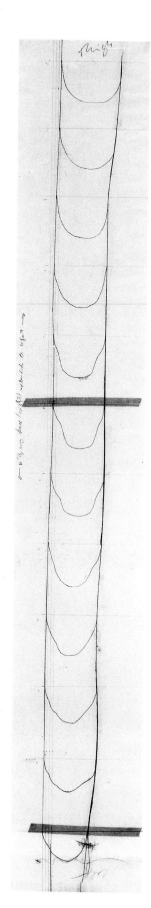

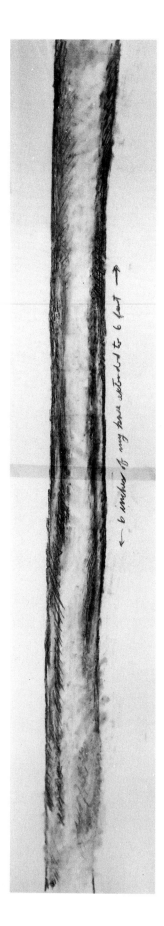

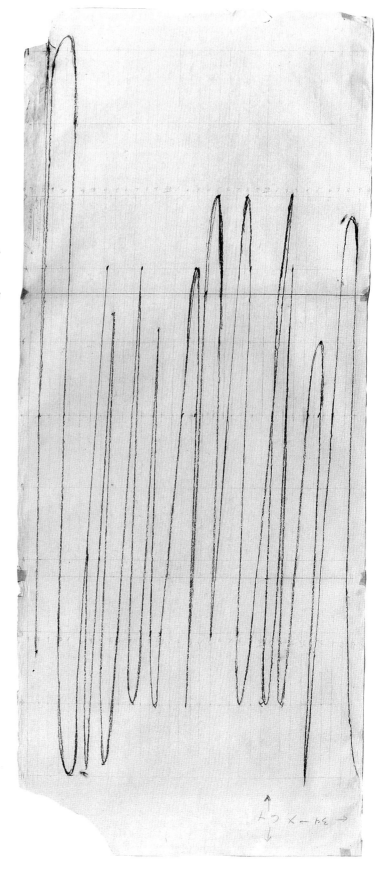

*My Last Name Exaggerated Fourteen Times
Vertically.* 1967
Neon tubing with clear-glass tubing
suspension frame
63 × 33 × 2″ (160 × 84 × 5 cm)
The Panza Collection, Milan

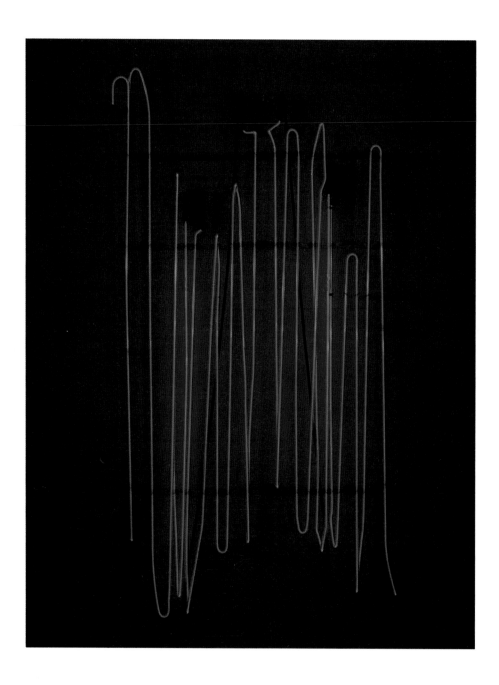

Tree Standing on Three Shoulder Joints. 1967–68
Plaster and tree branch
Destroyed

Tree Standing on Three Shoulder Joints. 1967
Ink and watercolor on paper
19 × 27¼" (48.3 × 69.2 cm)
Collection Joseph A. Helman, New York

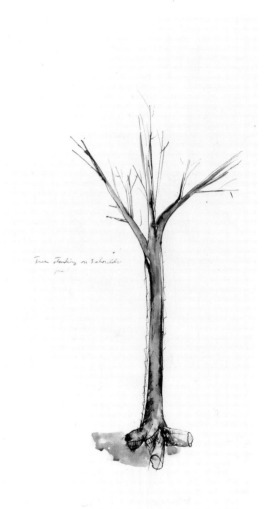

Large Knot Becoming an Ear (Knot Hearing Well). 1967
Pencil on paper
34⅛ × 27⅜" (86.5 × 69.5 cm)
Oeffentliche Kunstsammlung, Basel
Donation Capsugel AG

H. C. WESTERMANN
The Big Change. 1963–64
Laminated-pine plywood
56 × 12 × 12" (142.2 × 30.5 × 30.5 cm)
Private collection, New York

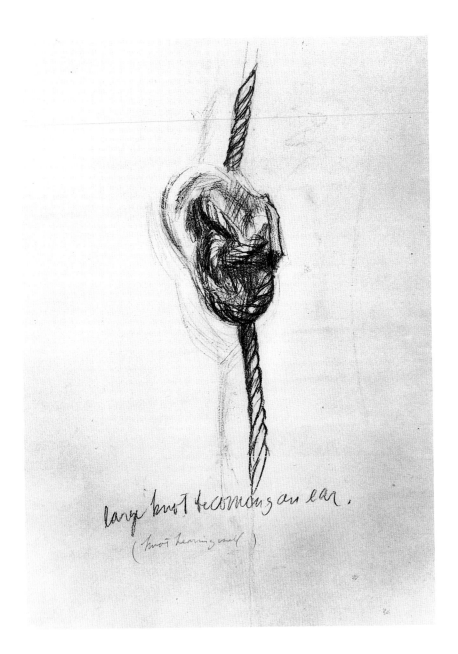

Letter to Bill Allan: Three Well-Known
Knots (Square Knot, Bowline, and
Clove Hitch). 1967
Photographs mounted on paper
Archives of American Art,
Smithsonian Institution, Washington, D.C.
William George Allan Papers

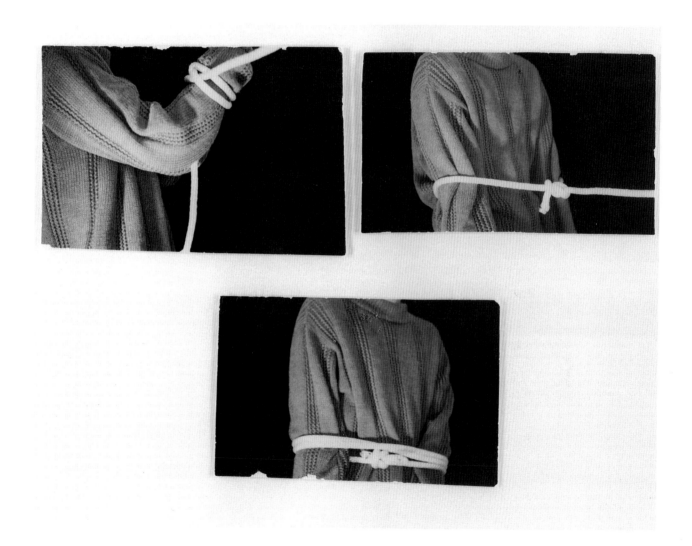

Square Knot (H. C. Westermann). 1967
Charcoal on paper
26¾ × 27¼″ (68 × 69.5 cm)
Private collection, Geneva

Untitled (Square Knot). 1967
Charcoal and watercolor on paper
27½ × 30¼″ (69.8 × 76.8 cm)
Private collection, New York

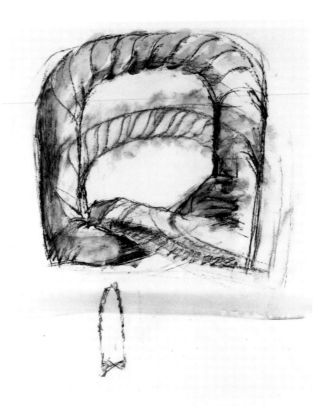

Untitled. 1967
Rope and wax over plaster
17 × 26 × 4½″ (43.2 × 66 × 11.4 cm)
Courtesy Thomas Ammann, Zürich

Westermann's Ear. 1967
Plaster and rope
Ca. 8'6" × 6" (259 × 15.2 cm)
Museum Ludwig, Cologne, West Germany

TOP LEFT:
Seated Storage Capsule (for H. M.). 1966
Pastel and acrylic on paper
42 × 35¾" (106.7 × 90.8 cm)
Collection Elizabeth and Michael Rea,
New York

TOP RIGHT:
Study for *Henry Moore Trap*. 1966–67
Crayon and acrylic on paper
42 × 33" (106.7 × 83.8 cm)
Present location unknown

BOTTOM LEFT:
HENRY MOORE
Crowd Looking at a Tied-Up Object. 1942
Chalk, crayon, watercolor, and pen and
ink on paper
17 x 22" (42.2 x 55.9 cm)
The Henry Moore Foundation

BOTTOM RIGHT:
H. C. WESTERMANN
The Mysteriously Abandoned New Home
1958
Pine
50½" (128.3 cm) high
The Art Institute of Chicago

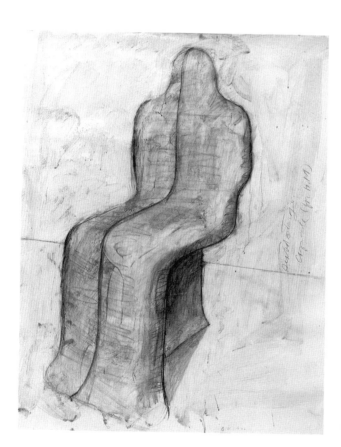

Henry Moore Trap. 1966
Pencil on paper
42 × 30″ (106.7 × 76.2 cm)
Hallen für neue Kunst,
Schaffhausen, Switzerland
Crex Collection

Seated Storage Capsule for H. M.
Made of Metallic Plastic. 1966
Pencil and crayon on paper
40 × 35″ (101.6 × 88.9 cm)
Hallen für neue Kunst,
Schaffhausen, Switzerland
Crex Collection

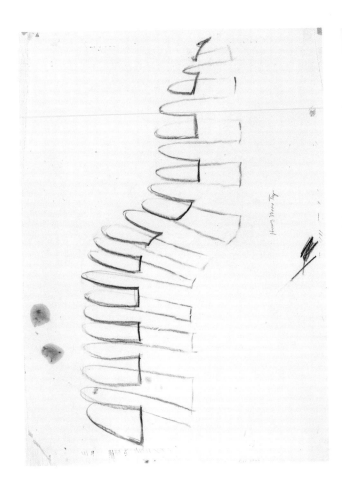

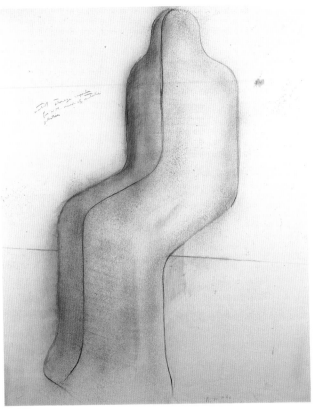

Bound to Fail. 1966
Charcoal on paper
Present location unknown

Henry Moore Bound to Fail. 1967 (cast 1970)
From an edition of nine
Cast iron
$25\frac{1}{2} \times 24 \times 2\frac{1}{2}''$ (64.8 $\times$ 61 $\times$ 6.4 cm)

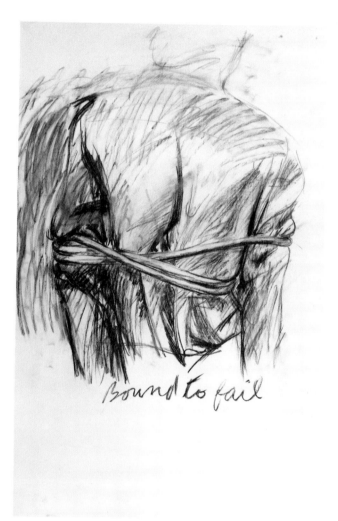

Light Trap for Henry Moore, No. 1. 1967
Black-and-white photograph
67 × 40″ (170.2 × 101.6 cm)
Present location unknown

Light Trap for Henry Moore, No. 2. 1967
Black-and-white photograph
67 × 40″ (170.2 × 101.6 cm)
Hallen für neue Kunst,
Schaffhausen, Switzerland
Crex Collection

William T. Wiley or Ray Johnson
Trap. 1967
Black-and-white photograph
67 × 40″ (170.2 × 101.6 cm)
Collection Cy Twombly, Rome

Failing to Levitate in the Studio. 1966
Black-and-white photograph
20 × 24″ (50.8 × 61 cm)
Collection the artist

Love Me Tender, Move Te Lender. 1966
Pencil on paper
38 × 25″ (86.5 × 63.5 cm)
The St. Louis Art Museum

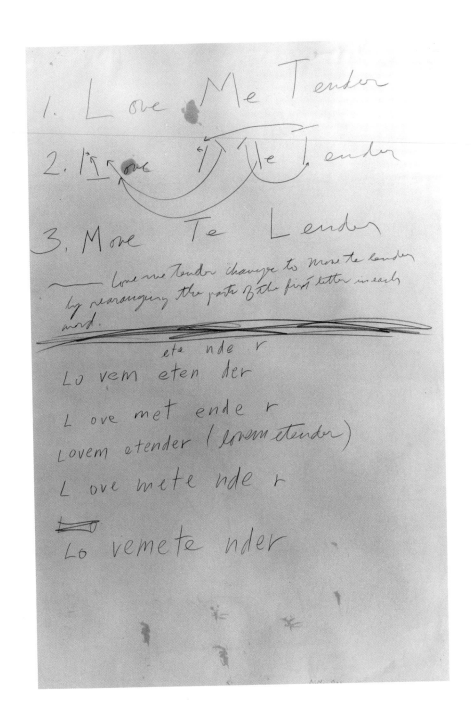

TOP:
Sugar Ragus, Racus Sugar (detail). 1973
Pencil and collaged Presstype on paper
$23\frac{1}{8} \times 29''$ (58.8 × 73.7 cm)
Collection Sonnabend, New York

BOTTOM:
Sugar Ragus (detail). 1972
Pencil on paper
18 × 24″ (45.7 × 60.9 cm)
Private collection, Switzerland

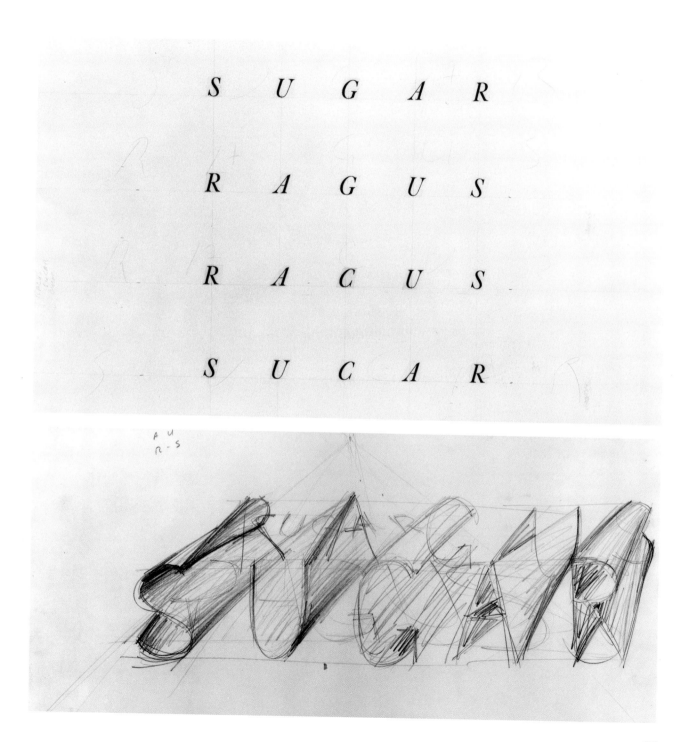

** B S T * T U **. 1967–68
Inscribed: "Stars are black, letters
are white or clear/ * * B S T * T U * *."
Watercolor on paper
Destroyed

None Sing Neon Sign. 1970
From an edition of six
Neon tubing
None Sing: 5⅝ × 23¾ × 1⅝″ (14.3 × 59.4
× 4.2 cm); Neon Sign: ca. 6 × 23¾ × 1½″
(15.2 × 59.4 × 4.2 cm)

Suite Substitute. 1968
From an edition of three
Neon tubing with clear-glass tubing
suspension frame
5¼ × 30 × 3″ (13.2 × 127 × 12.7 cm)

Sweet Suite Substitute. 1968
From an edition of three
Neon tubing with clear-glass tubing
suspension frame
$5\frac{1}{4} \times 29\frac{3}{4} \times 4\frac{3}{4}''$ (13.3 × 75.6 × 12 cm)

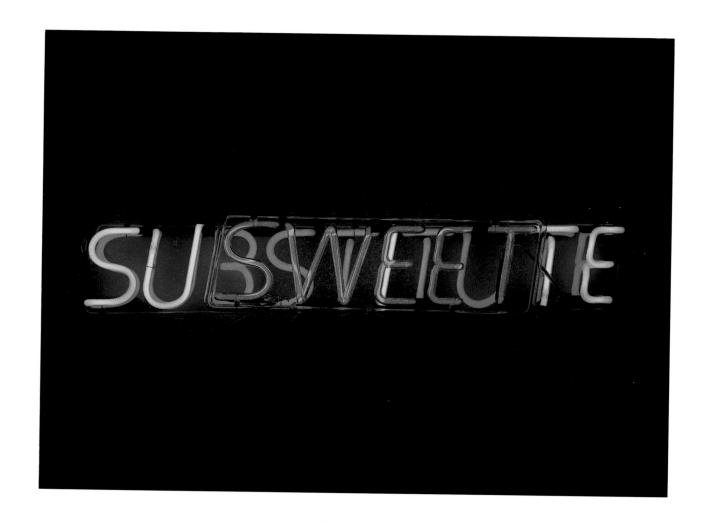

Raw War. 1968
Inscribed: "WAR 1/ WAR 2/ WAR 3/ Sign to hang when there is a war on—/ This size or up to 6 feet long./ ~~Sequence-is-~~ 1+2+3+off+1+2+3+-off+1—etc.— ~~About-1-see-or-so-moves-½-½-see.~~ Or ½ sec or less flash on 1 then off then flash 2 then off then flash 3 then/ off and repeat etc./ 'Off' should be about 2 seconds or more."
Pencil, colored pencil, and watercolor on paper
30 × 22″ (75.5 × 55.8 cm)
Private collection, Munich

OPPOSITE:
Raw War. 1970
From an edition of six
Neon tubing with clear-glass tubing suspension frame
6½ × 17⅛ × 1½″ (16.5 × 43.5 × 3.8 cm)

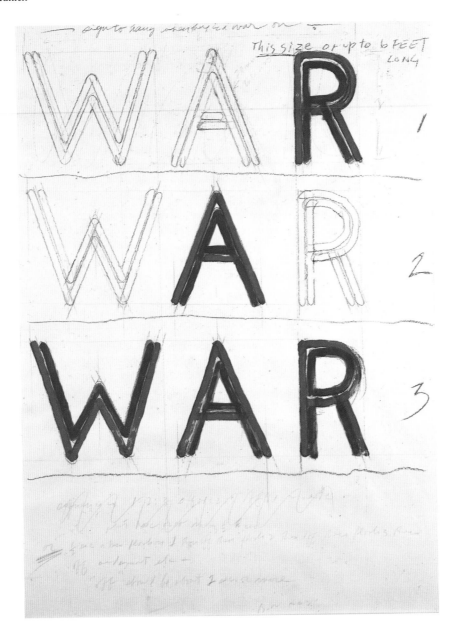

Four phases from *American Violence*
1981–82
Neon tubing with clear-glass tubing
suspension frame
6'6" × 62" × 3¼" (198.1 × 157.5 ×
7.9 cm)
Collection William J. Hokin, Chicago

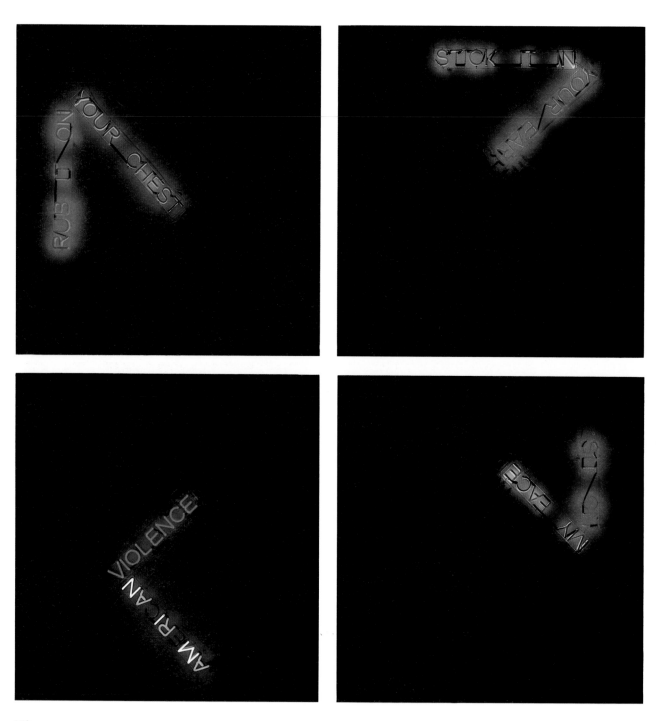

Life Death, Knows Doesn't Know. 1983
Neon tubing with clear-glass tubing
suspension frame
Ca. 8'11½" × 8'11" (273 × 271.8 cm)
The Saatchi Collection, London

TOP:
Violins Violence Silence. 1982
Inscribed: "VIOLINS VIOLENCE SILENCE/ not
particularly to scale/ about 1:3. Colors
approximate."
Pencil, chalk, and colored pastel on taped
paper
$26\frac{1}{2} \times 8'10\frac{1}{2}''$ (67.4 × 270.5 cm)
Collection Angela Westwater, New York

BOTTOM:
Violins Violence Silence (Exterior Version)
1981–82
Neon tubing with clear-glass tubing
suspension frame
Letters 48″ (122 cm) high
The Baltimore Museum of Art
Gift of Leo Castelli Gallery and
Sperone Westwater Fischer, Inc.,
New York

One Hundred Live and Die. 1984
Neon tubing with clear-glass tubing
suspension frame, mounted on four panels
9'10" × 11'1¼" × 21" (299.7 × 33.9 ×
53.3 cm)
Collection Susan and Lewis Manilow,
Chicago

Study for *A Rose Has No Teeth*. 1966
Inscribed: " 'A Rose Has No Teeth.'/ Lead
or bronze plaque to be attached/ to a tree
in the woods so that it will/ be grown
over."
Pencil on paper
18⅞ × 24″ (47.9 × 60.9 cm)
Collection Sonnabend, New York

RIGHT:
A Rose Has No Teeth. 1966
Lead plaque
12 × 12 × 4″ (30.6 × 30.6 × 10.2 cm)
Courtesy Thomas Ammann, Zürich

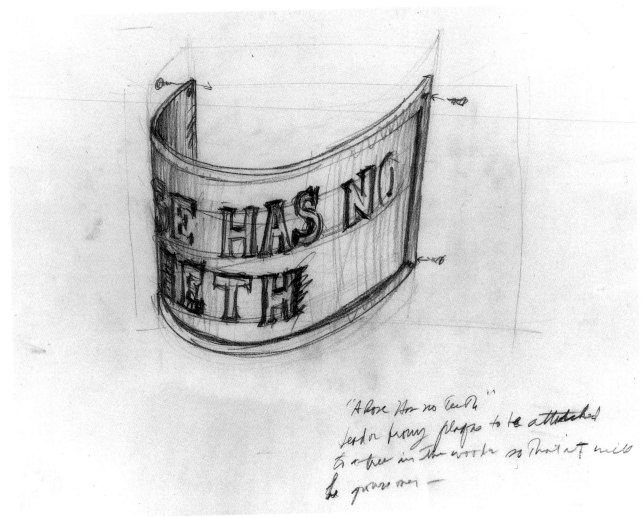

162

The Negative Shape of the Right Half of My Body Carved into a Living Tree. 1966–67
Inscribed: "The negative shape of the right/ half of my body carved into a living tree./ The cut should be sealed so the tree will not/ die. In some years the tree will grow/ at least partly closed./ (If I were to stand in the/ spot for several years, my body would be partly closed in by the tree and I could/ not get away.)"
Ink and wash on paper
Present location unknown

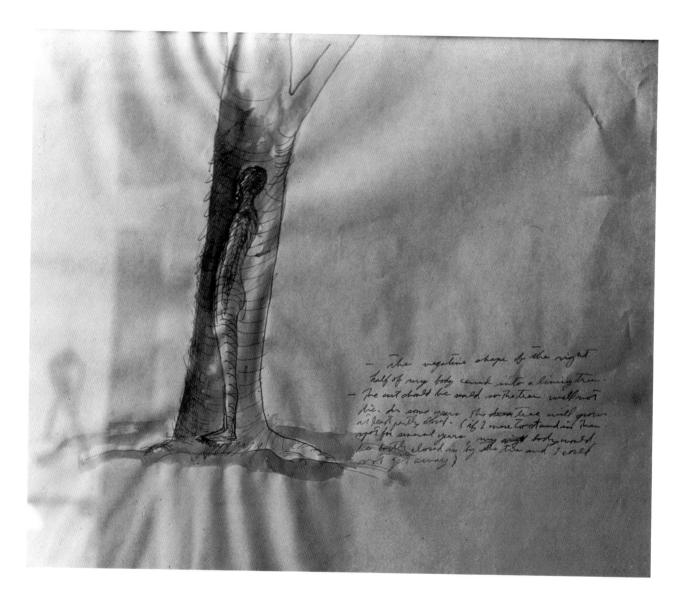

First Poem Piece. 1968
Engraved: "You May Not Want to Be
Here . . ."
Steel plate
Ca. $\frac{1}{2}$ × 60 × 60″ (1.8 × 152.4 ×
152.4 cm)
Rijksmuseum Kröller Müller,
Otterlo, the Netherlands
Formerly collection Martin Visser

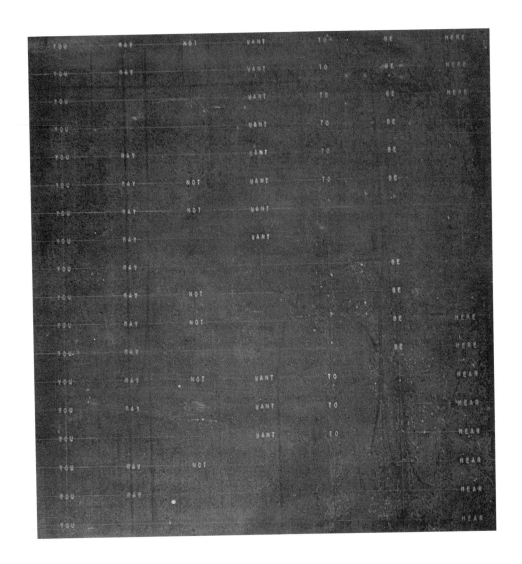

Second Poem Piece. 1969
Engraved: "You May Not Want to Screw
Here . . ."
From an edition of three
Steel plate
$\frac{1}{2}$ × 60 × 60″ (1.8 × 152.4 × 152.4 cm)

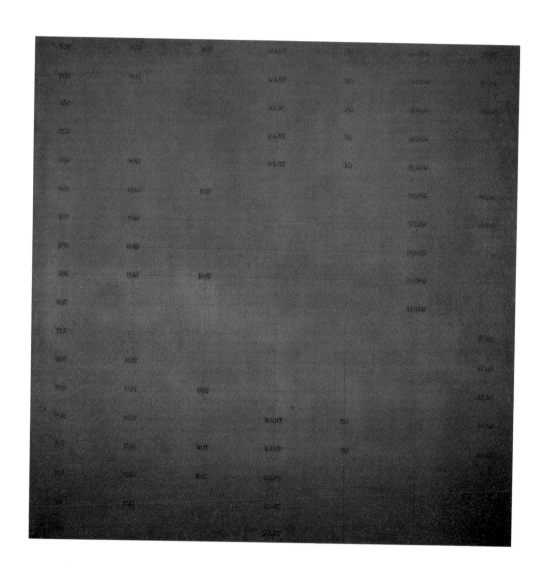

TOP TO BOTTOM:
Studies for *Seven Virtues and Seven Vices.*
1983
Collection Martin Visser,
Bergeijk, the Netherlands

Avarice Justice, Gluttony Temperance
Pencil, conté crayon, and charcoal on four
sheets of paper taped together
30¼″ × 13′4″ (76.8 × 406.5 cm)

Pride Prudence
Ink on two sheets of paper taped together
30¼″ × 6′8″ (76.8 × 203.3 cm)

Faith Lust, Hope Envy, Charity Sloth
Pencil and wash on four sheets of paper
taped together
30¼″ × 13′4″ (76.8 × 406.5 cm)

Fortitude Anger
Pencil and ink on two sheets of paper
taped together
30¼″ × 6′8″ (76.8 × 203.3 cm)

TOP TO BOTTOM AND OVERLEAF:
Five stones from *Seven Virtues and
Seven Vices.* 1984
Carved granite
Edward R. Broida Trust, Los Angeles

Faith Lust
$23\frac{3}{4} \times 47\frac{1}{4}''$ (60.3 × 120 cm)

Justice Avarice
$23\frac{3}{4} \times 60\frac{5}{8}''$ (60.3 × 154 cm)

Hope Envy
$23\frac{3}{4} \times 47\frac{1}{4}''$ (60.3 × 120 cm)

Seven Virtues and Seven Vices. 1984
Carved granite
Edward R. Broida Trust, Los Angeles

Temperance Gluttony
$23\frac{3}{4}'' \times 7'10\frac{1}{4}''$ (60.3 × 240 cm)

Fortitude Anger
$23\frac{3}{4}'' \times 6'8\frac{3}{4}''$ (60.3 × 205.1 cm)

Five stones from *Seven Virtues and Seven Vices.* 1984
Installation view, Sperone Westwater,
New York, October 6–November 3, 1984

TOP LEFT:
Study for *A Cast of the Space under My Chair.* 1968
Inscribed: "Space under my (steel) chair in Düsseldorf/ (from 1965–68)/ for Geertjan Visser."
Ballpoint pen on paper
$23\frac{3}{4} \times 16\frac{3}{4}''$ (60.5 × 42.5 cm)
Collection Geertjan Visser, on loan to the Rijksmuseum Kröller-Müller,
Otterlo, the Netherlands

TOP RIGHT:
A Cast of the Space under My Chair. 1966–68
Concrete
$17\frac{1}{2} \times 15\frac{3}{8} \times 14\frac{5}{8}''$ (44.5 × 39 × 37 cm)
Collection Geertjan Visser, on loan to the Rijksmuseum Kröller-Müller,
Otterlo, the Netherlands

BOTTOM LEFT:
MARCEL DUCHAMP
Why Not Sneeze Rose Sélavy? 1921
Readymade: painted metal birdcage, marble cubes, thermometer, and cuttlebone
$4\frac{1}{2} \times 8\frac{5}{8} \times 6\frac{3}{8}''$ (11.4 × 21.9 × 16.2 cm)
Philadelphia Museum of Art
Louise and Walter Arensberg Collection

BOTTOM RIGHT:
JASPER JOHNS
Painted Bronze. 1960
Bronze $5\frac{1}{2} \times 8 \times 4\frac{3}{4}''$ (14 × 20.3 × 12 cm)
Museum Ludwig, Cologne, West Germany

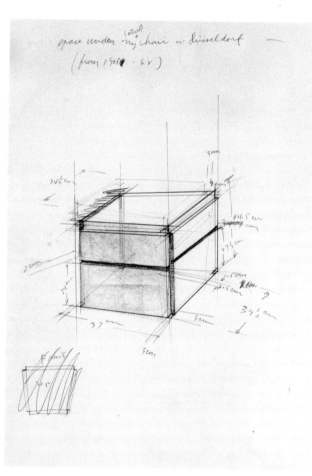

Film with Sound: 1. Stamping,
2. Beckett Walk? 1968–69
Pencil and colored pencil on paper
11 × 8½″ (28 × 21.6 cm)
Private collection, New York

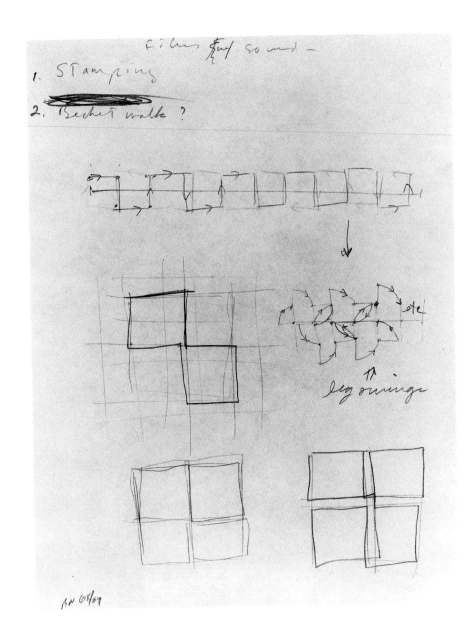

TOP:
Untitled (Study for *Slow Angle Walk*).
1968–69
Inscribed: "Right leg swings and steps/
left leg pivot and/ step/ first/ swing
to r 3 times/ then L 3 times/ Repeat."
Pencil and colored pencil on paper
8½ × 11″ (21.6 × 28 cm)
Collection the artist

BOTTOM:
Still from *Playing a Note on the Violin
While I Walk around the Studio.* 1968
Film, 16 mm, black and white, sound,
8–10 min., ca. 400′

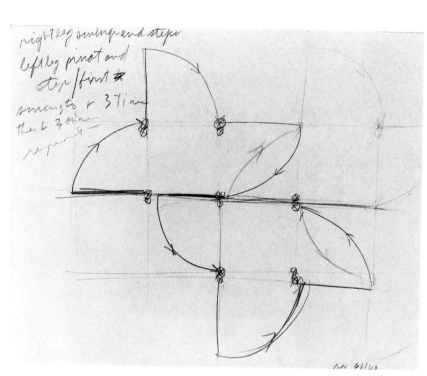

Stills from *Slow Angle Walk*. 1968
Videotape, black and white, sound,
60 min.

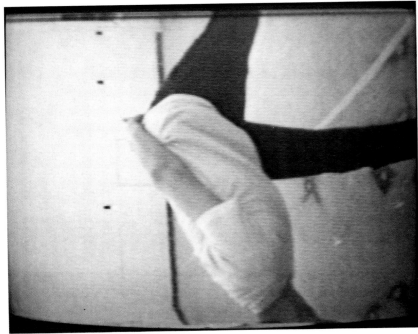

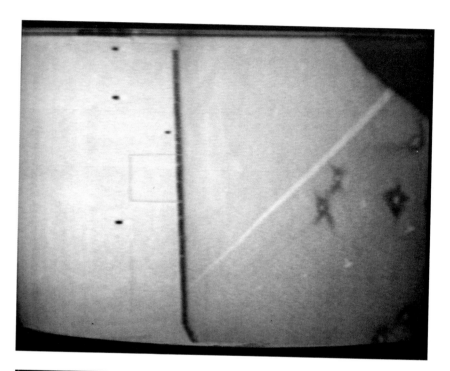

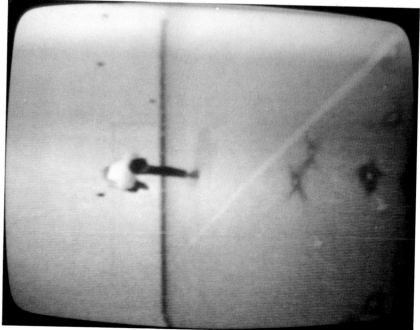

A Cubic Foot of Steel Pressed between My Palms. 1968
Steel
24 × 24 × 3" (61 × 61 × 7.6 cm)
Leo Castelli Gallery, New York

Untitled (Study for Unfinished Sculpture)
1968
Inscribed: "Cubic foot of/ steel pressed
between/ my palms/ Cubic foot/ of steel/
Cubic foot/ of steel pressed/ between
2 cubic'/ of steel/ Cubic foot/ of steel/
For Konrad—Dorothee/ unfinished/
Sculpture, 1968."
Pencil on paper
11⅝ × 8¼" (29.5 × 21 cm)
Collection Dorothee and Konrad Fischer,
Düsseldorf, West Germany

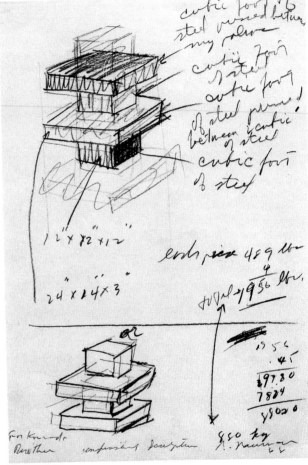

LEFT:
Untitled (Study for Unfinished Sculpture)
1968
Inscribed: "Plain/ steel plate/ steel plate
squeezed between my palms/ some (soft)
things from my pocket/ photo of 2 balls/
photo of my violin/ photo of my face/
several 60 cm sq × 3 cm thick steel
plates/ with things between them—/ each
plate 122 kg./ unfinished sculpt. drawing/
For Konrad + Dorothee, 1968."

Ballpoint pen and pencil on paper
19¾ × 15¾" (50 × 39 cm)
Collection Dorothee and Konrad Fischer,
Düsseldorf, West Germany

RIGHT:
Untitled (Study for Unfinished Sculpture).
1968
Inscribed: "5. Steel block/ 4. steel block
pressed/ between my palms/ 3. steel block/
2. steel block pressed between/ two steel

blocks/ 1. steel block/ For Konrad/ and
Dorothee/ unfinished sculpt. drawing,
1968."
Pencil on paper
11¾ × 8¼" (29.5 × 21 cm)
Collection Dorothee and Konrad Fischer,
Düsseldorf, West Germany

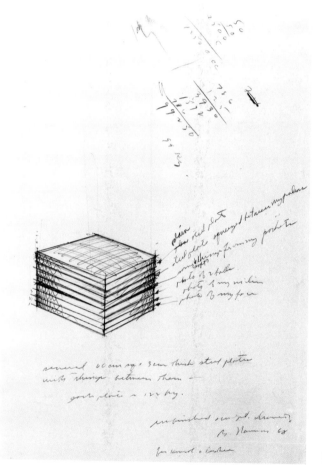

TOP:
Untitled (After *Corridor Installation with Mirror*). 1971
Inscribed: "Mirrors 5'5" high/ 16'/ walls 12' high (to/ ceiling)/ No light inside piece from/ above: all reflected through front of corridors./ 34'/ San Jose installation— May 1971."
Pencil on paper
23 × 29" (58.4 × 73.6 cm)
Collection the artist

BOTTOM:
Untitled (Study for *Corridor Installation with Mirror*). 1970
Inscribed: "Wall 8' high/ Mirror 4' high only/ Black lines indicate walls/ Red lines indicate reflected image in mirror."
Pencil and felt-tipped pen on paper
23 × 29" (58.4 × 73.6 cm)
Collection the artist

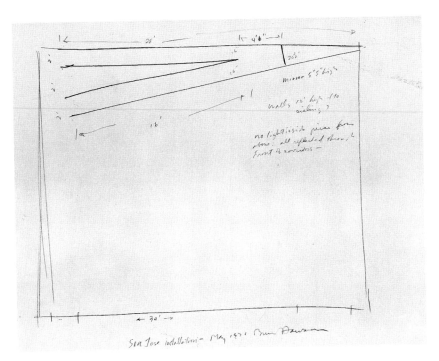

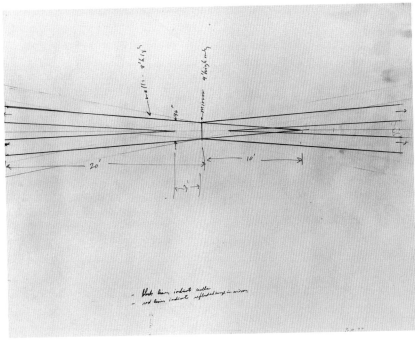

Corridor Installation with Mirror. 1970
Installed San Jose State College,
San Jose, California, May 1970
Plasterboard, wood frame, and mirror
Wall, 8′ (243.84 cm) high; mirror,
54″ (137.16 cm) high
Destroyed

Kassel Corridor: Elliptical Space. 1972
Reconstructed Museum of Contemporary
Art, Los Angeles, 1986
Two curved wood-and-wallboard walls
Outer: 12 × 47′ (365.8 × 1,432.6 cm);
inner: 12 × 46′6″ (365.8 × 1,417.3 cm);
at center, 27″ (68.6 cm) apart, tapering
to 4″ (10.2 cm) at either end
The Panza Collection, Milan

TOP AND BOTTOM:
House Divided. 1983
Cement structure
14′3″ × 30′ × 20′ (434.3 × 914.4 × 609.6 cm)
Nathan Manilow Sculpture Park, Governors State University, University Park, Illinois

TOP:
Untitled (Three Circular Tunnels I). 1977
Inscribed: "Open where ○ meets surface/
(off drawing)."
Charcoal and crayon on two sheets of
paper taped together
63″ × 6′11″ (150 × 211 cm)
Rijksmuseum Kröller Müller,
Otterlo, the Netherlands

BOTTOM:
Untitled (Three Circular Tunnels II). 1977
Inscribed: "Connected circular/ tunnel
ramp/ with △ cross sections/ entrance to
tunnel/ surface."
Pencil and charcoal on two sheets of paper
taped together
62¹⁄₈″ × 7′¼″ (158 × 214 cm)
Rijksmuseum Kröller-Müller,
Otterlo, the Netherlands

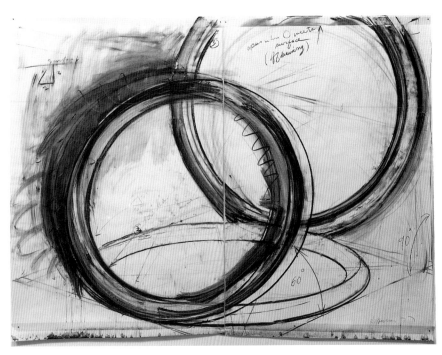

Untitled (Study for Trench, Shaft, and
Tunnel). 1977
Inscribed: "Tunnel entrance/ open/ top/
surface/ entrance to tunnel."
Pencil and charcoal on two sheets of paper
taped together
$61\frac{3}{8}'' \times 7'1\frac{1}{4}''$ (156 × 214 cm)
Rijksmuseum Kröller-Müller,
Otterlo, the Netherlands

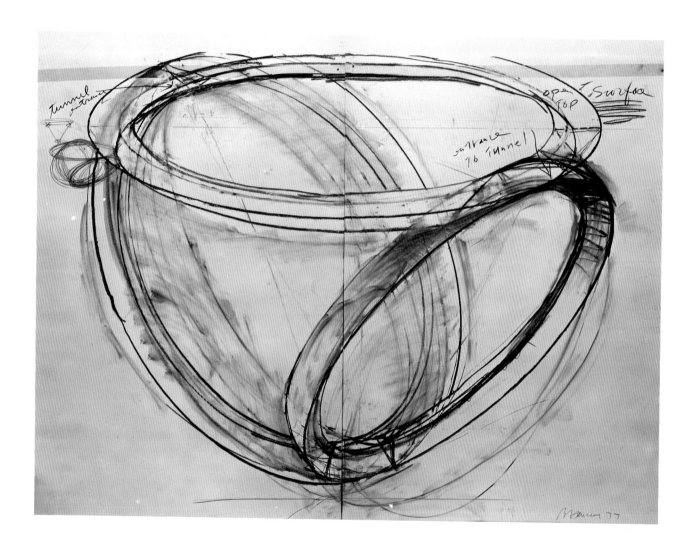

Model for Trench, Shaft, and Tunnel. 1978
Fiberglass
9'10⅛" × 9'10⅛" × 10'9⅞" (300 × 300 × 330 cm)
Hallen für neue Kunst,
Schaffhausen, Switzerland
Crex Collection

Untitled (Model for Trench, Shaft, and
Tunnel). 1978
Fiberglass
10'9⅞" × 9'10⅛" × 9'10⅛" (330 × 300 ×
300 cm)
The Saatchi Collection, London

Untitled (Study for *Musical Chairs: Studio
Version*). 1983
Inscribed: "A + D hang about 1′ apart/
V vertical dist.)/ Welded square.
Take/ chair from dream passage/ Cast iron
chair from South America?"
Charcoal on paper
37¾ × 49¼″ (95 × 125 cm)
Collection Franz Meyer, Basel

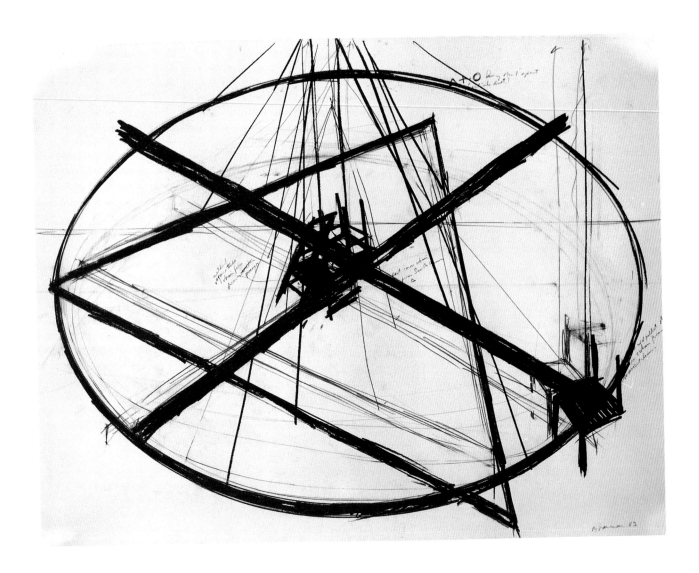

Musical Chairs: Studio Version. 1983
Installed Galerie Konrad Fischer,
Düsseldorf, November 1983
Wood, aluminum, three chairs,
and steel cable
$51\frac{1}{8}''$ × $13'9\frac{3}{8}''$ × $13'9\frac{3}{8}''$ (130
× 420 × 420 cm)
Hallen für neue Kunst,
Schaffhausen, Switzerland
Private collection

Punch and Judy: Kick in the Groin, Slap in the Face. 1985
Neon tubing with clear-glass tubing suspension frame, mounted on aluminum panel
6′5″ × 61″ × 14″ (195.6 × 154.9 × 35.6 cm)
Collection Claude Berri, Paris

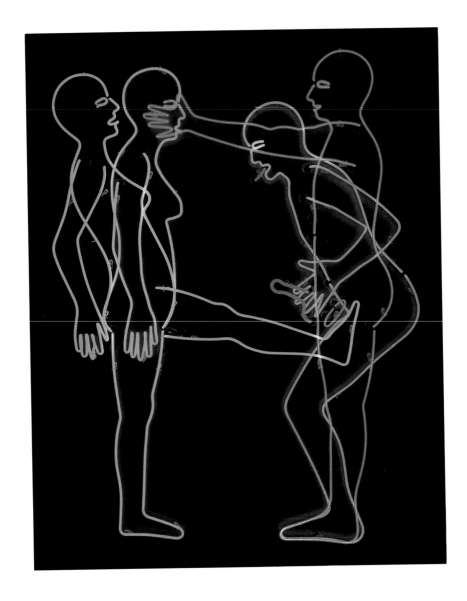

Crime and Punishment (Study for *Punch and Judy*). 1985
Pencil, charcoal, and watercolor on paper
6'5" × 60⅝" (195.6 × 154 cm)
Oeffentliche Kunstsammlung, Basel

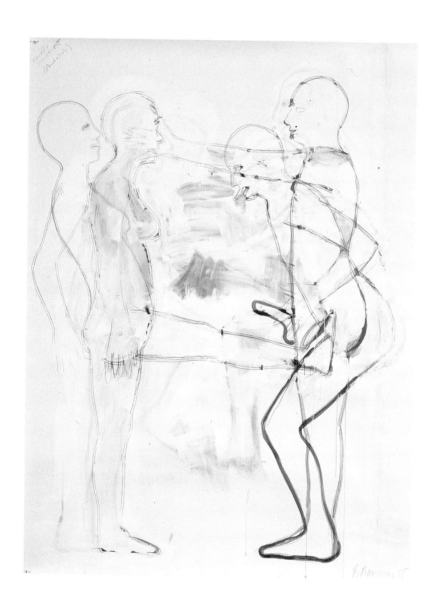

Neon Porno Chain. 1984
Inscribed: "Neon Porno chain/ Figures life
size. Frieze is about 4' high × 25' long/
Butt moves and tongue moves/ butt moves
up + down/ arm moves in asshole/ etc./
tongue moves/ head moves on/ penis/
pelvis moves/ (+ penis)/ hands/ move/
on/ tits/ toe moves in/ vagina/ Chain Left
to Right or Right to Left/ Female: 2/ 6/ 7/
1/ Male: 1/ 3/ 4/ 5."
Ink on paper
11 × 8½" (28 × 21.6 cm)
Private collection, Basel

Antonio Pollaiuolo
Battle of Ten Naked Men. 15th C.
Engraving
The Metropolitan Museum of Art,
New York
Purchase, 1917, Joseph Pulitzer Bequest

Circle of Death? 1986
Inscribed: "Circle of death?/ Death by
mob violence/ (baseball bats)/ Film or
video/ (Dance?)/ 6 figures + victim/
Figures step forward and/ hit with bats—/
grunt at same time/ in/ 1. clockwise order/
2. counterclockwise/ 3. all pairs/ 4. all
together/ 5. random/ (or a rondelet/ in
music—)/ (counterpoint/ Victim flashes
+/ rolls over? (or/ mob violence w/
baseball bats./—, △, □, ○—victim in a
bag.)/ or—choreograph—1 person—
another enters + joins/ + another etc. 1,
pair, △, ○, □, mob/ or—2 gangs—no
individual victim. 'Greek phalanx.' "
Ink and ballpoint pen on two sheets of
paper taped together
17 × 11″ (43 × 27.9 cm)
Private collection, Basel

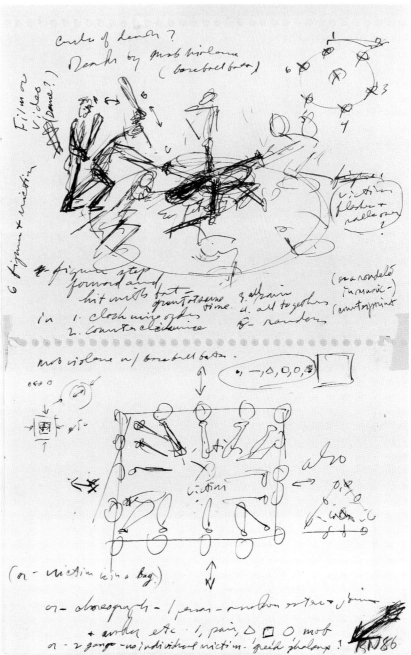

Stills from *Violent Incident*. 1986
Videotape from installation with four
videotapes and twelve monitors
The Saatchi Collection, London

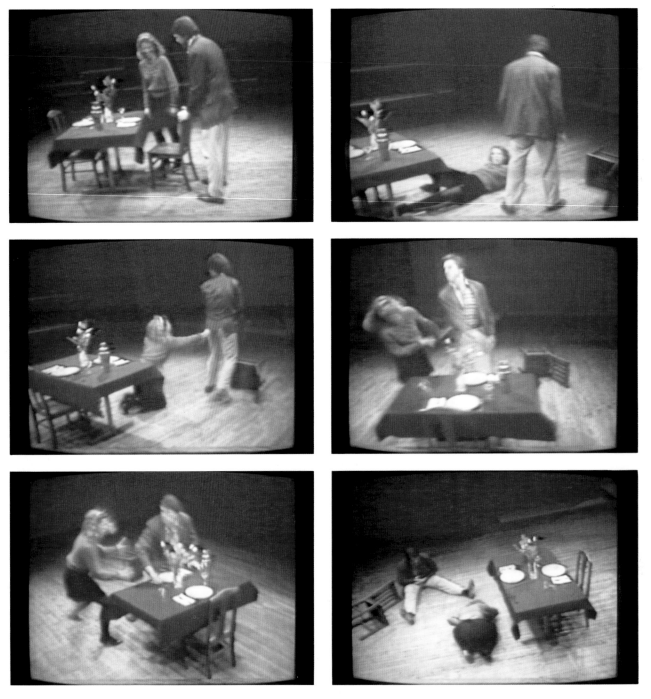

Left or Standing, Standing or Left Standing

During the first half of the 1970s, Nauman created several installations for which he wrote accompanying texts. These writings appeared in exhibition or else formed the invitation for the show. As in some of his earlier corridors and later tunnels, Nauman set up a polarity in these installations between public and private spaces, using the resulting tension to achieve an edge. "When you are alone, you accept the space by filling it with your presence," he would say in the 1979 *Vanguard* interview, but "as soon as someone else comes into view, you withdraw and protect yourself."[1] The visitor at such an installation, getting drawn into the game of exposure and withdrawal and trying to discover the rules set by the artist, usually became even more confused upon reading the accompanying text. Nauman's writings functioned as independent, lyrical entities by themselves, yet played with the mind in their seeming relationship to the physical and mental experiences one got from walking through the installations. The match-up was not parallel but skewed; texts and installations were analogous on one level, but deviated on all others, much in the way Nauman played with the viewer's expectations by setting up discrepancies between poetic titles and sculptures, shifting between what one knows and does not know.

In making a poster for the exhibition of *Installation with Yellow Lights* (p. 199) in 1971 at the Leo Castelli Gallery, 420 West Broadway, New York, Nauman found it necessary to use words rather than a picture or sketch of the room to define the work; he composed *Left or Standing, Standing or Left Standing* (p. 198). "Perhaps the space was insufficient," he explained. "In a way it's a poem that's stands by itself, next to the space, without describing it. The writing is about language; it includes a kind of anxiety that the space seemed to generate." Nauman designed the space

before he wrote the text. Walking into the gallery, one entered a wedge-shaped area, at the end of which one passed through a doorway into a trapezoidal room. Its space was broken up by pillars, and because only two sides of the room were parallel, different angles were created. Just walking through the space aroused disconcerting feelings because of the intense yellow fluorescent light, which fatigued the eyes with its purple flashes and black afterimages. Written as it is in the third person, from an observer's point of view, *Left or Standing, Standing or Left Standing* seems detached in comparison to the direct involvement of the yellow-lit room. Yet the text correlates states of mind and activities that evoke specific fears, while the anxiety evoked by the room stays completely undefined and abstract. According to Nauman, the mood of the piece was suggested by John Steinbeck's *East of Eden* (1952). He recalls becoming interested in the uncertainty evoked by the heroine of the novel, the madam of a whorehouse, who developed the skill of giving perverse sexual and psychological pleasure to her customers by touching their skin with a razor blade, leaving a barely noticeable impression. It is, of course, another one of Nauman's creative misreadings. Nothing exactly like that occurs in the book, but among several incidents of scarring, there is a passage, deviating from Nauman's description, that contains a similar but more violent kind of suspense. It reads: "She advanced slowly toward him, and Mr. Edwards overcame his impulse to edge away. He was afraid of her but he sat still. Directly in front of him she drank the last champagne in her glass, delicately struck the rim on the table, and jammed the jagged edge against his cheek."[2]

In both the installation with yellow fluorescent lights and *Left or Standing, Standing or Left Standing,* Nauman is

193

once more after "an art that puts you on an edge; it forces you into a heightened awareness of yourself and the situation. Often without you knowing what it is that you're confronting and/or experiencing. All you know is that you're being pushed into a place that you're not used to and that there's an anxiety involved in that."[3]

FLOATING ROOM, 1973

To accompany the installation *Floating Room* at the uptown Leo Castelli Gallery in March 1973, Nauman wrote an instructional text by the same name (p. 200). As in performance pieces such as *Body as a Cylinder* and *Body as a Sphere,* both from 1970, Nauman did not perform himself but gave others a set of instructions to be executed. The text for *Floating Room* was applicable to more than the Castelli installation, however; a similar set of instructions was displayed in an empty room of the Whitney Museum of American Art, New York, in 1973 during Nauman's one-man exhibition there.

Placed within a darkened gallery, the brightly lit *Floating Room* (reconstructed in 1980, p. 201) was installed high enough off the floor so that the center of the room was above the center of one's body, giving a sense of levitation; gravity seemed to be defied and the room appeared to float. Nauman explained: "The *Floating Room* was about not being able to control the space around you; the space inside the lit room floats to the outside, where it is dark."

The unspoken fear generated by being in such an uncontrollable situation is more immediate and primitive than the intellectual, refined activity explored in the text of finding the center of something or the self-examining activity of discovering the center of one's body. Because of their emotional disparity, the writing and the piece worked against rather than with each other. Yet the room functioned in such a way that despite the seeming irrelevancy of the instructional text, one still ended up in the center of the space. "The more time you spent in the room, the harder it was to think about leaving," Nauman said. "It became much safer to stay in the center of the room, because you became anxious about the dark space outside of it." He compared the experience to the dilemma of a child who is lying in bed and drops an arm over the edge. Withdrawing the arm may stir up something unknown under the bed that can grab it. But it is too scary to jump up and run out the room into the dark. The only way out is to slowly withdraw the arm and wait comfortably within the safe middle of the bed until the sun rises.

FLAYED EARTH, FLAYED SELF: SKIN SINK, 1974

The installation *Flayed Earth, Flayed Self: Skin Sink* (p. 206) at the Nicholas Wilder Gallery, Los Angeles, in 1974, was so spare that one can scarcely decipher any clues to its substance without examining the accompanying text (pp. 204–05). Starting at the center of the floor of the rectangular space, spiraling pieces of masking tape divided the floor and walls into six equal parts like sections of a peeled orange. The lines of tape distorted the flatness and rectangularity of the space, disorienting the visitor. Nauman's intention was "to relate that peeling to the surface of the earth and to the surface of one's body. Imagine having to expand yourself to fill the earth, and the earth filling yourself, then, having become equivalent to the earth, being flayed or peeled." The writing alludes in a poetic, lyrical tone to the earth turning on its axis and revolving about the sun. In *Flayed Earth, Flayed Self: Skin Sink,* the physical existence of the place is reduced to almost nothing, a bare hint at the writing, which has become the essential element in understanding the piece.

194

CONES COJONES, 1974–75

The *Cones Cojones* project (pp. 208–13), executed in 1975 at the Leo Castelli Gallery, 420 West Broadway, New York, was based on the premise that there are "cones of different diameters starting from the center of the earth and passing on to the universe. It's a two-dimensional allegory, all you really can do is to imagine it." One is left with little information, and even that is further confused by the accompanying text. To avoid explanations of the theme, the writing was kept deliberately fragmentary, obliging one to move from one disjunctive thought to another. In applying deconstruction, disconnection, permutation, and rearrangement of phrases, Nauman was able to provide shards of information and wordplays, leaving all options open and avoiding logical connections that add up to only one story line. Nauman compared the text to "a bunch of fortune cookies lying on a dinner table." At first sight their messages might be incoherent, yet as a group they tell their own story.

CONSUMMATE MASK OF ROCK, 1975

The writing of *Consummate Mask of Rock* (pp. 214–17) took place in 1975 while Nauman was working on an installation of stone blocks for the Albright-Knox Art Gallery in Buffalo. He called the installation *The Mask to Cover the Need for Human Companionship,* but later retitled it after his text (p. 218). In this case, Nauman did not want to separate the text from the installation but wanted to accentuate the complexity of both kinds of information. For the installation, two sizes of sandstone block, the larger one 15 inches square and the smaller 14 inches square, were grouped in eight pairs around the perimeter of a large room. The configuration of the stones and their positions in diagonal relationships to one another caused a confusion in perspective. The floor no longer appeared to be flat; when one moved around the space it looked twisted. The calm, classical space of the Albright-Knox Art Gallery contrasted with the rigorous, sculptural presence of the stones and with their rough texture and sharp gashes. The discrepancies in scale between the small units and the large room gave one the impression of looking at a maquette of a city; yet by applying the text to the installation, a lyrical dimension was added. The contrast between the logical, formal exposition of the work and poetic quality of the written text allowed more vulnerable thoughts to surface. In the months following the Buffalo exhibition, Nauman embarked on a series of exhibitions involving similar installations: the proportions of the room were used to determine the placement of stones. Called *Forced Perspective, Enforced Perspective, Diamond Mind, White Breathing,* and *Consummate Mask of Rock,* these installations were built upon analogies to mathematics. However, the logical systems once again gradually came apart and absurdities began to surface through the making of analogies between one system and another, through cheating along the way, and through mixing up the systems, much in the way of the 1968–69 Poem Pieces.

The text for *Consummate Mask of Rock* unfolds around a circular argument derived from the children's game "Scissors cuts paper, rock breaks scissors, and paper covers rock." After counting to three, two children each open one hand at the same time. At that moment they either display "paper," by opening the hand; "scissors," by holding up two fingers; or "rock," by making a fist. If at the count of three one holds up two fingers and the other displays an open hand, "scissors" cuts "paper" and thus wins the round. Nauman used the game as the basis for another group of symbols relating to human needs, among them the need to hide oneself. The writing addresses the moral dilemma of the artist's needs and his position within the culture. The text starts with lists summing up human relationships, which by being divided up and restricted lead to the making of more complex lists, which in their turn cancel each other out. In a parody on Wittgenstein, the seven parts are put together in a weird imitation of logic that is difficult to analyze. In *Consummate Mask of Rock,* Nauman exposes his vulnerability as an artist, alternately following his impulse to tell the truth, hide behind a mask, and seek out human companionship: "The artist feels the need to expose himself in any kind of social situation, and at the same time he needs to hold some of that back, because it's so painful."

Nauman originally explored the theme of hiding behind a mask in his *Art Make-Up* films, 1967–68 (pp. 197, 222), and in the videotape *Flesh to Black to White to Flesh,* 1968. By alternately putting on white and black masks, Nauman breaks social taboos. Shifting back and forth between objectification and illusion, he takes on different roles, paradoxically

exposing himself and covering up out of fear of rejection. As he explained: "Make-up is not necessarily anonymous but it's distorted in some way, it's something to hide behind. It's not quite giving, not quite exposing. The tension in the work is often about that. You're not going to get what you're not getting." Make-up does not pretend to be more of a formal problem than it is, a direct acting out of an allegory, on the one hand a seductive masquerade and on the other the unveiled truth. Often we live without an understanding of who we are; as Jorge Luis Borges once said: "I dream of a mirror. I see myself with a mask, or I see in the mirror somebody who is me but whom I do not recognize as myself."

Notes

1. *Ian Wallace and Russell Kaziere, "Bruce Nauman Interviewed,"* Vanguard 8, *no. 1 (February 1, 1979):16*
2. *John Steinbeck,* East of Eden *(New York: Viking Press, 1952), p 110.*
3. *This quotation and others that follow come from a series of interviews with the author between June 1985 and April 1986.*

Still from *Art Make-Up, No. 1:*
White. 1967
Film, 16 mm, color, silent,
8–10 min., ca. 400′

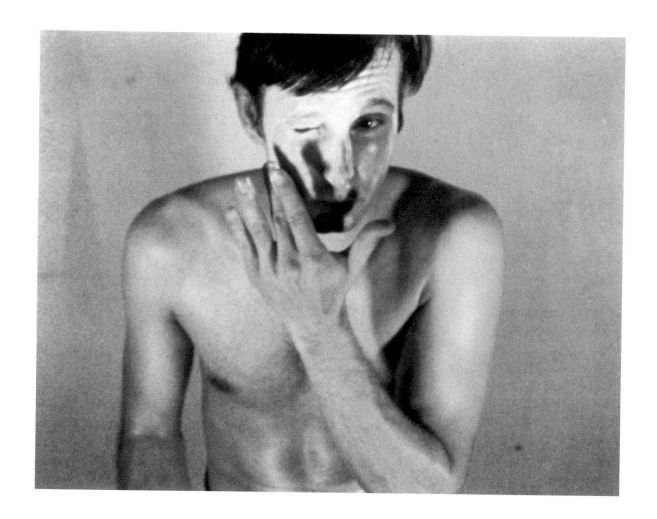

Left or Standing

His precision and accuracy
suggesting clean cuts, leaving
a vacancy, a slight physical
depression as though I had been
in a vaguely uncomfortable place
for a not long but undeterminable
period; not waiting.

Standing or Left Standing

His preciseness and acuity left
small cuts on the tips of my
fingers or across the backs of
my hands without any need to
sit or otherwise withdraw.

Installation with Yellow Lights. 1971
Installed Leo Castelli Gallery, New York,
November–December 1971
Wallboard and fluorescent tubes
Size variable

Floating Room

We are trying to get to the center of some place: that is,
exactly halfway between each pair of parts.

We want to move our center (some measurable center) to coincide
with such a point.

We want to superimpose our center of gravity on this point.

Save enough energy and concentration to reverse.

(The center of most places is above eyelevel)

Floating Room: Lit from Inside. 1972
Wallboard and fluorescent tubes
10 × 16 × 16′ (305 × 488 × 488 cm);
6″ (15.2 cm) above floor
Hallen für neue Kunst,
Schaffhausen, Switzerland
Crex Collection

Floating Room: A Version (Dark Inside,
Light Outside). 1972
Pencil and ink wash on paper
29 × 23″ (73.7 × 58.4 cm)
Present location unknown

Floating Room: B Version (Light Inside,
Dark Outside). 1972
Pencil and ink wash on paper
29 × 23″ (73.7 × 58.4 cm)
Present location unknown

BRUCE NAUMAN

FLAYED EARTH/FLAYED SELF
(SKIN/SINK)

NICHOLAS WILDER GALLERY

8225½ Santa Monica Blvd., Los Angeles 90046 (213) 656-0770

December 17 - January 11. Open Tuesday through Saturday: 11 A.M. to 5 P.M.

FLAYED EARTH/FLAYED SELF
(SKIN/SINK)

Peeling skin peeling earth - peeled earth
raw earth, peeled skin
The problem is to divide your
skin into six equal parts
lines starting at your feet and
ending at your head (five lines to make six
equal surface areas) to twist and spiral
into the ground, your skin peeling off
stretching and expanding to cover the surface
of the earth indicated by the spiraling
waves generated by the spiraling twisting
screwing descent and investiture (investment
or investing) of the earth by your swelling body.

Spiraling twisting ascent descent screwing in
screwing out screwing driving diving
invest invert convert relent relax control
release, give in, given. Twisting driving down.
Spiraling up screwing up screwed up screwed
Twisted mind, twist and turn, twist and shout.
Squirm into my mind so I can get into
your mind your body our body
arcing ache, circling warily then
pressed together, pressing together,
forced.

Surface reflection, transmission, refraction-
surface tension absorption, adsorption
Standing above and to one side of your-
self- schizoid - not a dislocation, but a
bend or brake (as at the surface of water or a
clear liquid - quartz or a transparent crystal)
(transparent crying)
I HAVE QUICK HANDS MY MIND IS ALERT
I HOLD MY BODY READY FOR INSPIRATION
ANTICIPATION ANY SIGN RESPIRATION
ANY SIGH I THINK NEITHER AHEAD NOR
BEHIND READY BUT NOT WAITING NOT
ON GUARD NOT PREPARED.

Rushing:
I AM AN IMPLODING LIGHT BULB
(imagine a more perfect abstract sphere)
Draw in energy rushing toward you -
toward your center.
(Fools rush in - Russian fools)
Try to get it down on paper - try to
get it in writing (try to get it written down -
try to write it down): Some evidence of a
state - a mark to prove you were there: Kilroy
(make a mark to prove you are here)
Suspension of belief, suspension of an object
object of suspension - to hang.

Talking of a particular space - the space a
few inches above and below the floor and within
the area bounded by and described by the taped
lines.
NOW INFORMATION RUSHING AWAY FROM THE CENTER
TOWARD THE PERIMETER A FEW INCHES ABOVE THE FLOOR.
A kind of vertical compression of space or do you
see it as a lightening or expanding opening in
space - just enough to barely let you in - not
so you could just step into it but so that you might
be able to crawl into it to lie in it to bask in it
to bathe in it.
Can it crush you - very heavy space - (gravity is
very important here) (or for important read strong)

You want to turn at an ordinary rate, as though
you want to speak to someone there, behind you
but you want not to speak, but to address yourself to a situation. (everything will feel the
same and it will not have a new meaning THIS
DOES NOT MEAN ANYTHING ANYWAY) but now there
is either a greater density or less density
and if you turn back (when you turn back)
the change will be all around you. Now you
cannot leave or walk away. Has to do with your
ability to give up your control over space. This
is difficult because nothing will happen - and
later you will be no better or worse off for it.
This is more than one should require of another
person. THIS IS FAR TOO PRIVATE AND DANGEROUS
BECAUSE THERE IS NO ELATION NO PAIN NO KNOWLEDGE
AN INCREDIBLE RISK WITH (BECAUSE) NOTHING IS
LOST OR GAINED NOTHING TO CATCH OUT OF THE
CORNER OF YOUR EYE - YOU MAY THINK YOU FELT SOME-
THING BUT THAT'S NOT IT THAT'S NOT ANYTHING
YOU'RE ONLY HERE IN THE ROOM:
MY SECRET IS THAT I STAYED THE SAME FOR A SHORT TIME.

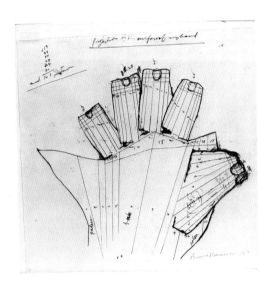

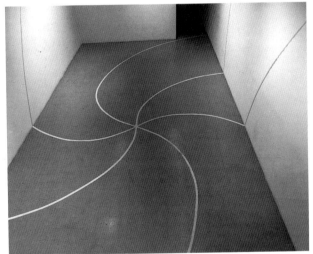

Untitled. 1974
Inscribed: "Sketch for/ self playing/ earth
investing—/ 6 part division of surface/
investing the core/ 2 rates."
Pencil on paper
30 x 40″ (76.2 x 101.6 cm)
Sperone Westwater, New York

Study for *Flayed Earth Flayed Self:
Skin Sink.* 1974
Pencil and collage with typewriting
on paper
40⅛ × 30⅛″ (101.9 × 76.3 cm)
Leo Castelli Gallery, New York

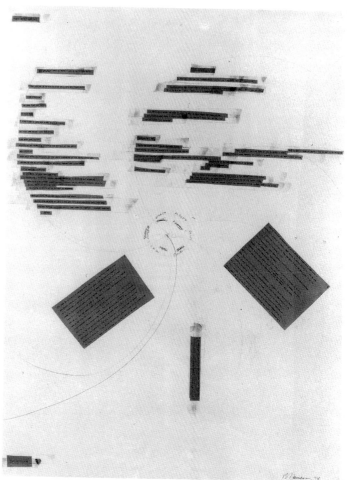

Cones

Floater: Rising time/count-up sequence.

A finite number of concentric circles not equally spaced: starting at the outside and measuring inward, the distances between circumferences is a geometric progression (expanding or contracting).

Concentric circles becoming progressively closer either from their center or measured from the outer circumference, describing the intersection of the plane through your center parallel to the floor and a very large but finite series of concentric cones whose common center is located through the center of the earth at a distant place in the universe.

The point of the universe which is the apex of a countable number of concentric cones whose intersection with the plane parallel to the floor passing through your center describing an equal number of concentric circles, appear to radiate, inward or not, that point, moving with the universe, expanding, and so changing, the shape, of the cones, and circles, at this rate.

Earth Moves

The massive center moves about tides.

Black hole functions: contraction, concentration, compression, collapse, contour inversion, contour immersion, inverse/diverse/divest.

Thinking feeling.

Sinking, feeling.

Expansion Ethics

Release the gas and the container is contained.

Free thinking free thinker; free thinker thinking free.
Floater flauting flauter floating.

Fit into an enormous space where a great deal of time is available as the
continually rapidly expanding distances are enormous. Stay inside the cone; avoid
the walls; compact yourself; avoid compression. Now time is short.

(You can't get there from here but you can get here from there if you don't mind
the t left over.)

What I mean is everything is finite, every thing is closed, *nothing touches.*

It doesn't mean anything to say there are no spaces in between.

It is meaningless to say there are spaces between.

As though the water had recently been removed.
As though water had emptied.

Cojones

I want to get the whole. I'm trying to get everything, accurate.

I want to get the whole,
Here is every.
Here is the whole, everything, accurate, precise:

Imagine accidentally coming upon a line and adjusting yourself so that the center
of your body lies on that line. When you accomplish this there is no next step.

Take my meaning not my intention.

You will just have to do something else.

Here is every.

Here is my precision.
Here is everything.
Apparently this is my hole.
Apparently this is my meaning.

(I have precise but mean intentions.)

Ere he is very.

1. Let's talk about control.
2. We were talking about control.
3. We are talking about control.

There is no preparation for this occurrence.

There is no excuse for this occurrence, there is no reason, no need, no urgency, no . . .

Apparently this is what I mean, although it's not what I intended.

This *accuracy* is not my intention.

Oh, my shrinking, crawling skin

and the need within me to stretch myself to a point.

This accuracy is my intention. *Placate my art.*

Cones Cojones. 1973–75
Installed Leo Castelli Gallery, New York,
January 1975
Masking tape on floor
50′ (1,219.2 cm) diameter

Untitled (Study for *Cones Cojones*). 1973
Pencil on paper
28¾ × 41⅜ (72 × 105 cm)
Hallen für neue Kunst,
Schaffhausen, Switzerland
Private collection

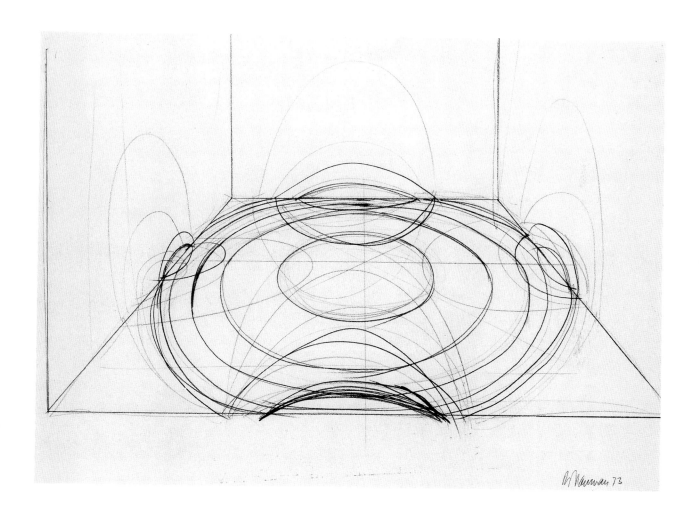

The Consummate Mask of Rock

1. mask
2. fidelity
3. truth
4. life
5. cover
6. pain
7. desire
8. need
9. human companionship
10. nothing
11. COVER REVOKED
12. infidelity
13. painless
14. musk/skum
15. people
16. die
17. exposure.

2

1. This is my mask of fidelity to truth and life.
2. This is to cover the mask of pain and desire.
3. This is to mask the cover of need for human companionship.
4. This is to mask the cover.
5. This is to cover the mask.
6. This is the need of cover.
7. This is the need of the mask.
8. This is the mask of cover of need.
   Nothing and no
9. No thing and no mask can cover the lack, alas.
10. Lack after nothing before cover revoked.
11. Lack before cover
    paper covers rock
    rock breaks mask
    alas, alack.
12. Nothing to cover.
13. This is the mask to cover my infidelity to truth.
    (This is my cover.)
14. This is the need for pain that contorts my mask conveying the message of truth and fidelity to life.
15. This is the truth that distorts my need for human companionship.
16. This is the distortion of truth masked by my painful need.

17. This is the mask of my painful need distressed by truth and human companionship.
18. This is my painless mask that fails to touch my face but floats before the surface of my skin my eyes my teeth my tongue.
19. Desire is my mask.
    (Musk of desire)
20. Rescind desire
    cover revoked
    desire revoked
    cover rescinded.
21. PEOPLE DIE OF EXPOSURE.

3

CONSUMMATON/CONSUMNATION/TASK

(passive)
paper covers rock

(active–threatening)
scissors cuts paper

(active–violent)
rock breaks scissors

1. mask   4. desire
2. cover   5. need for human companionship
3. diminish   6. lack

desire covers mask

need for human companionship masks desire

mask diminishes need for human companionship

need for human companionship diminishes cover

desire consumes human companionship

cover lacks desire

THIS IS THE COVER THAT DESIRES THE MASK OF LACK THAT CONSUMES THE NEED FOR HUMAN COMPANIONSHIP.
THIS IS THE COVER THAT DESPISES THE TASK OF THE NEED OF HUMAN COMP.
THIS IS THE TASK OF CONSUMING HUMAN COMP.

5

1. some kind of fact
2. some kind of fiction
3. the way we behaved in the past
4. what we believe to be the case now
5. the consuming task of human companionship
6. the consummate mask of rock

(1.) Fiction erodes fact.
(2.) Fact becomes the way we have behaved in the past.
(3.) The way we have behaved in the past congeals into the consummate mask of rock.
(4.) The way we have behaved in the past contributes to the consuming task of human companionship.
(5.) The consuming task of human comp. erodes the consummate mask of rock.
However (2.) Fact becomes the way we have behaved in the past may be substituted
into (3.) and (4.) so that
(6.) Fact congeals into the consummate mask of rock.
But (5.) the consuming task of human comp. erodes the consummate mask of rock or
the consuming task of human comp. erodes fact, then from (1.) it follows that
THE CONSUMING TASK OF HUMAN COMPANIONSHIP IS FALSE.

6

THE CONSUMMATE MASK OF ROCK HAVING DRIVEN THE WEDGE OF DESIRE
THAT DISTINGUISHED TRUTH AND FALSITY LIES COVERED BY PAPER.

7

1. (This young man, taken to task so often, now finds it his only sexual relief.)

2. (This young man, so often taken to task; now finds it his only sexual fulfillment.)

3. (This man, so often taken to task as a child . . .)

4. (This man, so often taken to task, now finds it satisfies his sexual desires.)

                                          arouses   needs
5. This man, so often taken as a child, now wears the consummate mask of rock and uses it to drive his wedge of desire into the ever squeezing gap between truth and falsity.

6. This man, so often taken as a child, now uses his consummate mask of his rock to drive his wedge of his desire into his ever squeezing (his) gap between his truth, his falsity.

7. (This) man, (so often) taken as (a) child, finding his consummate mask of rock covered by paper, he finding his wedge being squeezed (from) between his desired truth (truth desired) and his desireless falsity (falsity desireless), he unable to arouse his satisfaction, he unable to desire his needs, he proceeds into the gap of his fulfillment his relief lacking the task of human companionship.

Moral
Paper cut from rock, releases rock to crush scissors.
Rock freed from restrictions
of paper/scissors/rock, lacking context proceeds.

TOP:
Untitled (Study for *Forced Perspectives*).
1975
Inscribed: "FORCED PERSPECTIVES:/ OPEN
MIND/ CLOSED MIND/ PARALLEL MIND/
EQUAL MIND/ DIAMOND MINED/ DIAMOND
MIND/ A/B combinations of stone blocks/
(Rhomboids)."
Pencil and pasted paper on paper
$29\frac{1}{8} \times 63\frac{7}{8}''$ (74 × 162.2 cm)
The Panza Collection, Milan

BOTTOM:
Forced Perspective. 1975
Installed Galerie Konrad Fischer,
Düsseldorf, December 1975–January 1976
Plaster
64 blocks
Städtisches Museum Abteiberg,
Mönchengladbach, West Germany

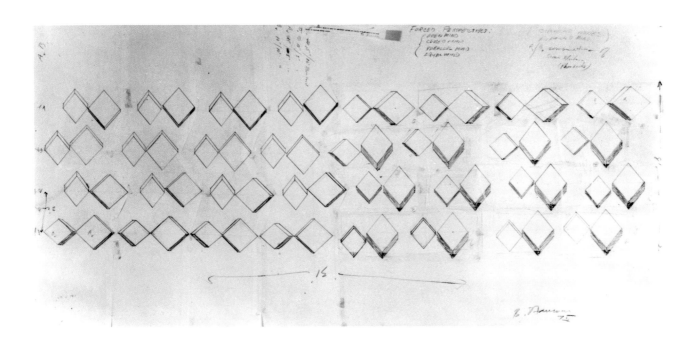

TOP:
Diamond Mind. 1975
Installed Galerie Konrad Fischer,
Düsseldorf, December 1975–January 1976
Stone
Private collection, Belgium

BOTTOM:
Diamond Mind, No. 2. 1975
Installed Sperone Westwater Fischer, New
York, October–November 1976
Plaster
Twelve blocks, $14\frac{1}{2} \times 17\frac{3}{4}''$ (37 × 45 cm)
each
Original destroyed; reconstructed in
Maulbrunner sandstone
Rijksmuseum Kröller-Müller,
Otterlo, the Netherlands

TOP:
Untitled (Study for *Diamond Mind*). 1975
Inscribed: "Diamond mind/ circle of tears/
fallen all around me./ pressed board + hot
glue."
Pencil on paper
30 × 40″ (76.2 × 101.6 cm)
Ace Gallery, Los Angeles

BOTTOM:
Untitled (Study for *Diamond Mind*). 1975
Inscribed: "DIAMOND MIND/ CIRCLE OF
TEARS/ FALLEN ALL AROUND ME/ FALLEN
MIND/ MINDLESS TEARS/ CUT LIKE A DIAMON
LAYOUT/ 12 pc. stone 7½″ RHOMBOIDS/
GRANITE 15″ ON A SIDE."
Pencil on paper
30⅝ × 39⅞″ (77.8 × 101.3 cm)
Present location unknown

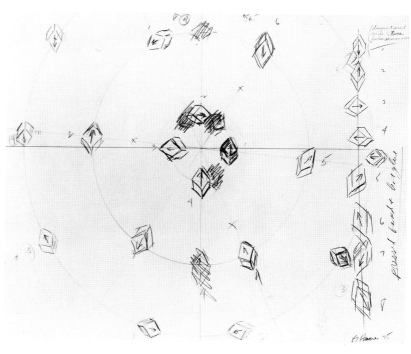

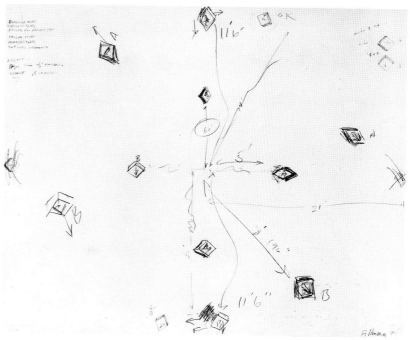

Stills from *Art Make-Up, No. 4:*
Black. 1967–68
Film, 16 mm, color, silent, 8–10 min.,
ca. 400′

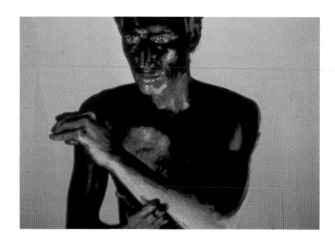

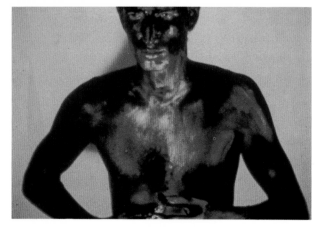

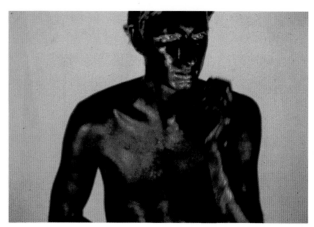

Black Marble with Yellow Light. 1981
Installed Galerie Konrad Fischer,
Düsseldorf, August–September 1981
Enamel-painted wood blocks and
fluorescent tubes
Sixteen 15″ (31.8 cm) cubes;
sixteen 13¾″ (34.9 cm) cubes
Konrad Fischer, Düsseldorf,
West Germany

Untitled (Drawing No. 1 for White Breathing). 1976
Inscribed: "DRWG #1/ #1 of 3 Drawings/ THE STEEL BLOCKS/ ARE NOT ALL SHAPED/ THE SAME AS THE/ PLASTERS IN THESE/ PHOTOS—BUT ARE NUMBERED/ AND 'AIMED'/ IN THE SAME DIRECTIONS. [aligned corner to corner at bottoms]/ [aligned corner to corner at top]/ Room size was 21'8" ×

28'4½"/ White Breathing/ Bruce Nauman/ 1976./ Plaster for stone/ or steel/ (cast iron?)/ (edge to edge and corner to/ corner radial progression, then/ repeated 3/ 2/ 2/ as shown]/ etc. [aligned edge to edge at top]/ BLOCKS ARE STAMPED WITH NUMBERS NEAR/ THE TOP CENTER/ AND ALSO NEAR THE BOTTOM OF ONE SIDE/ 3 shapes/

Rhombohendrons/ gap is always ¼"/ [aligned edge to edge at bottoms]/ BN. 1976 Oct. Sperone Westwater Fischer/ Installation/ additions + corrections."
Pencil and taped photographs on paper 32½ × 28½" (82.5 × 72.3 cm)
Collection Annick and Anton Herbert, Ghent, Belgium

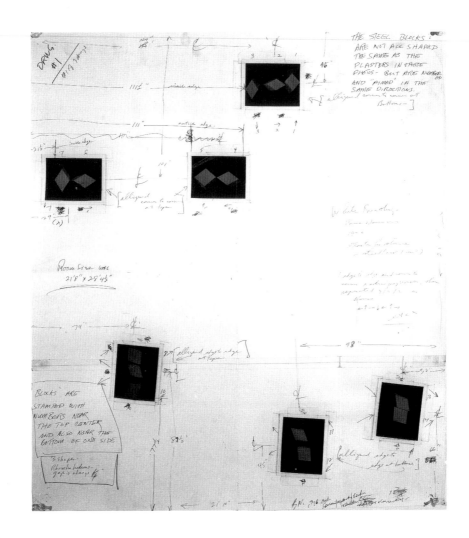

Sounddance

Nauman's first films, made in 1965–66, are about seeing: "I wanted to find out what I would look at in a strange situation, and I decided that with a film and camera I could do that."[1] These early films are about how an artist makes his choices: what objects or events in the visual field to focus on, what to include in the frame and what to crop out, and, in general, how to handle the camera. Nauman later remarked that it was Man Ray's films that had made him aware of the conceptual possibilities to be achieved through the manipulation of the camera. For him, the most original aspect of Man Ray's film work was that act of throwing the camera in the air while the film was running, not what he chose to record with the camera; it did not matter if the event took place in a room or outdoors. To Nauman, the use of film—which he considered an optical illusion—was a way to see the artist in direct relation to his ideas, unencumbered by the existence of an object whose physical presence might distract from those ideas. Another advantage of using film or photography was that they both would be accepted as "truthful records," without the question being asked of whether or not they were art. The closest Nauman came to "just making a film without considering it art" was one he made with William Allan, *Fishing for Asian Carp,* 1966.

Around 1966–67, working alone in his studio in San Francisco and in William T. Wiley's studio in Mill Valley, Nauman began to develop a strong body awareness, which resulted in his making casts of parts of his body. He not only focused his attention on individual body parts, as in *Device for a Left Armpit,* 1967 (p. 133), but also used his body as a standard for measuring his surroundings. For instance, in a series of drawings from 1966, Nauman literally applied the rule, taught in every art school, that the human body is ideally about seven heads

tall. One study from this series shows a human figure neatly divided into a stack of seven units of equal height; it also shows three units consisting of cross-sectional slices of a torso. Still another, from 1967, *Wax Templates of My Body Arranged to Make an Abstract Sculpture* (p. 244), shows seven such slices piled up to form a teetering "column-body." Nauman's complex vision of the human body seems to relate neither to a keen interest in human anatomy nor to the humanistic ideal of self-definition. Instead it addresses controversial comparisons between the human body and machines that have been made since the latter part of the nineteenth century. A watercolor from 1966, *Glass Templates of the Left Half of My Body Separated by Cans of Grease* (p. 242), makes a correlation between the organic character of machines and the rigid mechanism of the human frame. Another study, *Templates of the Left Half of My Body Every Ten-Inches, Spaced Out to Twenty-Inch Intervals (Doubling My Height),* also 1966 (p. 244), would stretch the figure across the floor of a room. In the 1967 *Wax Templates of My Body Arranged to Make an Abstract Sculpture,* each of the templates is given the name of the body part with which it is associated: head, shoulder, chest, waist, thigh, knee, and calf. Here Nauman disassembles the human body according to abstract industrial production techniques; each disjointed part has to be examined in order to understand how the whole works. The various body parts can still be identified in the abstract templates, but they have lost their uniqueness; they can now be replaced by spare parts. In a related sketch from 1967, on which Nauman wrote "7 wax templates of the left half of my body spread over 12 feet," the human body is divided into seven separate templates that expand in space. The effect in this work is similar to that of a production line: the whole is dis-

mantled and laid out for eventual reassembly. In a related idea, Nauman abstracted a specific body part by physically stretching it in a pair of drawings, both entitled *Six Inches of My Knee Extended to Six Feet,* 1967 (p. 136); he used a similar tactic in pieces such as *My Last Name Extended Vertically Fourteen Times,* 1967 (p. 137). In another work he extended his first name by repeating each letter horizontally ten times: *Bbbbbbbbbbrrrrrrrrrruuuuuuuuuu-cccccccccceeeeeeeeee.* Next he taped together the sheets with the different letters written on them, laid them out on the floor of the studio, and photographed them in many segments. By varying the distance between the camera and the paper, photographing from farther away at the ends and from a lesser distance at the center of the stretched name, Nauman created the impression that the letters are lying on a curved surface. This piece, *My Name As Though It Were Written on the Surface of the Moon,* 1967 (p. 245), recalls the photographs sent back to earth by the five lunar orbiters that were launched by the United States between 1966 and 1968 (the neon version, *My Name As Though It Were Written on the Surface of the Moon* [pp. 246–47], appeared in the latter year). Here again Nauman created a suggestive work by combining widely disparate pieces of information—one of which, about the surface of the moon, had just come into reach. In his essay "Woman in a Mirror," Marshall McLuhan writes that the "artistic discovery for achieving rich implication by withholding the syntactical connection" was stated as a principle of modern physics by A. N. Whitehead, who wrote in *Science and the Modern World*: "In being aware of the bodily experience, we must thereby be aware of aspects of the whole spatio-temporal world as mirrored within in the bodily life. . . . My theory involves the entire abandonment of the notion

225

that simple location is the primary way in which things are involved in space-time."[2]

My Name As Though It Were Written on the Surface of the Moon also emanates from an attitude that, as Nauman explains it, "I adopt sometimes to find things out—like turning things inside out to see what they look like." In this case, he said, "it had to do with doing things that you don't particularly want to do, with putting yourself in unfamiliar situations, following resistances to find out why you're resisting, like therapy."[3] A prime example of that attitude is Nauman's photographic work *Flour Arrangements,* 1967 (p. 248). An aesthetic precedent for the activity of arranging flour on one's studio floor has been established by *Dust Breeding,* 1920 (p. 249), a photograph made by Marcel Duchamp and Man Ray in New York of Duchamp's *Large Glass* lying flat, showing "the accumulation of dust in the region of the Sieves," as Arturo Schwarz described it in his monograph on Duchamp. Schwarz also notes that Duchamp had alluded to this collecting of dust in *The Green Box,* 1934: "For the Sieves in the glass—allow dust to fall on this part, a dust of 3 or 4 months and wipe well around it in such a way that this dust will be a kind of color (transparent pastel)." Man Ray's photograph was made in Duchamp's New York studio on Sixty-seventh Street during the dinner hour, by artificial light. Man Ray told Schwarz that "he and Marcel went out for a snack leaving the camera to take a very long exposure; when they came back the photo was ready."[4]

However much Nauman admired the casual, conceptual attitude of Man Ray and Duchamp, with *Flour Arrangements* he wanted to stress the physical activity involved in being an artist and at the same time test himself, to see if he really was "professional" in his work. For Nauman, being a professional artist en-

tails having "the powerful, almost moral attitude most West Coast artists have, which requires going to the studio every day and doing work." He said in an interview with Willoughby Sharp, "I took everything out of my studio, so that *Flour Arrangements* became an activity which I could do every day, and it was all I would allow myself to do for about a month. Sometimes it got pretty hard to think of different things to do every day."[5]

After a month Nauman selected seven of the most interesting photographs from this project, intending to put them together in a loose configuration on the wall. However, he cropped the fragments carefully because he also wanted each to be a "beautiful aesthetic photograph," in order to transform the project, with its documentary character, into art. That year, after he had made composite photos for *My Name As Though It Were Written on the Surface of the Moon,* Nauman produced *Composite Photo of Two Messes on the Studio Floor,* 1967 (p. 249), a parody of his flour arranging. This time he recorded the debris left over from several sculptures he was working on as evidence of his ongoing activity in the studio. It was also a kind of artistic economy—he didn't want to leave any idea or material unused. In this piece Nauman again uses what does and does not belong to a piece, just as he did in 1966 when he exhibited the plaster mold of the Slant Step in two parts (p. 131), and, later, when he included a mold in one of his fiberglass pieces (p. 34). Dislocated from their original context, the remnants of the sculptures are given weight by being turned into photographs, which are arranged in a specific configuration. As Jane Livingston pointed out in 1972 in her essay on Nauman, this work has certain similarities to Barry Le Va's distributional sculptures. But *Composite Photo of Two Messes on the Studio Floor*

echoes the acceptance of chance that Duchamp demonstrated in using the crack that developed in the *Large Glass,* as well as the dust that collected on top of it, as part of the creative process. "Duchamp allowed the object to take on a life of its own rather than forcing it to be an illustration of an idea that can't be changed," Nauman said. Another related photographic piece, in which an activity was to be recorded over a period of time, was intended for a show at the gallery of the University of California at Davis in January 1970. A number of artists had been invited to carry out a work on site, within a period of twenty-four hours. Nauman's idea was to record the activities in a stop-action film, using a camera set up to shoot one frame a minute, but in the end he was unable to complete it.

With *Flour Arrangements* and *Composite Photo of Two Messes on the Studio Floor* Nauman made his first attempt to move away from making static objects. These pieces, which emphasize the remnants of an activity rather than sculptural qualities of objects or artistic photography, were transitional pieces between Nauman's sculptural objects and later works in which the activity itself became the piece. The latter could be arbitrary and absurd—for example, the film *Playing a Note on the Violin While I Walk around the Studio,* 1968 (p. 253); in fact, Nauman did not know how to play the violin. The activity could also be more logical, such as "pacing or rhythmic stamping around the studio." Nauman remembers at the time telling a friend who was a philosopher that he imagined him spending most of his time at a desk, writing. But in fact his friend did his thinking while taking long walks during the day. This made Nauman conscious of the fact that he spent most of his time pacing around the studio drinking coffee. And so he decided to film that— just the pacing. During the winter of

Dance or Exercise on the Perimeter of a
Square. 1968
Film, 16 mm, black and white, sound,
8–10 min., ca. 400′

1967–68 Nauman made four black-and-white films of activities carried out in a studio in Mill Valley that he had sublet from his teacher William T. Wiley, while Wiley was traveling: *Playing a Note on the Violin While I Walk Around the Studio; Bouncing Two Balls between the Floor and Ceiling with Changing Rhythms* (p. 250); *Walking in an Exaggerated Manner around the Perimeter of a Square* (p. 251); and *Dance or Exercise on the Perimeter of a Square* (p. 252). The activities recorded in these films and the videotapes Nauman made in New York during the following winter were originally intended as performances. However, at the time there was no situation in which to perform them. Nauman felt that notes were not sufficient to preserve his ideas, so he made these inexpensive short films (each lasting no more than ten minutes) and hour-long videotapes both as a record of his studio activities and as a form of art.

In the film *Dance or Exercise on the Perimeter of a Square*, Nauman performs a simple dance step: starting from one corner of a square formed by masking tape fastened to the studio floor, he moves around the perimeter. He turns alternately into the square and out toward the wall, with either his face or his back turned to the camera (the back view allows more anonymity). His movements are regulated by the beat of a metronome. In the silent film *Walking in an Exaggerated Manner around the Perimeter of a Square*, a larger square is taped to the floor outside the first one. With great concentration Nauman, shown in profile, puts his feet carefully down on the line of the outer square, one foot in front or in back of the other; at the same time he shifts weight onto a hip in an exaggerated manner. At times a reflection of this exercise in contrapposto balance, showing the figure from a different angle, can be seen in a mirror leaning against the back wall. From time to time the performer is completely absent from the screen, because the frame cuts off part of the square; at those times Nauman seems to be paradoxically stressing the artist's isolation within the double entrapment of his studio and the frame. Nauman's method of escape from this imprisonment, stepping out of the picture, also takes him out of reach of the viewer, which creates a strong sense of remoteness. This exaggerated dance exercise was the forerunner of another performance, executed only on videotape in 1969, the hour-long *Walk with Contrapposto* (p. 274). In this work the artist, his hands clasped behind his neck, walks slowly, with his arms and legs akimbo, toward and away from the camera, along an extremely narrow, 20-foot-long corridor. Nauman's exaggerated movements, mostly taking up lateral space, appear cramped within the narrow corridor. The artist explained: "The camera was placed so that the walls came in at either side of the screen. You couldn't see the rest of the studio, and my head was cut off most of the time. The light was shining down the length of the corridor and made shadows on the walls at each side of me."[6]

These three dance exercises are based on a daily activity, walking, but, by breaking it up into detached motions, they distort its ordinariness. For instance, by emphasizing the hip movement, Nauman lavishly covers space, stressing his presence in the corridor; by turning the step into a balancing act he lifts it out of its everyday context. The disjunction of motion into a series of fragments echoes the multiple frames of Eadweard Muybridge's sequential photographs of people and animals in action, causing tension between movement and rest. The use of the square on the floor is somewhat arbitrary—it could have been a circle or a triangle, or the pieces could have been performed around the edges of the room—but it serves to direct the movements and to formalize the exercises, giving them more importance as dances than they would have had if Nauman had just wandered aimlessly. For instance, in taking one convenient step forward in *Dance or Exercise on the Perimeter of a Square*, Nauman reaches precisely the middle of a side of the square. In *Walking in an Exaggerated Manner around the Perimeter of a Square*, the framing of the image is accentuated by cropping off a part of the square, so that the field of action becomes restricted. The lopping off of the performer's limbs or head serves to objectify the human body.

Nauman practiced these dance exercises extensively before filming them. "An awareness of yourself comes from a certain amount of activity and you can't get it from just thinking about yourself," Nauman stated in his interview with Willoughby Sharp.

You do exercises, you have certain kinds of awarenesses that you don't have if you read books. So the films and some of the pieces that I did after that for videotapes were specifically about doing exercises in balance. I thought of them as dance-problems without being a dancer, being interested in the kinds of tension that arise when you try to balance and can't. Or do something for a long time and get tired. In one of those first films, the violin film, I played the violin as long as I could. I don't know how to play the violin, so it was hard, playing on all four strings as fast as I could for as long as I could. I had ten minutes of film and ran about seven minutes of it before I got tired and had to stop and rest a little bit and then finish it."[7]

By reading the psychologist Frederick Perls's book *Gestalt Theory*, Nauman was stimulated to place himself in an unfamiliar situation "where you can't relax following resistances," and to turn to the root of one's problems as a way to make art. However, no matter how much Nauman enjoyed reading in psy-

Walk with Contrapposto. 1969
Videotape, black and white, sound, 60
min., taped in *Performance Corridor,* 1969

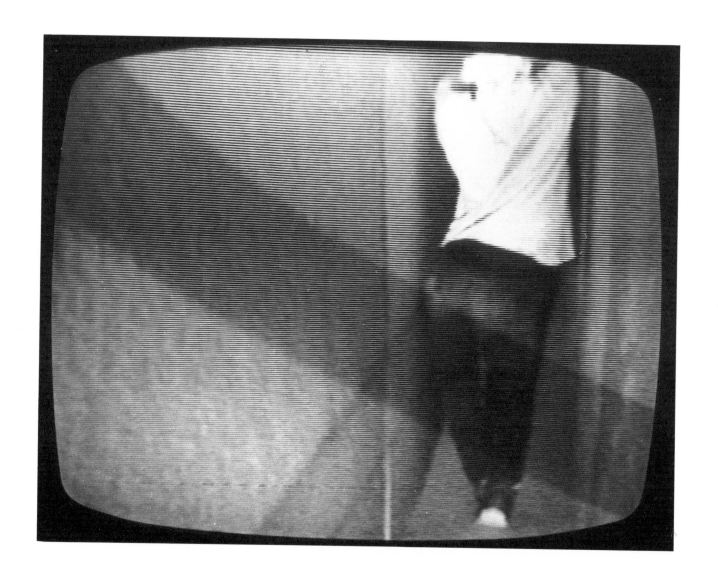

chology, it did not provide a methodology for his performances or the installation pieces he made during the first half of the 1970s. He explained that many laboratory tests have shown that specific physiological changes occur in particular situations, and that we react in certain ways in certain situations. You can set up those situations as if they were experiments, he reasoned, "but I don't think any of my pieces really function that way. They're much more intuitive . . . It somehow has to do with intuitively finding something or some phenomenon and then later relating it to art . . . But the approach always seems to be backwards."[8] Nauman never seems "to get there" from knowing the result he will achieve beforehand or from working off a previous experiment. Perls's book provided a rationale for Nauman in his work, and helped clarify what he had been doing in making art from simple everyday activities.

In San Francisco in 1968 Nauman met the dancer-choreographer Meredith Monk. She had seen some of his films on the East Coast, and she assured him that his "amateur" method need not be an obstacle to turning his body awareness into art. This method as well as the spatio-temporal structure of Nauman's performances were suggested in part by the work of choreographer Merce Cunningham and the composer John Cage: "I guess I thought of what I was doing as a sort of dance because I was familiar with some of the things that Cunningham and others had done, where you can take any simple movement and make it into a dance just by presenting it as a dance. . . . I wasn't a dancer, but I sort of thought if I took things I didn't know how to do but was serious enough about them, they would be taken seriously."[9]

In making use of the tension between professionalism and dilettantism Nauman put into practice what Cunningham had applied, for example, in a group performance at the Brandeis University Creative Arts Festival in 1952; the choreographer had used students with little or no dance training in a performance with dancers he brought from New York. The students were asked to do "simple gestures they did ordinarily," such as washing their hands, filing their nails, combing their hair, and skipping. He commented, in describing this work: "These were accepted as movement in daily life, why not on stage?"[10] The students could execute with confidence those movements they were accustomed to, and thus had little stage fright.

Cunningham tried not "to separate the human being from the action he does, or the actions which surround him, but . . . [to] see what it is like to break these actions up in different ways, to allow the passion, and it is passion, to appear for each person in his own way."[11] In the same way that Nauman believed conventional tools tended to determine how art could be made, Cunningham was suspicious about relying totally on technique: "The danger with acquiring a technique is that it can constrict, *can make you think that's the way* you have to do it." It was Cunningham's experience that "movement is expressive, regardless of intentions of expressivity"; of his dancers he wrote that "in one way or another, what we thought we couldn't do was altogether possible, if only we didn't get the mind in the way."[12] Cunningham's attitudes toward dance indicated to Nauman that he could proceed as an "amateur," working intuitively rather than by aiming for technical perfection. The force of Nauman's performances stems from the tension of operating at the edges of "professionalism" where the warm-up exercises or rehearsals end and "dance" starts, as well as from the continuous threat of collapse, of losing his balance or otherwise failing technically, that comes from his amateur status in a professional field.

In other works Nauman blurs distinctions between music and noise, and again poses the question of where practice ends and the performance begins. In *Playing a Note on the Violin While I Walk around the Studio,* 1968, his original intention was "to play two notes very close together so that you could hear the beats in the harmonics . . . .The camera was set up near the center of the studio facing one wall, but I walked all around the studio, so often there was no one in the picture, just the studio wall and the sound of the footsteps and the violin."[13] The sound is fast, loud, distorted, and out of sync, but it is not noticeable until the end of the film. Nauman quietly walks out of the frame in the knowledge that, as John Cage put it, "There is no such thing as an empty space or an empty time. There is always something to see, something to hear."[14] It was again Cage who made Nauman aware of the possibilities of playing with sounds "that are notated and those that are not." In his book *Silence,* Cage explained that "those that are not notated appear in the written music as silences, opening the doors of the music to the sounds that happen to be in the environment."[15] When Nauman steps outside the frame, the viewer's sense of his own environment is heightened, while the action in the film is reduced to "white noise," vaguely present in the background; the involvement of the spectator with the performance is nearly broken.

When he made this film, Nauman did not know how to play the violin, which he had bought only a month or two earlier. "I play other instruments, but I never played the violin and during the period of time that I had it before the film I started diddling around with it." A year later, during the winter of 1968–69, Nauman made the videotape *Violin Tuned D E A D* (p. 268). "One thing I was interested in was playing," Nauman stated in the already mentioned interview with Willoughby Sharp. "I wanted to set up a problem where it wouldn't matter whether I knew how to play the violin or not. What I did was to play as fast as I could on all four strings with the violin tuned D, E, A, D. I thought it would just be a lot of noise, but it turned out to be musically very interesting. It is a very tense piece."[16]

Nauman felt strongly that the important thing in doing these performances was to "recognize what you don't know, and what you can't do," and as an amateur never to allow himself to slip into traditional music, theater, or dance, where he would put himself in the position of being compared with professional performers in those fields. Nauman believed that if he chose the right set of circumstances and structure, was serious enough about his activities, and worked hard at it, his performance would have merit. His intentions and attitude would turn the performance into art. John Cage's *Pieces for Prepared Piano* of 1940 gave Nauman additional insight into the reinvention of how to play the violin. For this piece Cage had changed the sound of a piano in order to produce music suitable for the dancer Syvilla Fort's performance of *Bacchanale*. First Cage had placed a pie plate on the strings, but it bounced around because of the vibrations. Nails, which he had placed inside the piano as well, slipped down between the strings; however, screws and bolts worked out. In this way, Cage wrote, "two different sounds could be produced. One was resonant and open, the other was quiet and muted."[17]

By playing the notes D, E, A, D, on the violin as fast as he could, Nauman created a rhythmic structure and notational pattern that, because of its repetition, provided a certain monotonous continuity. Because of the frenetic tempo, the performance was very intense; Nauman's screechy manner of playing lacked any melodic inflection, and the

sounds picked up by the cheap equipment gave the piece a harsh electronic character. Nauman got the idea of playing as fast as he could from the aleatoric directions in certain musical compositions by Karlheinz Stockhausen, especially his 1955–56 *Zeitmasse* ("Tempi") for Woodwind Quintet. As Peter S. Hansen has written, Stockhausen's Quintet "employs various kinds of 'time.' Some are metronomic (in specified tempi), while others are relative. These are 'as fast as possible' (dependent on the technique of the players); from 'very slow to approximately four times faster' and from 'very fast to approximately four times slower.' "[18] In *Violin Tuned D E A D,* Nauman created a specific kind of environment through sound, and at the same time turned the act of playing the violin into a physical activity that is itself interesting to watch. By turning the camera on its side and his back to the camera, in a static, medium-long shot of the studio, Nauman portrayed himself as an anonymous figure floating horizontally across the screen in defiance of gravity.

The performance in *Violin Tuned D E A D* would have been a continuous activity were it not for the unintentional mistakes, accentuations, and moments of faltering and tiredness that slowed the tempo from time to time. In a similar way, the sound in the film *Bouncing Two Balls between the Floor and Ceiling with Changing Rhythms,* 1968 (p. 250), in which Nauman performs a sort of athletic version of the children's game of jacks, appears at first to be only incidental but turns out to be the focus of the piece, sustaining the structure and rhythm of the performance. In the interview with Willoughby Sharp Nauman recalls:

At a certain point I had two balls going and I was running around all the time trying to catch them. Sometimes they would hit something on the floor or the

ceiling and go off into the corner and hit together. Finally I lost track of them both. I picked up one of the balls and just threw it against the wall. I was really mad, because I was losing control of the game. I was trying to keep the rhythm going, to have the balls bounce once on the floor and once on the ceiling and then catch them, or twice on the floor and once on the ceiling. There was a rhythm going and when I lost it that ended the film. My idea at the time was that the film should have no beginning or end: one should be able to come in at any time and nothing would change."[19]

Rather than attempting to pick up objects while the balls were bouncing (as in a real game of jacks), Nauman stressed physical force by throwing the balls as hard as he could; this made them bounce more unpredictably. He compared the effect to an incident that happened when he was playing baseball as a kid: "Once I got hit in the face, totally without expecting it, as I was leaving the field; it knocked me down. I was interested in that kind of experience you can't anticipate—it hits you, you can't explain it intellectually." In both his films and his videotapes Nauman starts from certain rules he has invented and then lets events take their own course. He waits for chance to come along to change those rules, and when it does he allows the unexpected to take over. As a parallel to his intuitive approach of making up rules and breaking them, he cites the African game Ngalisio, which is played by the Turkana men at any time, with a constantly varying number of players. The men dig two rows of small, shallow holes in the ground, and then place stones in each. The players gather around the holes and squat down, and then one at a time move the stones in different combinations from hole to hole. The objective seems to be for each player to gather as many stones as possible, but no player ever seems to win. The game appears to be not so much about winning as about the act of playing. New rules are made up silently and are adopted or discarded with the understanding and consent of the other players, so that there is never a consistent pattern in the way the men move the stones. In *Bouncing Two Balls between the Floor and Ceiling with Changing Rhythms,* the discontinuous noises which structure both the time of the performance and the rhythm of the film can be heard by the spectators even after they have walked away from the monitor. By using the natural noises resulting from his activities Nauman found a clever way to let sounds be themselves rather than, in Cage's words, "vehicles for man-made theories or expressions of human sentiments."[20]

The first time Nauman gave directions for particular sounds to be incorporated as an element in a sculptural work was in a concept for a piece that was never executed but is preserved in a drawing of 1966 (p. 254). On it he noted: "Cry to me, cry to me, yellow neon at bottom pile of felt pads with letters cut out—neon light at bottom; if pad is say 5' or 6' square, can't see light at bottom except what light shining up from the holes—(could be lead rather than felt); need 7" of felt, ⁵⁄₁₆" per layer, say 22 layers; if 6 sq. cost $8 for 9 x 12, or $4 per layer, cost $88 for sufficient felt." Instead of presenting a piece of information, he employed an imperative that could be a fragment of a rock and roll lyric, as he had in *Love Me Tender, Move Te Lender* (p. 150), the pun on the title of the Elvis Presley song. Nauman recalls that at a symposium he attended in Santa Barbara at the time, a sculptor defended her right to use bread as a material, while a well-known critic argued that to do so was unethical since so many people were starving. "This confirmed to me that I could use anything I wanted, whatever was around," Nauman said. "I could use

it even if it did not appear to be appropriate to somebody else." Nauman also observed other artists, such as Joseph Beuys and H. C. Westermann, using "poor" materials at that time. In 1966 the publication of Robert Morris's "Notes on Sculpture" stimulated discussions about what sculpture should be. In this piece Morris argued that cubes, pyramids, and simple, irregular polyhedrons, such as beams or inclined planes, are relatively "easy to visualize and sense as wholes." Those simple forms "create strong Gestalt sensations. Their parts are bound together in such a way that they offer a maximum resistance to perceptual separation."[21] Nauman shared an interest in Gestalt psychology, but disagreed with what he felt was Morris's narrowing of its definition. For Nauman, the idea of "completion" meant arriving at a more complex physical and emotional experience through a Gestalt. The use of light, sound, and "poor" materials as sculptural elements became his means of getting away from reductivist statements. His approach is exemplified by the drawing *Cry to Me,* in which he charged elementary geometric forms with strong emotional and evocative content that is reinforced by the title, the hidden light, and the suggestion of the muffled sound buried beneath the pile of felt.

In 1968 Nauman realized a piece with hidden sound and described it in a drawing (p. 254) with this notation: "Tape recorder with a tape loop of a scream wrapped in a plastic bag and cast into the center of a block of concrete; weight about 650 pounds or 240 kg." The theatrical gesture of the muffled scream offsets the minimal form of this piece. The idea shows similarities with Nauman's time-capsule pieces, such as *Storage Capsule for the Right Rear Quarter of My Body,* 1966 (p. 255). A reversal of expectations occurs as the volume of air enclosing the recorded

scream is solidified in concrete, giving the piece a sculptural presence. By sealing off the sound, Nauman forces the spectator to imagine the concept and therefore to think about the piece rather than simply be attracted by its formal qualities. This proposal and another from the same year—for an unrealized stack piece that would conceal memorabilia from his own life, such as photographs and pocket things, between heavy steel plates—bring to mind Marcel Duchamp's *With Hidden Noise,* 1916. This work, made in New York during Easter of that year, is an "assisted" readymade, which consists of a ball of twine sandwiched between two brass plates; inside the ball is a small secret object that rolls around—the "hidden noise" of the title—added by the collector Walter C. Arensberg.

In *Six Sound Problems for Konrad Fischer* (pp. 256–57), a piece done in the summer of 1968 at the Galerie Konrad Fischer in Düsseldorf, Nauman again set up discrepancies between what one knows and what one sees. This piece mixed recorded sounds with the natural noises of the environment. On the plan for this work (drawn first backwards and then correctly), Nauman noted, "6 sound problems for Konrad Fischer—(6 day week)/ 1. walk/ 2. balls/ 3. violin 4. violin w. walk/ 5. violin w./ balls/ 6. balls w/ walk/ must be short can be very short/ loop 1/ monday/ 2 tuesday/ wednesday 3/ thursday 4/ friday 5/ saturday/ loop 5/ loop 4/ loop 3/ on tape/ recorder/ loop 6/ loop 2/ 11 cm, 1968." Nauman started by repeating his earlier performance activities—walking around, playing the violin, and rhythmically bouncing two balls—which he performed for the occasion in Fischer's gallery, again by himself, making the space his studio. Then he physically cut the tapes to lengths that fit the physical layout of the space. On each of six days a different loop of sound tape was both played and shown in the gallery space. On the first day of the piece, a visitor entering the gallery was confronted with a scene that might have been a stage set for a production of Samuel Beckett's *Krapp's Last Tape*; there was nothing in the space but a chair and a table, placed off center in the room. On top of the table was a tape recorder playing the smallest loop of sound tape. On following days, however, a visitor would find, strung diagonally across the space, ever-longer loops of sound tape, at one end threaded through the recorder head and at the other wound loosely around a pencil fastened to the chair with masking tape. Each day the chair would be located in a different spot, with the tapes eventually forming a radiating pattern.

Six Sound Problems for Konrad Fischer summarized central aspects of Nauman's sculptural and performance activities. In incorporating his own memories and experiences into his sculptural works— as he had also done in some of his 1968 stack pieces—Nauman eliminated the distance between his work and himself, just as Beckett had in the trilogy *Molloy, Malone Dies,* and *The Unnamable* where one hears the author's voice, as the first-person narrator, alongside the fictional main characters'. Both Beckett and Nauman transform their experiences into anonymous, timeless events. Nauman kept his performances from becoming too autobiographical by distancing himself from his audience through film and video. Through his use of framing and cropping he turned himself into an anonymous, abstract body.

During the winter of 1968–69 Nauman stayed in New York; while there he made several hour-long black-and-white videotapes, among them *Bouncing in the Corner No. 1* and *No. 2* (p. 269), *Lip Sync* (p. 268), *Revolving Upside Down* (p. 267); and *Pacing Upside Down* (p. 266). Then, in 1969, after returning to Los Angeles, he made a set of four

black-and-white silent films—*Black Balls* (p. 260), *Bouncing Balls* (p. 259), *Gauze* (p. 261), and *Pulling Mouth* (p. 263). Each of these so-called Slo-Mo films is less than ten minutes long; the four are shown together on one reel.

Nauman had originally intended to show his films from 1967–68 as loops, so that the audience could come in or leave at any time without feeling that they had missed something, but he never screened them that way. He wanted to set up a cyclic time structure because he felt that *Fishing for Asian Carp*, with its beginning and end, was a narrative; as such it became "too much like making movies, which I wanted to avoid, so I decided to record an ongoing process and make a loop that could continue all day or all week."[22] In these films the camera was stationary, placed at a low height and then pointed slightly downward in order to show the floor. The only camera manipulation consisted of the framing, which caused Nauman to be partly in and partly out of the picture as he performed. The technical flaws of the films were included in their aesthetics, as were the imperfections of Nauman's actions caused by fatigue and chance. For instance, Nauman explained that in both *Playing a Note on the Violin While I Walk around the Studio* and *Bouncing Two Balls between the Floor and Ceiling with Changing Rhythms*, he "started out in sync but there again, it is a wild track, so as the tape stretches and tightens it goes in and out of sync. I more or less wanted it to be in sync but I just didn't have the equipment and the patience to do it."[23] In contrast, Nauman had been able to rent a special industrial camera to make the four Slo-Mo films, which are shot in very slow motion. Speaking with Willoughby Sharp in 1970, Nauman described his process:
You really can't do it with the available video equipment for amateurs. I'm getting about four thousand frames per second.

I've made four films so far. One is called Bouncing Balls, *only this time it's testicles instead of rubber balls. Another one is called* Black Balls. *It's putting black make-up on testicles. The others are [*Pulling Mouth *and* Gauze], *and in the last one I start out with about 5 or 6 yards of gauze in my mouth, which I then pull out and let fall on the floor. These are all shot extremely close up.*[24]

Each film took from six to twelve seconds to shoot, depending on the frame speed, which varied between a thousand and four thousand frames per second, depending on how well the area in which the activity staged was lit. "The action is really slowed down a lot," Nauman said; "sometimes it is so slow that you don't really see any motion but you sort of notice the thing is different from time to time."[25]

In his films from 1967–68 Nauman had objectified his activities through the endless repetition of sound and broken-up movements, and through the cropping of the body by the frame. In some of the slow-motion films, the suspension of time and gravity caused by the slowed filming abstracts the action. The viewer stops looking for recognizable objects; the absence of sound forces one to concentrate even more intently on the nearly arrested motion of the picture. Nauman compares the effect to that of watching silent, slow-motion films of atomic bomb explosions, "where you become fascinated with the weightless cloud formations unfolding like giant flowers. You have to know what the images are in order to understand their morbid implications." In *Bouncing Balls* and *Black Balls* the nearly static images alternately take the form of movie stills, kinetic sculpture, and "stillnesses"—Cunningham's term for static positions held by dancers—stressing not so much the breaking up of motion but of the relationships that exist between movements.

Precedents for these slow-motion

233

works can be found in a film Nauman made in 1967 entitled *Thighing* (p. 258), and, specifically for *Pulling Mouth* (p. 263), a series of holograms he produced entitled *Making Faces*, 1968 (p. 264). In *Thighing* Nauman distorted his thigh by pinching and pulling it, while confusing the viewer with a sound track of his breathing loudly. That same year he made a drawing of five poses of unnaturally twisted lips (p. 262); they suggest both children's games and aberrant behavior. On this drawing he carefully noted: "Both lips turned out; mouth open, upper lip push[ed] up by right thumb and lower lip pulled down by right forefinger; both lips pulled in tight over teeth—mouth open. As above but mouth open. Both lips squeezed together from the side by the thumb and forefinger right hand." In the series of holograms called *Making Faces* (p. 264), Nauman contorted, stretched, and pulled his face into exaggerated and formal facial arrangements, ending in absurdity. "I guess I was interested in doing a really extreme thing," he revealed. "It's almost as though if I'd decided to do a smile, I wouldn't have had to take a picture of it. I could just have written down that I'd done it, or made a list of things that one could do. There was also the problem with the holograms of making the subject matter sufficiently strong so that you wouldn't think about the technical side so much."[26] Of the four slow-motion films, *Gauze* (p. 261) is the most ethereal. "When I pulled the gauze out of my mouth, I had no idea what it was going to be like," Nauman remembers. "Watching it afterwards, you are left with beautiful images of falling gauze. All kinds of allusions had slipped in which I had not intended, but certainly had allowed to be there." *Gauze* was filmed with the camera upside down, giving the activity a sense of weightlessness. This quality combines associations that range from the yogi who purifies the

digestive tract with a length of wet string, to the magician who pulls a seemingly endless string of handkerchiefs from his mouth.

Both the idea of the suspension of gravity, which reduces the sense of the physicality of the scenes, and the omission of references to scale, which forces the spectator to use his or her imagination, return in Nauman's Film Sets: *Spinning Spheres* and *Rotating Glass Walls*, both 1970 (pp. 270, 271), 8- and 16-millimeter film loops that are projected simultaneously onto four walls. Nauman has described the projects as follows:

Film Set A: Spinning Spheres

A steel ball placed on a glass plate in a white cube of space. The ball is set to spinning and filmed so that the image reflected on the surface of the ball has one wall of the cube centered. The ball is center frame and fills most of the frame. The camera is hidden as much as possible so that its reflection will be negligible. Four prints are necessary. The prints are projected onto the walls of a room (front or rear projection; should cover the walls edge to edge). The image reflected in the spinning sphere should not be that of a real room but of a more idealized room, of course empty, and not reflecting the images projected on the other room walls. There will be no scale references in the films.

Film Set B: Rotating Glass Walls

Film a piece of glass as follows: glass plate is pivoted on a horizontal center line and rotated slowly. Film is framed with the center line exactly at the top of the frame so that as the glass rotates one edge will go off the top of the frame as the other edge comes on the top edge of the frame. The sides of the glass will not be in the frame of the film. Want two prints of the glass rotating bottom coming toward the camera and two prints of bottom of plate

going away from camera. The plate and pivot are set up in a white cube as in Set A, camera hidden as well as possible to destroy any scale indications in the projected films. Projection: image is projected from edge to edge of all four walls of a room. If the image on one wall shows the bottom of the plate moving toward the camera, the opposite wall will show the image moving away from the camera."[27]

In contrast to *Gauze*, the videotapes Nauman made during the winter of 1968–69 record such commonplace studio activities as pacing or walking, and therefore have a more down-to-earth character. Nevertheless, because of Nauman's manipulations of the camera, these tapes are no less absurd or abstract. Here the camerawork has become "a bit more important," Nauman noted; he used a wide-angle lens to distort the image, or he turned the camera on its side or upside down. "As I became more aware of what happens in the recording medium I would make little alterations," he said. For *Stamping in the Studio*, 1968, (p. 266), which records Nauman stamping his feet in different rhythms, the camera was stationary but placed in an upside-down position. The rhythms of the stamping become more and more complex, moving, as Nina Sundell describes it, "from a steady one-two one-two to a syncopated ten-beat phrase. . . . Nauman crosses the studio horizontally and then diagonally, and then moves in expanding and contracting spirals, covering the entire floor area, his path often taking him off-screen."[28] In *Revolving Upside Down*, 1969 (p. 267), the camera is also inverted. The action in this tape is related to that of *Slow Angle Walk*; Nauman complicates and extends the process of getting "from here to there" by making a series of complicated leg movements in a manner that seems alternately logical and illogical, first raising one leg while standing on the other, then revolving a quarter-circle by turning his

Gauze. 1969
Film (slow motion), 16 mm, black and
white, silent, 8 min.

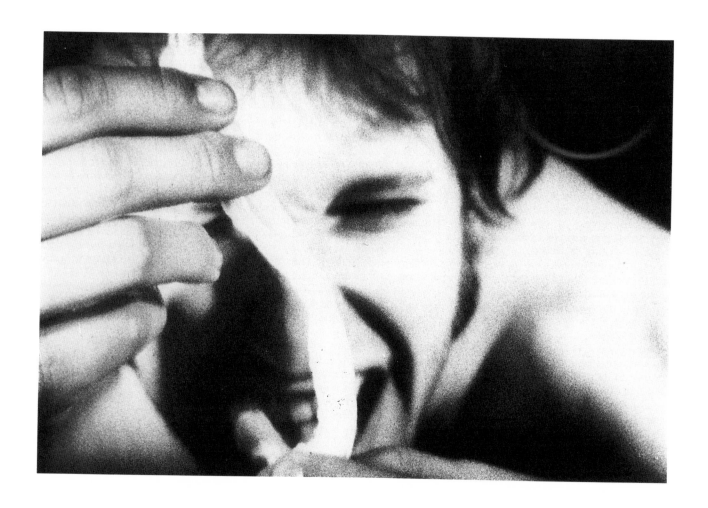

heel, then completing the step. While Nauman made this sort of multidirectional movement part of his video vocabulary, it had been Merce Cunningham who had emphasized this idea, in applying chance to space: "Rather than thinking in one direction, i.e., to the audience in a proscenium frame, direction could be foursided and upside down," he wrote.[29]

Lip Sync, 1969 (p. 268), in which the camera is again upside down, focuses on Nauman's mouth, chin, and throat as he repeats the words "lip sync" over and over, articulating them in an exaggerated manner. Nauman hears the words through the earphones that he wears, and then repeats them; but the rhythm of the soundtrack on which he says the phrase is not synchronized with the movements of the lips on the screen—which are made even harder to comprehend because of their inversion. The lips and sound go in and out of sync. In contrast to the grainy, lyrical images of his films of 1967–68, which suggest a visual field on which one is free to impose one's imagination, this video image separates what one hears from what one sees, forcing the viewer to try to match up sound and image.

Nauman did his last live performance in 1969, during the exhibition "Anti-Illusion: Procedures/Materials," held at the Whitney Museum of American Art in New York from May 19 to July 6. For an hour, the performers in the piece—Nauman, his wife Judy, and the dancer Meredith Monk—stood in different corners of the space, facing the audience. Over and over they let themselves fall back, then pushed themselves off the walls of the corner, a foot and a half away, bouncing back to the point where they would nearly lose their balance. The effect of this rigorous, physically exhausting exercise was intensified by the thumping sound it produced. Because the performers could not see each other,

they were in varying degrees in and out of sync both with each other and with the pounding sounds they produced. Nauman employed a similar effect in his 1985 neon pieces on sex and power. For instance, in *Mean Clown Welcome* (p. 100), the sequence in which the various parts of the piece flash on and off is the same for each pair of figures, but they flash at different speeds, going out of phase and back into it over a period of five minutes. Basically the two pairs of figures are programmed to "stand, step forward (hand and arm reach out, limp penis becomes erect penis), and shake hands (when hand is up, erect penis is on, when hand is down, limp penis is on)," as Nauman described it. The figures on the left flash at a rate "about that of a brisk handshake," while the figures on the right flash faster and thus go out of phase, so that the limbs no longer align with each other, creating confusion and complexity. Nauman compares his procedure of taking events in and out of synchronization to the composer Steve Reich's use of a similar technique in *Violin Phase,* 1967, and *It's Gonna Rain,* 1965. In the latter, several sound tracks are played at a slightly different rate so that the phrase, "It's gonna rain," repeated over and over, is altered at the points where the tracks don't align. This not only causes the cadence to change but also breaks the sequence of the words, giving them a different meaning, somewhat in the manner of Nauman's *First Poem Piece,* 1968, and *Second Poem Piece,* 1969 (pp. 164, 165). It interested Nauman, too, that Reich had picked up the phrase from a man voicing his opinion in New York's Central Park. This was in accordance with his own practice of using the titles of popular songs, as in the drawing *Love Me Tender, Move Te Lender,* 1966 (p. 150), and in his neon piece *Suite Substitute,* 1968 (p. 154). In 1972 he took an exhortation, sprayed in red letters

about five feet high on an overpass in Pasadena, California, for his yellow and pink neon piece *Run from Fear, Fun from Rear* (p. 101).

Nauman met Reich in 1968 at the University of Colorado, where he was visiting William T. Wiley. Wiley and Reich were collaborating on a performance they entitled *Overevident Falls,* and Nauman became interested in Reich's working methods while observing him as he recorded over the course of two days. Wiley recalls that Reich suspended a pair of microphones from a swing. Each time the swing passed in front of a set of amplifiers feedback was produced—a shriek, followed by a kind of howling sound when the swing reached the height of its motion before swinging back in the opposite direction. Meanwhile, Wiley poured soap flakes on the swing; these fluoresced under a black light and softly drifted down to form a pile beneath the swing. Later that same year Reich used a similar device for his piece *Pendulum Music,* performed at the Whitney Museum of American Art.

In the winter of 1968–69, before his own performance at the Whitney during the "Anti-Illusion" exhibition, Nauman had made two tapes called *Bouncing in the Corner No. 1* and *No. 2* (p. 269) based on the same idea as the Whitney piece. These works are more remote and sculptural than the live performance, which was direct and theatrical. In the first tape the camera is held sideways, in the second upside down; in the second tape, one especially perceives an abstract, swaying image positioned carefully at the edge of the frame. Through the repetitious cadence, the dislocating cropping of the image, the apparent defiance of gravity, and the use of reductive black-and-white tones, the performer is changed into a hypnotic, undulating visual field.

Performing at the Whitney Museum with two people made Nauman realize

236

that he could involve others in his performances if he gave them specific instructions. Before this he had found it difficult to carry out a performance even once, let alone repeat it. He figured that he could "make a situation where someone else has to do what I would do," he could go into the studio and do whatever he was interested in doing, and then "try to find a way to present it so that other people could do it without too much explanation." But he felt he had to set up a "very strict kind of environment or situation so that even if the performer didn't know anything about me or the work that goes into the piece, he would be able to do something similar to what I would do." After the Whitney evening, and throughout the first half of the 1970s, Nauman no longer performed himself but sent specific performance instructions to exhibitions in which he was invited to participate. A typical set of instructions was published in 1970 in *Artforum*:

Hire a dancer or dancers or other performers of some presence to perform the following exercises for one hour a day for about ten days or two weeks. The minimum will require one dancer to work on one exercise for ten to fourteen days. If more money is available two dancers may perform, one dancer performing each exercise at the same time and for the same period as the other. The whole may be repeated on ten or fourteen day intervals as often as desired.

(A) Body as a Cylinder

Lie along the wall/floor junction of the room, face into the corner and hands at sides. Concentrate on straightening and lengthening the body along a line which passes through the center of the body parallel to the corner of the room in which you lie. At the same time attempt to draw the body in around the line. Then attempt to push that line into the corner of the room.

(B) Body as a Sphere

Curl your body into the corner of a room. Imagine a point at the center of your curled body and concentrate on pulling your body in around that point. Then attempt to press that point down into the corner of the room. It should be clear that these are not intended as static positions which are to be held for an hour a day, but mental and physical activities or processes to be carried out. At the start, the performer may need to repeat the exercise several times in order to fill the hour, but at the end of ten days or so, he should be able to extend the execution to a full hour. The number of days required for an uninterrupted hour performance of course depends on the receptivity and training of the performer.[30]

These performances and a related one about attempting to make the center of the room and the center of one's body coincide are to a large extent mental exercises in which the audience observes no action. In the first place, it is virtually impossible to locate the perfect center of a room, even with incredibly precise measurements. In these works Nauman again explores the discrepancies between idea and reality, between what one observes and what one theoretically knows. Again, the conceptual process prevails over physical details. In 1969, Nauman had used the idea of finding a center in a sculptural piece, *Dead Center* (p. 272), in which he cut a hole through the center of a steel slab with a blowtorch. In this case the violence of the act, with its allusion to the deadly precision of shooting through the bull's-eye of a target, is combined with the absurd literalness Nauman had used in other works—for instance, *From Hand to Mouth* (p. 90). Discrepancies between seeing and knowing return in two videotapes of performances done in 1973, *Elke Allowing the Floor to Rise Up over Her, Face Up* and *Tony Sinking into the Floor, Face*

Up and Face Down (both p. 273), forty and sixty minutes long, respectively. For these tapes Nauman instructed each performer to lie motionless on the floor—and had told each one to practice this diligently before the taping. Furthermore, he had told the first performer to imagine that the molecules of her body would mix with those in the floor, and that slowly she would lose herself and become a part of something else. Under the pressure and tension of the actual performance, she lost her sense of time and became frightened; three times she had to sit up because she felt that she was filling up with the molecules of the floor and was therefore becoming unable to breathe.

Nauman intended these performances as mental exercises, the realization of a concept that already was implicit in his slow-motion films. Slowing down the performer's movements in these earlier films made the muscular contractions seem weaker; the performer appeared to be perfectly still. The internal process did not necessarily show on the outside. Thus in 1973 it occurred to Nauman that he could make a tape in which a person who was concentrating very hard would appear the same as someone taking a nap on the floor. In these tapes Nauman's presence is felt behind the camera, something that is not true of the videotapes from 1968–69, where as the performer he was in front of the camera. In these later works, for instance, at five-minute intervals he dissolves between two images of the body, seen from different angles, and he sets up the time structure of the works by panning and moving the camera. By restricting a situation in this way Nauman ensured that whatever variation the performer invented spontaneously would remain within the framework of his instructions. It was through this kind of reasoning that, in the spring of 1969, Nauman hit upon the idea that by creating a sculptural installation in a sufficiently specific manner he could "make a participation piece without the participants being able to alter the work." Thus he would bridge in one piece his sculptural and performance activities. An example of this is *Performance Corridor* (p. 274), first used as a prop in his videotape *Walk with Contrapposto* (p. 274) and then exhibited by itself in the "Anti-Illusion" show at the Whitney Museum of American Art. "I began to think about how you relate to a particular place, which I was doing by pacing around," Nauman wrote.

That was an activity which took place in the studio. Then I began thinking about how to present this without making it a performance, so that somebody else would have the same experience instead of just having to watch me have that experience. The earliest pieces were just narrow corridors. The first one I used was a prop for a piece that was taped. It was presented as a prop for a performance and was called that, without any description of what the performance was. It was just a very narrow, gray corridor, and all you could do was walk in and walk out. It limited the kind of things you could do, because I don't like the idea of free manipulation, of putting a bunch of stuff out there and letting people do what they want with it. I really had more specific kinds of experience in mind, and without having to write out a list of what people should do, I wanted to make play experiences unavailable just by the preciseness of the area.[31]

By giving no instructions, Nauman left it up to the visitor to decide whether or not to enter the corridor and become a performer in the piece. Another piece from that time, *Lighted Performance Box*, 1969 (p. 275), consists of a tall welded-aluminum box, open at the top, to which there was clamped a theatrical light. The idea of this work may be that one is to climb into the box and stand under the bright light. Here again the performer-spectator is made aware of the physical limitations the artist has imposed; for one thing, it is very nearly impossible to enter the box.

In December 1969, Nauman constructed his first Acoustic Wall at the Galerie Ileana Sonnabend in Paris. "It was a large *L*-shaped piece covering two walls of her Paris gallery," Nauman explained. "It was flush with the wall of the gallery, and had very thin speakers built into it. Two different tapes were played over the speakers: one was of exhaling sounds, and the other alternated between pounding and laughing. You couldn't locate the sound. That was quite a threatening piece, especially the exhaling sounds."[32] The false wall, 9 feet high and 12 feet long on each wing of the *L* shape, served no support function and so was built roughly to create a sculptural presence in the room.

In most of the Acoustic Wall installations, sound is used not only to disorient but also to impart a psychological impact to otherwise neutral surroundings. The advantage of using sound in this way is that it does not cover up "true" materials, something that must be done to create a sculptural presence in the gallery. To reinforce both their tactility and their ambiguity—are these false walls art, or are they part of construction work being done in the gallery?—most of these walls are smooth on the inside but rough and unfinished on the outside. In the 1969–70 *Acoustic Wall* (p. 276), Nauman shifts the emphasis from visual experience to physical involvement. He explained his intent in such works: *When the corridors had to do with sound damping, the wall relied on soundproofing material which altered the sound in the corridor and also caused pressure on your ears, which is what I was really interested in: pressure changes that occurred while you were passing by the material. And then one thing to do was to make a V. When you are at the open end of the V there's not too much effect, but as you walk into the V the pressure increases quite a bit, it's very claustrophobic.[33]*

In her article "PheNAUMANology," published in *Artforum* in 1970, Marcia Tucker writes that "Nauman has pointed out an analogous situation existing in nature, when certain winds or approaching storms can create even minute massive changes in the atmosphere, which are said to account for widespread emotional instability and increased suicide rates in a given area."[34] As hard as it is to measure the impact of "emotional overload" on the participants, it is as senseless, in accordance with Nauman's intent, to attempt to describe the Acoustic Wall pieces which "rely on words less and less." Already in 1970 Nauman had written that "it has become really difficult to explain the pieces. Although it's easier to describe them now, it's almost impossible to explain what they do when you're there. Take *Performance Corridor*. . . . It's very easy to describe how the piece looks, but the experience of walking inside it is something else altogether which can't be described. And the pieces increasingly have to do with physical or physiological responses."[35] Information from two sources, touching and hearing, disorients and confuses the participants in the Acoustic Wall installations. Sometimes these sources are inseparable; at other times they do not align at all. The artist can then restrict the participants physically, guiding their experiences. On the other hand, the "cooler" the empty spaces become the more emotionally loaded the pieces are, leaving the artist in a vulnerable position as well: "I think when you attempt to engage people that way—emotionally—in what you're doing," Nauman told Tucker, "then it's difficult because you never know if you succeed or not, or to what extent. In other words, it is easier to be professional, because then you can step outside the situation. When you bring things to a personal level, then you're just much less sure whether people can accept what's presented."[36]

In 1985, after a hiatus of about ten years, Nauman returned to video; he made two videotapes in color, one featuring a man and the other a woman, and together they constitute *Good Boy Bad Boy* (p. 282). Each performer repeats the same one hundred phrases. In a later interview he explained why he had returned to this medium:

I think it's because I had this information that I didn't want to put into a neon sign; I didn't know what to do with it. . . . I could write it and publish it, print it or whatever. . . . It took a long time, but I finally decided to do it as a video. I had thought about presenting it as a performance, but I have never felt comfortable with performance. And so video seemed to be a way to do it. It was very interesting for me when we made the tapes—I used professional actors. The man had done mostly live, stage acting, so he was much more generous and open in his acting. The woman had done a lot of television acting, mostly daytime, in commercials and some soap operas. So a lot of her acting is in her face—she didn't use her hands much. I liked that difference. What interests me is the line that exists between others. Because the performers are actors, the material's not autobiographical. It's not real anger; they're pretending to be angry— and they are pretty good at it, but not really convincing. I like all these different levels, not knowing quite how to take the situation, how to relate to it.[37]

Good Boy Bad Boy was conceived as a didactic, moral statement. Both actors address the viewer, looking straight into the camera. They appear in close-up, like news announcers, as each one tries to convince the audience of the truth of his or her message. "It involves you by talking to you—'I was a good boy—you were a good boy!' " Nauman said. "It's

not a conversation; you are not allowed to talk. But you are involved simply by virtue of the fact that someone uses that form of address."[38] An artificial relationship is set up not only between the actor and the audience, but also between the man and the woman—although they act and speak at the same time, they do so at a psychological and physical distance from each other, framed within their own separate monitors. Each time they repeat the hundred phrases, both actors become more emotionally intense in their delivery. In the course of going through the phrases five times (during which they are shown in tighter and tighter close-ups), the actors change from inflections that are neutral and cheerful to those that show irritation and anger. Gradually the emotional differences between the actors (within their methods of acting) begin to show up more and more. Their sentences don't match up any longer, the cadence keeps going out of sync—once more, the scheme of the action breaks down.

Later that same year *Good Boy Bad Boy* returned as part of an installation in Haus Esters, Krefeld, West Germany (p. 282). In this work Nauman attempted to suggest the atmosphere of his studio, in which one thing leads to another, connecting through a process of free association, taking on a variety of ambiguous meanings. He was working against the atmosphere of the museum, in which works of art tend to be defined hierarchically and to be categorized uncomfortably. In his 1970s corridor installations, Nauman had set up a confusion between works under construction, sculptures, and installation pieces, in an attempt to escape the elimination of possibilities that the act of selection implies. Other ways in which he has attempted to avoid categorization have included putting plaster pieces from two different sculptures together in one work, as in the *Studio Piece* of 1978–79

(p. 63), and reassembling dispersed works again in a new context, as in the *Six Sound Problems for Konrad Fischer,* 1968 (p. 257). Another example of this tactic is the Haus Esters installation of 1985, which combined in three rooms the 1985 neon *Hanged Man* (pp. 280– 81); a sound recording of the text for the 1984 neon piece *One Hundred Live and Die* (p. 283); and the 1985 video work *Good Boy Bad Boy* playing on two monitors. This installation can be seen as part of Nauman's epos on the themes of war and peace, or perhaps as his version of the medieval dance of death. The *Hanged Man,* flashing on and off in a simple sequence, epitomizes ambiguity. The implicit question of whether it was the "good boy" who made the "bad boy" hang, or vice versa, is left unanswered. In any case, death is the result. Several associations are suggested by this installation, including the hanging of criminals, lynchings by the Ku Klux Klan, and images from such movies as Ingmar Bergman's *Seventh Seal* or John Ford's Westerns—as well as Nauman's own dangling chair pieces in the Diamond Africa and South America series. Once again a reference is made to a children's game—in this case, Hangman, in which one has to guess the letters of a word; when one misses, part of a gallows is drawn. The game continues until one player has either guessed the word or completed a gallows with a hanging figure. In the Haus Esters installation, *Hanged Man* keeps dangling between good and evil, accompanied by the sound of the chanting of the phrases "kill and die" and "kill and live," "fall and die" and "fall and live," and "spit and die" and "spit and live." At the same time the two actors address us with, "I was a good boy, . . . that was good, I was a bad boy . . . that was bad"; "I don't want to die, you don't want to die, we don't want to die, this is fear of death."

Notes

1. *Unless otherwise noted all quotations from Bruce Nauman in this chapter come from a series of interviews and discussions with the author held between June 1985 and August 1986.*

2. *Quoted in Marshall McLuhan,* The Mechanical Bride *(Boston: 1967), p. 80.*

3. *Quoted in Willoughby Sharp, "Nauman Interview,"* Arts Magazine, *March 1970: 27.*

4. *Quoted in Arturo Schwarz,* The Complete Works of Marcel Duchamp *(London: 1969), p. 483.*

5. *Quoted in Sharp, "Nauman Interview": 24.*

6. *Quoted in Sharp, "Nauman Interview": 23.*

7. *Quoted in Willoughby Sharp, "Bruce Nauman,"* Avalanche 2 *(Winter 1971): 27.*

8. *From an unpublished interview with Lorraine Sciarra, Pomona College, January 1972, quoted by Jane Livingston, in* Bruce Nauman: Works from 1965 to 1972, *Los Angeles County Museum of Art, 1972, pp. 16, 21.*

9. *Quoted in Sciarra interview. It was Jasper Johns who asked Bruce Nauman to make a stage set for Merce Cunningham. Johns recalls meeting Nauman for the first time when they had dinner in a Japanese restaurant after Nauman's first New York show, organized by David Whitney at the Leo Castelli Gallery in 1968. Later, they saw each other several times in Los Angeles, where Johns was making prints at Gemini G.E.L. According to Johns, when he asked Nauman to do the set for* Tread *(first performed in January 1970), Nauman told him to get a lot of fans and put them on a rail across the stage. Nauman's idea was that the Cunningham dance group would not have to carry the fans with them during their tour, but could rent them wherever they went. In a 1968 drawing Nauman had first proposed a kind of scaffolding on wheels, about 4½ feet high, with rows of fluorescent lights on it. The scaffolding was to move back and forth, from left to right, gradually illuminating the stage. The dancers would not only have to work around the patterns of light and dark on the stage but also around the scaffolding itself, which would be moving. However, Robert Morris had already designed a moving light fixture the height of the stage, and it was thought that the designs were too similar. Nauman then came up with* the idea of fans, blowing first toward the dancers, then toward the audience.

10. *From Merce Cunningham,* Changes: Notes on Choreography *(New York: Something Else Press, 1968), n.p.*

11. *Ibid, n.p.:*

12. *Ibid, n.p.*

13. *Sharp, "Bruce Nauman": 29.*

14. *From* Silence: Lectures and Writings by John Cage, *(Middletown, Connecticut: Wesleyan University Press, 1976), p. 8.*

15. *Ibid.*

16. *Quoted in Sharp, "Bruce Nauman": 29.*

17. *Quoted in* Empty Words: Writings 1973–1978 by John Cage *(Middletown, Connecticut: Wesleyan University Press, 1981), p. 8.*

18. *Quoted in Peter S. Hansen,* An Introduction to 20th Century Music *(Boston: Allyn and Bacon, 1971), p. 391.*

19. *Quoted in Sharp, "Bruce Nauman": 28, 29.*

20. *Cage,* Empty Words, *p. 8.*

21. *Quoted in Robert Morris, "Notes on Sculpture,"* Artforum 4, no. 6 *(February 1966): 44.*

22. *Quoted in Sharp, "Nauman Interview": 26.*

23. *Quoted in Sharp, "Bruce Nauman": 28.*

24. *Quoted in Sharp, "Nauman Interview": 26.*

25. *Quoted in Sharp, "Bruce Nauman": 24.*

26. *Quoted in Sharp, "Nauman Interview": 26.*

27. *From "Bruce Nauman: Notes and Projects,"* Artforum 4, no. 4 *(December 1970): 44.*

28. *Quoted in* Castellli-Sonnabend Videotapes and Films, *ed. Nina Sundell (New York, 1974), p. 103.*

29. *Quoted in Merce Cunningham,* Changes.

30. *From "Bruce Nauman: Notes and Projects": 44.*

31. *Quoted in Livingston,* Bruce Nauman: Works from 1965 to 1972, *p. 23.*

32. *Quoted in Sharp, "Nauman Interview": 26.*

33. *Quoted in Sharp, "Bruce Nauman": 23.*

34. *Marcia Tucker, "PheNAUMANology,"* Artforum 4, no. 4 *(December 1970): 42.*

35. *Quoted in Sharp, "Nauman Interview": 25.*

36. *Tucker, "PheNAUMANology": 42.*

37. *In an interview with the author, Nauman stated that he did not plan to make a neon of Good Boy Bad Boy. Shortly thereafter, however, he changed his mind, and transformed his text, a listing of a hundred phrases, into a multicolored neon sign as well.*

38. *Quoted in Chris Dercon, "Keep Taking It Apart: A Conversation with Bruce Nauman,"* Parkett 10 *(1986): 55, 61.*

Tread. 1970
Set design for Merce Cunningham Dance Company

Stills from *Wall-Floor Positions.* 1968
Videotape, black and white, sound,
60 min.

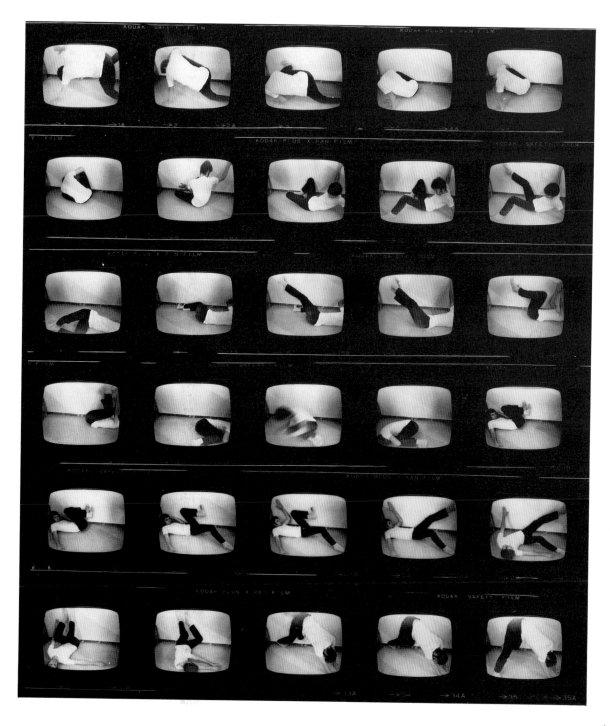

*Glass Templates of the Left Half of My
Body Separated by Cans of Grease.* 1966
Watercolor on paper
23¾ × 18⅞″ (60.3 × 47.9 cm)
Collection Joseph A. Helman, New York

Two views of *Wax Templates of the Left*
Half of My Body Separated by Cans of
Grease. Ca. 1967
Photographed artist's studio, San Francisco
Destroyed

Wax Templates of My Body Arranged to Make an Abstract Sculpture. 1967
Inscribed: "Head/ shoulder/ chest/ waist/ thigh/ knee/ calf/ wax templates of my body arranged to make an abstracted sculpture."
Ink on paper
25 × 19" (63.5 × 48.3 cm)
Washington Art Consortium
Bellingham, Washington

Templates of the Left Half of My Body Every Ten Inches, Spaced Out to Twenty-Inch Intervals (Doubling My Height). 1966
Ink and pencil on paper
18 × 22" (47.4 × 57.4 cm)
Present location unknown

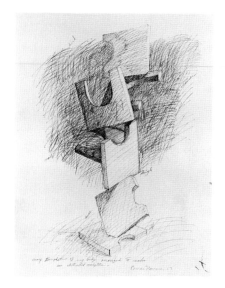

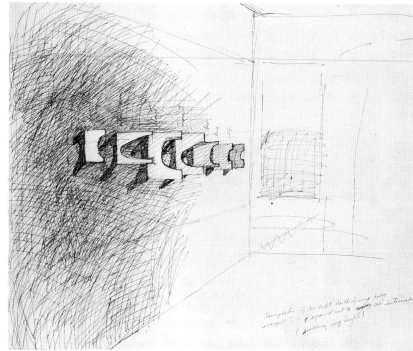

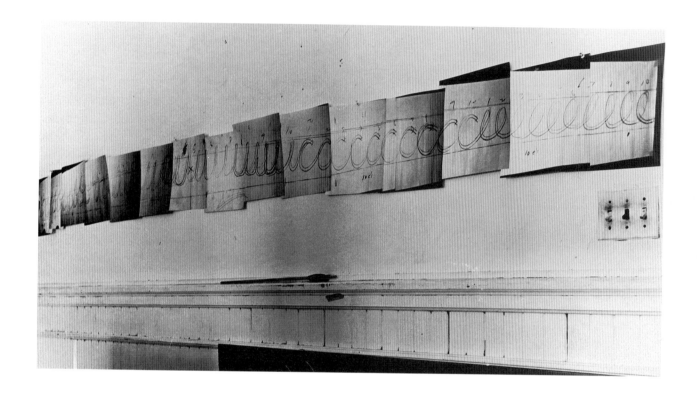

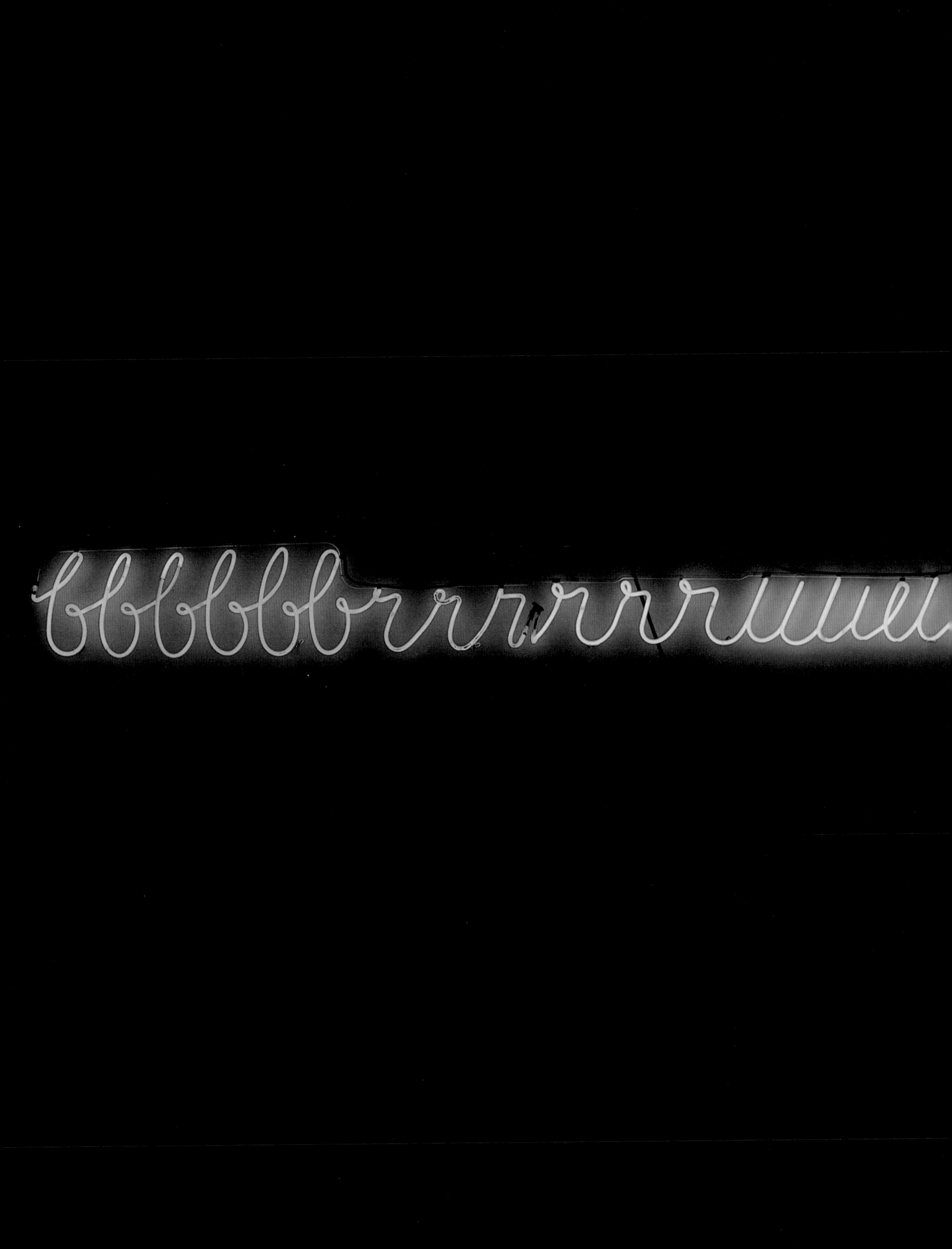

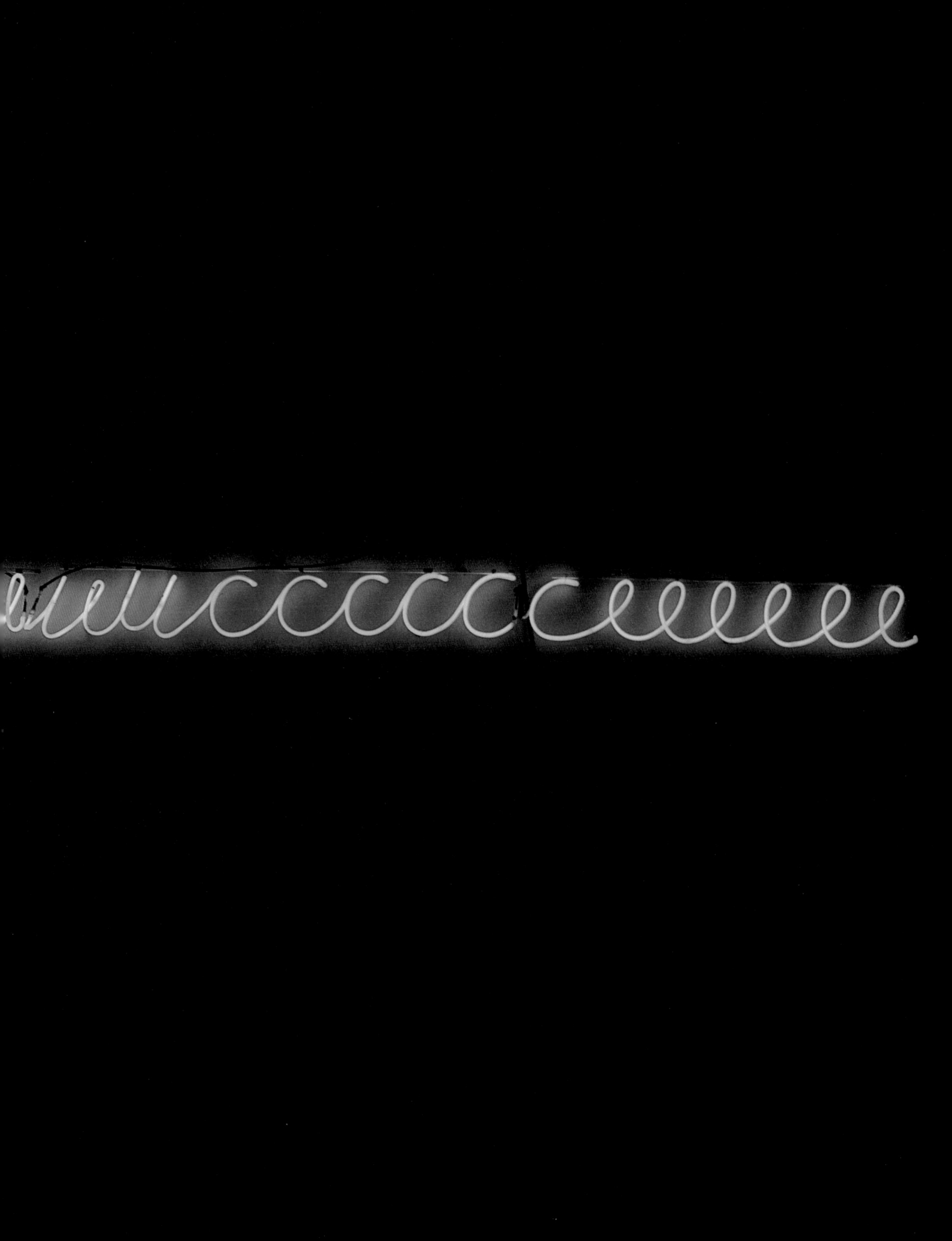

TOP:
Flour Arrangements. 1967
Seven black-and-white photographs with
color added
Sizes vary
Hallen für neue Kunst,
Schaffhausen, Switzerland
Crex Collection

BOTTOM:
Space under My Hand When I Write My Name. 1966
Wax
Ca. 8′ (244 cm) long
Destroyed

TOP:
*Composite Photo of Two Messes on the
Studio Floor.* 1967
Gelatin silver print
$40\frac{1}{2}''$ × 10'3" (101.6 × 312.2 cm)
The Museum of Modern Art, New York
Gift of Philip Johnson

BOTTOM:
MARCEL DUCHAMP
Dust Breeding. 1920
Photograph by Man Ray
$9\frac{1}{2}$ × 12" (24 × 30.5 cm)
Courtesy Timothy Baum, New York

Stills from *Bouncing Two Balls between the Floor and Ceiling with Changing Rhythms.* 1968
Film, 16 mm, black and white, sound, 9 min.

Stills from *Walking in an Exaggerated
Manner around the Perimeter of a Square.*
1968
Film, 16 mm, black and white, silent, 8–10
min., ca. 400′

Stills from *Dance or Exercise on the*
Perimeter of a Square. 1968
Film, 16 mm, black and white, sound,
8–10 min., ca. 400′

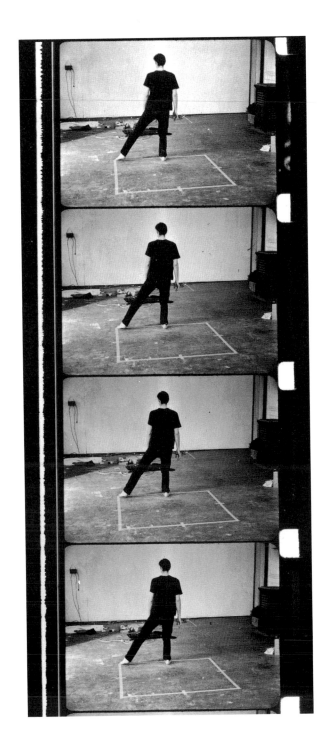

Stills from *Playing a Note on the Violin
While I Walk around the Studio.* 1968
Film, 16 mm, black and white, sound,
8–10 min., ca. 400′

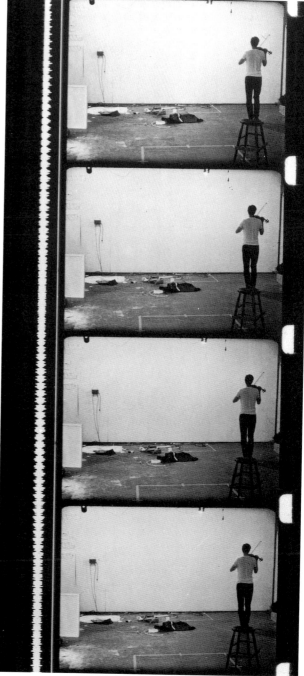

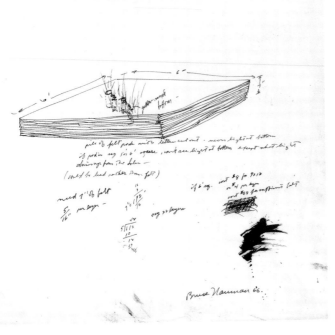

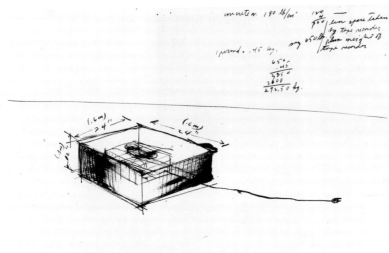

TOP:
Cry to Me. 1966
Inscribed: "Cry to me/ Cry to me/ yellow neon at/ bottom/ pile of felt pads with letters cut out—neon light at bottom/ if pad is say 5′ or 6′ square, can't see light at bottom except what light/ shining up from the holes—/ (could be lead rather than felt)/ need 7″ of felt/ $\frac{5}{16}$″ per layer/ say 22 layers/ if 6 sq. cost $8 for 9 × 12/ or $4 per layer/ cost $88 for sufficient felt."
Ink on paper
19 × 24″ (48.5 × 61 cm)
Oeffentliche Kunstsammlung, Basel
Depositum Emanuel Hoffmann Foundation

BOTTOM:
Tape Recorder with a Tape Loop of a Scream Wrapped in a Plastic Bag and Cast into the Center of a Block of Concrete. 1968
Inscribed: "Concrete w 180 lb/ in / 1 pound = .45 kg. Say 650 lb./ less space taken by tape recorder/ plus weight of tape recorder./ Tape recorder with a tape loop of a scream wrapped in a plastic bag and cast into the center of a block of concrete./ Weight about 650 pounds or 290 kg."
Ink on paper
Private collection, Kassel, West Germany

Storage Capsule for the Right Rear Quarter of My Body. 1966
Galvanized iron
6′ × 9½″ × 6″ (182.9 × 24.1 × 15.2 cm)
Oeffentliche Kunstsammlung, Basel

Study for *Storage Capsule for the Right Rear Quarter of My Body.* 1966
Pencil, charcoal, and watercolor on paper
38 × 24¾″ (96.5 × 62.9 cm)
The Museum of Modern Art, New York
Partial gift of Alexis Gregory and Purchase

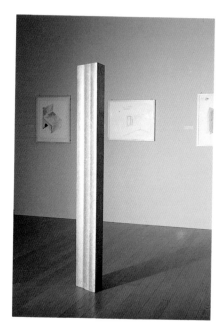

Study for *Six Sound Problems for Konrad Fischer.* 1968
Inscribed: "6 sound problems for Konrad Fischer/ (6 day week)/ 1. walk/ 2. balls/ 3. violin/ 4. violin w/walk/ 5. violin w/balls/ 6. balls w/walk/ must be short/ can be very short; loop 1/ monday/ 2. tuesday/ wednesday 3/ thursday 4/ friday 5/ saturday/ loop 6/ loop 4/ loop 3/ on tape recorder/ loop 6/ loop 2/ 11 cm."
Pencil on paper
25 × 19¼" (63.5 × 49 cm)
Konrad Fischer, Düsseldorf

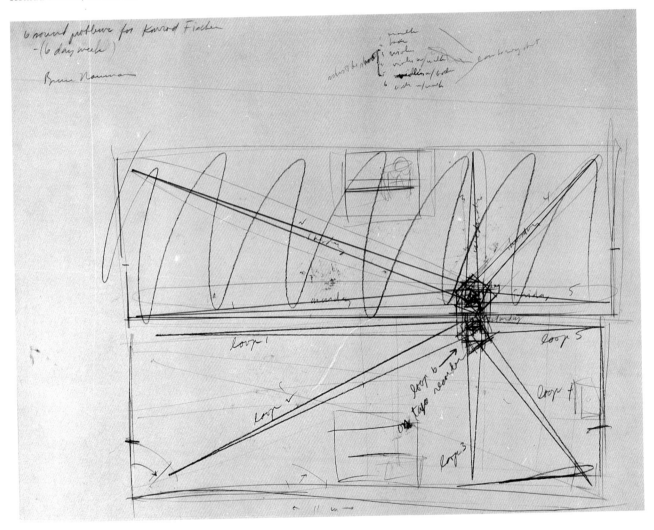

Six Sound Problems for Konrad Fischer.
1968
Installation at Galerie Konrad Fischer,
Düsseldorf, West Germany,
July–August 1968

Stills from *Thighing.* 1967
Film, 16 mm, color, sound, 8–10 min.,
ca. 400′

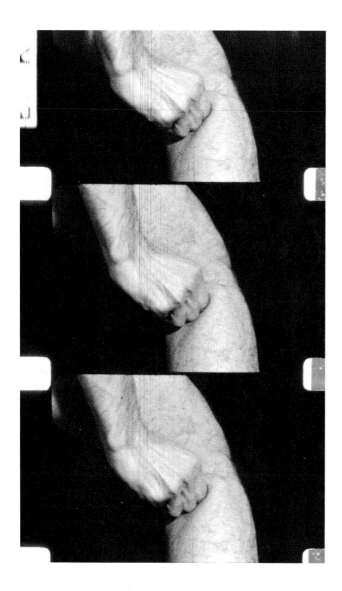

Stills from *Bouncing Balls*. 1969
Film (slow motion), 16 mm, black and
white, silent, 9 min.

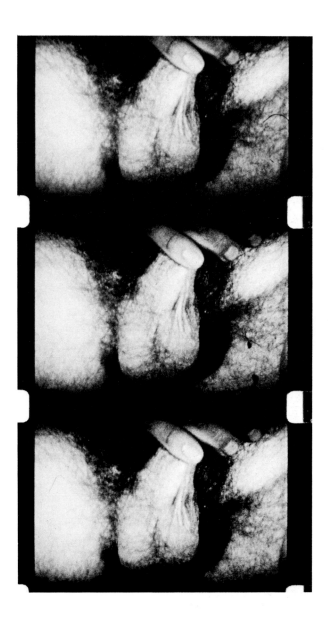

Stills from *Black Balls.* 1969
Film (slow motion), 16 mm, black and
white, silent, 8 min.

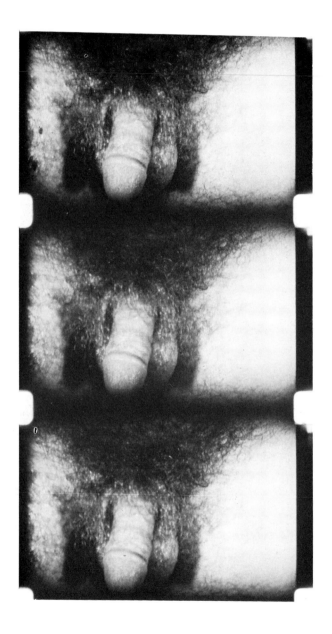

Stills from *Gauze.* 1969
Film (slow motion), 16 mm, black and
white, silent, 8 min.

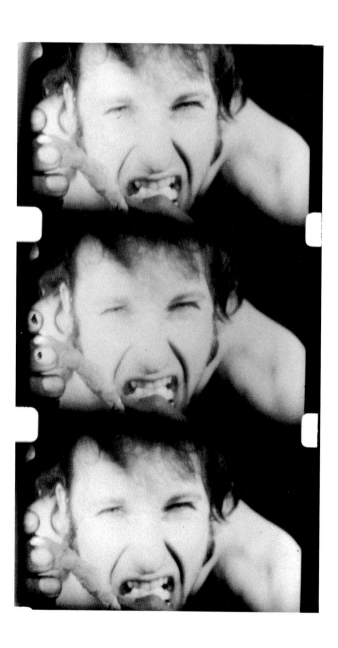

Untitled (Pulling Mouth). 1967
Inscribed: "Upper lip push up by right/
thumb and lower lip pulled down by right
forefinger/ As above but mouth open./
both lips turned out/ mouth open./ both
lips pulled in tight/ over teeth—mouth
open./ both lips squeezed together from/
the side by the thumb/ and forefinger right
hand."
Pen and wash on paper
27¼ × 19"
Collection Joseph A. Helman, New York

Still from *Pulling Mouth.* 1969
Film (slow motion), 16 mm, black and
white, silent, 9 min.

Making Faces. 1968
Holograms projected on glass
8 × 10″ (20.3 × 25.4 cm) each
Leo Castelli Gallery, New York

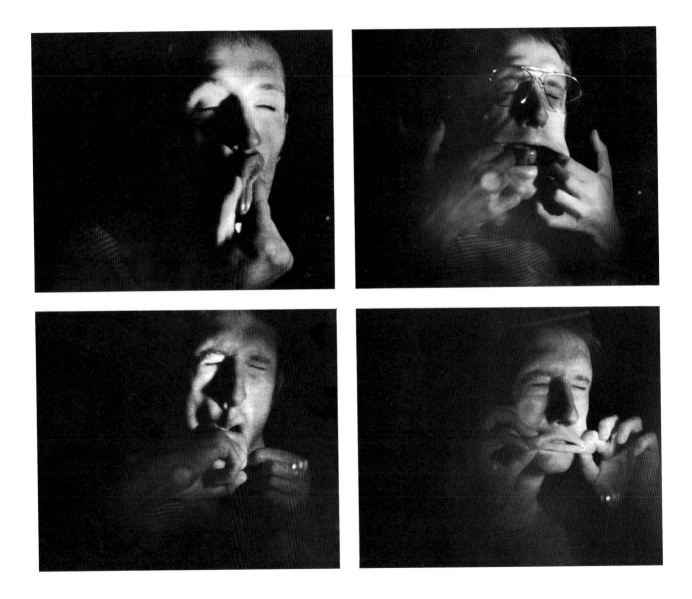

Full-Figure Poses. 1969
Holograms projected on glass
8 × 10″ (20.3 × 25.4 cm)
Leo Castelli Gallery, New York

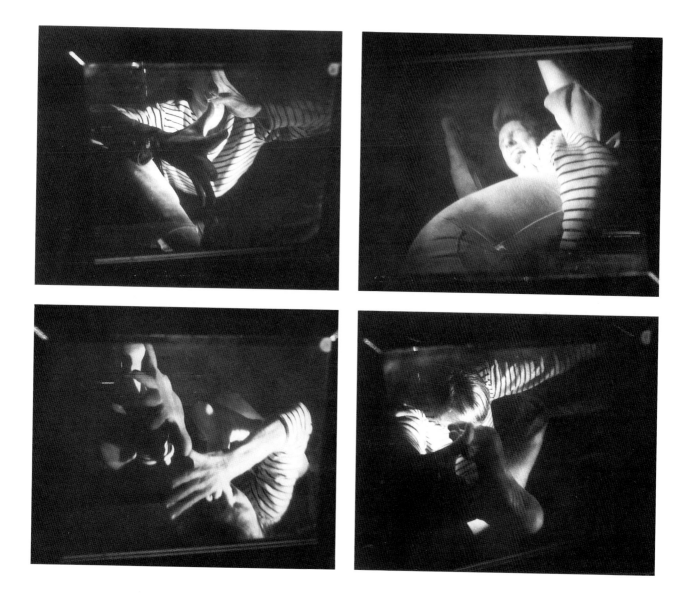

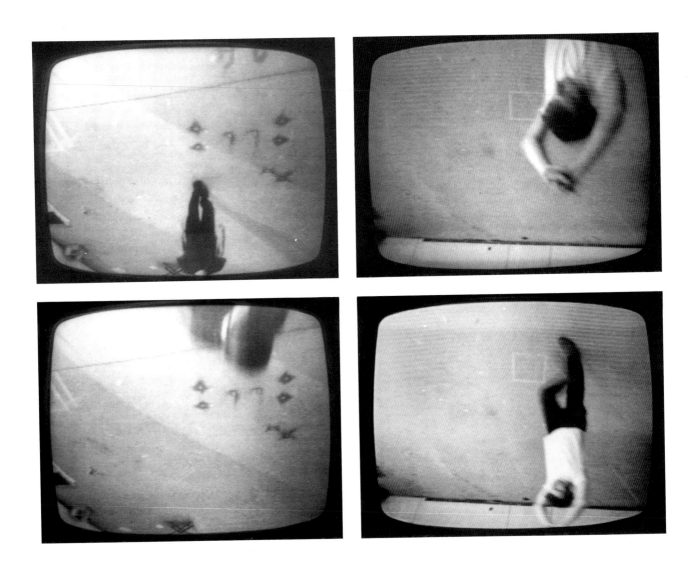

Stills from *Revolving Upside Down.* 1969
Videotape, black and white, sound,
60 min.

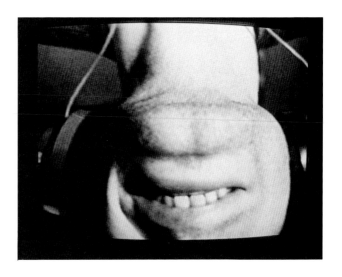

LEFT:
Still from *Bouncing in the Corner, No. 1.*
1968
Videotape, black and white, sound,
60 min.

RIGHT TOP AND BOTTOM:
Stills from *Bouncing in the Corner, No. 2:*
Upside Down. 1969
Videotape, black and white, sound,
60 min.

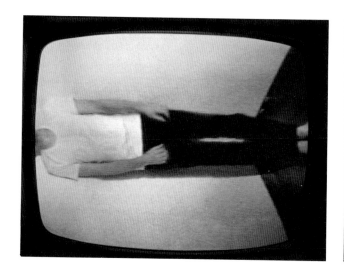

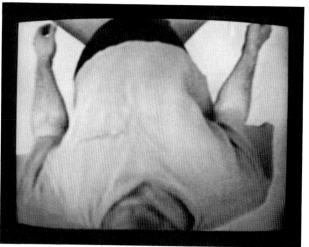

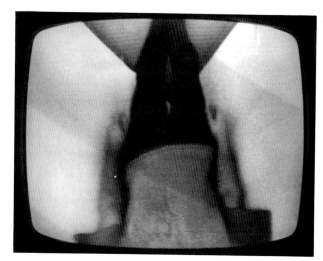

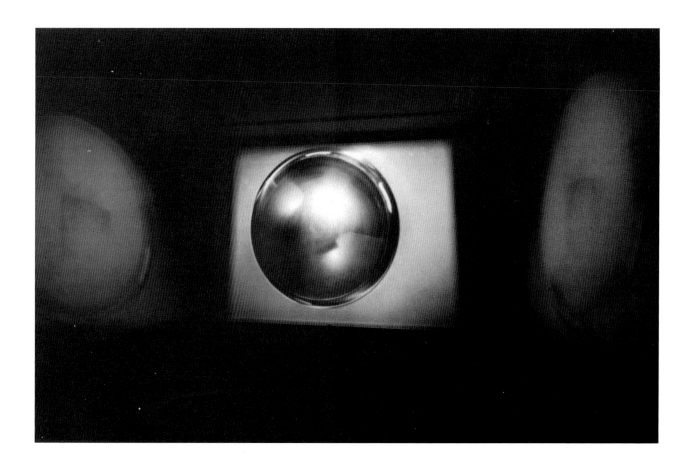

Rotating Glass Walls. 1970
16-mm film loops simultaneously projected
on four walls, Leo Castelli Gallery, New
York, February–March 1971
Courtesy Leo Castelli, New York

Dead Center. 1969
Steel
3 × 15 × 15″ (7.6 × 38.1 × 38.1 cm)
The Solomon R. Guggenheim Museum, New York
Gift of the Theodoron Foundation, 1969

TOP:
Still from *Elke Allowing the Floor to
Rise Up over Her, Face Up.* 1973
Videotape, color, sound, 40 min.

BOTTOM:
Still from *Tony Sinking into the Floor,
Face Up and Face Down.* 1973
Videotape, color, sound, 60 min.

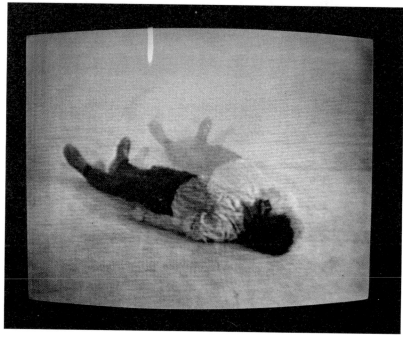

Performance Corridor. 1969
Wallboard and wood
Ca. 8′ × 20″ × 20′ (243.8 × 51
× 609.6 cm)
The Panza Collection, Milan

Still from *Walk with Contrapposto.* 1969
Videotape, black and white, sound,
60 min., taped in *Performance Corridor*

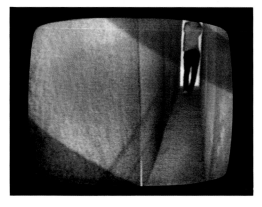

Lighted Performance Box. 1969
Aluminum box and spotlight
6'6" × 20" × 20" (198.1 × 50.8
× 50.8 cm)
The Panza Collection, Milan

Acoustic Wall. 1969–70
Installed Galerie Konrad Fischer,
Düsseldorf, February–March 1970
Wallboard covered with acoustic material
Ca. 8 × 35′ (243.8 × 1,065.8 cm)
The Panza Collection, Milan

Study for *Acoustic Wall.* 1969
Inscribed: "Diagonal wall covered with/
acoustic material./ B. Nauman for Konrad/
Fischer, December 1969."
Pencil on paper
Ca. 13½ × 10⅝" (34.5 × 28 cm)
The Panza Collection, Milan

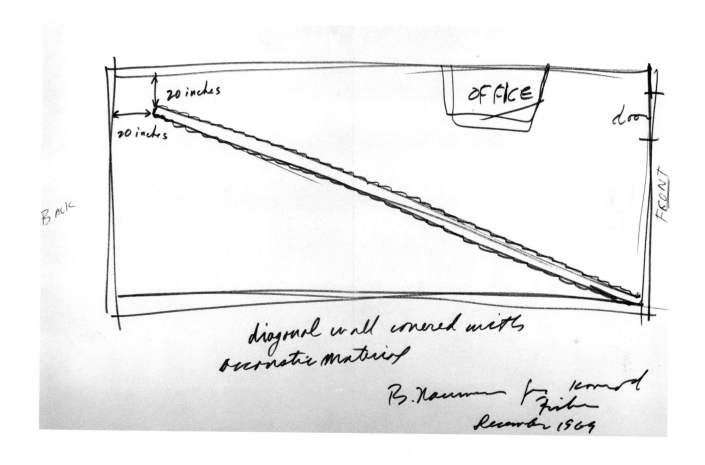

Acoustic Pressure Piece. 1971
Installed Leo Castelli Gallery, New York,
November–December 1971
Wallboard and acoustic material
Ca. 8′ × 48″ × 50′ (24.8 × 121.9 ×
1,524 cm)
The Panza Collection, Milan

Untitled (After *Acoustic Pressure Piece*)
1975
Inscribed: "Acoustic corridor approx.
made as installed at/ Castelli Gallery/
acoustic board framed by 2′ × 3′
lumber,/ acoustic material/ on floor/ Piece
may be constructed in/ one room in a
straight/ line, but angle the panel in the
larger section/ for additional acoustic-/
visual blocking."
Pencil and felt-tipped pen on paper
$30\frac{1}{8}$ × 40″ (76.5 × 101.5 cm)
The Panza Collection, Milan

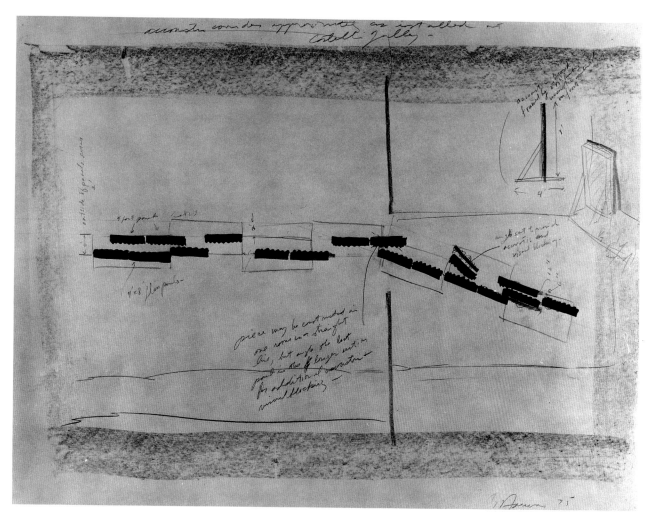

BELOW AND OPPOSITE:
Hanged Man. 1985
From an edition of three; first fabricated
for installation at Museum Haus Esters,
Krefeld, West Germany, September–
December 1985
Neon tubing with clear-glass tubing
suspension frame, mounted on wood
7'2⅝" × 55" (220 × 140 cm)

TOP:
Untitled (Haus Esters Installation). 1985
Inscribed: "Haus Esters Installation./
Speakers/ Video monitors/ Double/ video/
"Good Boy/ Bad Boy" Neon/ Neon/ B.
Nauman 85."
Pencil and collage on paper
40 × 50″ (101.6 × 127 cm)
Collection the artist

BOTTOM:
Stills from *Good Boy Bad Boy*. 1985
Videotapes from video, sound, and neon
installation at Museum Haus Esters,
Krefeld, West Germany, September–
December 1985

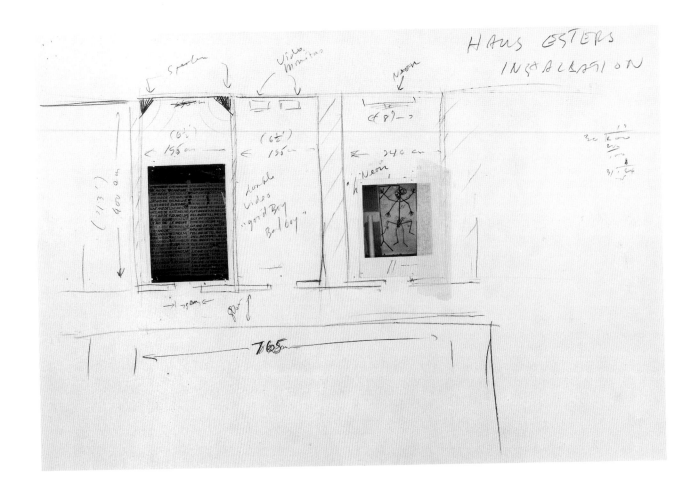

Museum Haus Esters Installation (detail).
1985
Room for playing sound piece *One
Hundred Live and Die*

Good Boy Bad Boy. 1986–87
Neon tubing with clear-glass tubing
suspension frame
11′5½″ × 18′2″ × 19″ (349.2 × 553.7
× 48.3 cm)
The Oliver-Hoffmann Family Collection,
Chicago

1 I WAS A GOOD BOY
2 YOU WERE A GOOD BOY
3 WE WERE GOOD BOYS
4 THAT WAS GOOD
5 I WAS A GOOD GIRL
6 YOU WERE A GOOD GIRL
7 WE WERE GOOD GIRLS
8 THAT WAS GOOD
9 I WAS A BAD BOY
10 YOU WERE A BAD BOY
11 WE WERE BAD BOYS
12 THAT WAS BAD
13 I WAS A BAD GIRL
14 YOU WERE A BAD GIRL
15 WE WERE BAD GIRLS
16 THAT WAS BAD
17 I AM A VIRTUOUS MAN
18 YOU ARE A VIRTUOUS MAN
19 WE ARE VIRTUOUS MEN
20 THIS IS VIRTUE
21 I AM A VIRTUOUS WOMAN
22 YOU ARE A VIRTUOUS WOMAN
23 WE ARE VIRTUOUS WOMEN
24 THIS IS VIRTUE

25 I AM AN EVIL MAN
26 YOU ARE AN EVIL MAN
27 WE ARE EVIL MEN
28 THIS IS EVIL
29 I AM AN EVIL WOMAN
30 YOU ARE AN EVIL WOMAN
31 WE ARE EVIL WOMEN
32 THIS IS EVIL
33 I'M ALIVE
34 YOU'RE ALIVE
35 WE'RE ALIVE
36 THIS IS OUR LIFE
37 I LIVE THE GOOD LIFE
38 YOU LIVE THE GOOD LIFE
39 WE LIVE THE GOOD LIFE
40 THIS IS THE GOOD LIFE
41 I PLAY
42 YOU PLAY
43 WE PLAY
44 THIS IS PLAY
45 I PLAY
46 YOU PLAY
47 WE PLAY
48 THIS IS PLAY
49 I'M HAVING FUN
50 YOU'RE HAVING FUN
51 WE'RE HAVING FUN
52 THIS IS FUN

53 I'M BORED
54 YOU'RE BORED
55 WE'RE BORED
56 LIFE IS BORING
57 I'M BORING
58 YOU'RE BORING
59 WE'RE BORING
60 THIS IS BORING
61 I HAVE SEX
62 YOU HAVE SEX
63 WE HAVE SEX
64 THIS IS SEX
65 I LOVE
66 YOU LOVE
67 WE LOVE
68 THIS IS OUR LOVE
69 I HATE
70 YOU HATE
71 WE HATE
72 THIS IS HATING
73 I LIKE TO EAT
74 YOU LIKE TO EAT
75 WE LIKE TO EAT
76 THIS IS EATING

77 I LIKE TO DRINK
78 YOU LIKE TO DRINK
79 WE LIKE TO DRINK
80 THIS IS DRINKING
81 I (LIKE TO) SHIT
82 YOU (LIKE TO) SHIT
83 WE (LIKE TO) SHIT
84 THIS IS SHIT(TING)
85 I PISS
86 YOU PISS
87 WE PISS
88 THIS IS PISS
89 I LIKE TO SLEEP
90 YOU LIKE TO SLEEP
91 WE LIKE TO SLEEP
92 SLEEP WELL
93 I PAY
94 YOU PAY
95 WE PAY
96 THIS IS PAYMENT
97 I DON'T WANT TO DIE
98 YOU DON'T WANT TO DIE
99 WE DON'T WANT TO DIE
100 THIS IS FEAR OF DEATH

1941
Born December 6 in Fort Wayne, Indiana.

1960–1964
Studies for B.A. at University of Wisconsin, Madison. At first concentrates on mathematics but later studies art.

1964–1966
Attends University of California at Davis, receiving M.F.A. in June 1966. During these years makes first fiberglass sculptures; also creates first performances and films.

1966
Moves to Vacaville, California. Studies under William T. Wiley.
First one-man exhibition, at Nicholas Wilder Gallery, Los Angeles.
During summer moves to San Francisco, joining faculty of San Francisco Art Institute. Collaborates with William Allan on several films.

1967
Moves to Mill Valley, California.

1968
First one-man exhibition in New York, at Leo Castelli Gallery.
First one-man exhibition in Europe, at Galerie Konrad Fischer, Düsseldorf, West Germany.
Receives National Endowment for the Arts grant; spends winter in Southampton, New York, making videotapes.

1969
Moves to Pasadena, California.

1970
Teaches sculpture at the University of California at Irvine.

1972–1974
Major retrospective at the Los Angeles County Museum of Art and Whitney Museum of American Art, New York; exhibition tours the United States and Europe.

1979
Moves to Pecos, New Mexico.

1986–1988
Major drawings retrospective at the Museum für Gegenwartskunst, Basel; exhibition tours West Germany, the Netherlands, and the United States.

An asterisk indicates that a work is available from Castelli/Sonnabend Tapes and Films, New York. Works for which no owner is listed are in the collection of the artist.

Manipulating the T-Bar. 1965–66
Film, 16 mm, black and white, silent, less than 10 min.

Opening and Closing. 1965–66
Film, 16 mm, black and white, silent, less than 10 min.

Revolving Landscape. 1965–66
Film, 16 mm, black and white, silent, less than 10 min.

WITH WILLIAM ALLAN
Abstracting the Shoe. 1966
Film, 16 mm, color, silent, 2:41 min.
Location: Richard Pervier farm, Muir Beach, California
Camera: Bruce Nauman
Participant: William Allan

WITH WILLIAM ALLAN
Building a New Slant Step. 1966
Film, 16 mm, black and white, silent, unfinished

WITH WILLIAM ALLAN AND ROBERT NELSON
Fishing for Asian Carp. 1966
Film, 16 mm, color, sound, 2:44 min.
Location: Putah Creek, near Woodland, California
Camera: Bruce Nauman
Sound: William Allan and Robert Nelson
Participant: William Allan

WITH WILLIAM ALLAN
Legal Size. 1966
Film, 16 mm, color, silent, 3:47 min.
Location: William Allan's studio, Muir Beach, California
Camera: Bruce Nauman
Participant: William Allan

WITH WILLIAM ALLAN
Span. 1966
Film, 16 mm, color, sound, 10:37 min.
Location: Muir Beach, California
Camera: Richard Pervier
Participants: Bruce Nauman, William Allan, and Richard Pervier

The Center of the Universe. 1988
Poured concrete
50 x 50 x 50′ (1,525 x 1,525 x 1,525 cm)
University of New Mexico, Albuquerque

*Art Make-Up, No. 1: White. 1967
Film, 16 mm, color, silent, 8–10 min.,
ca. 400'

*Thighing. 1967
Film, 16 mm, color, sound, 8–10 min.,
ca. 400'

*Art Make-Up, No. 2: Pink. 1967–68
Film, 16 mm, color, silent, 8–10 min.,
ca. 400'

*Art Make-Up, No. 3: Green. 1967–68
Film, 16 mm, color, silent, 8–10 min.,
ca. 400'

*Art Make-Up, No. 4: Black. 1967–68
Film, 16 mm, color, silent, 8–10 min.,
ca. 400'

*Bouncing Two Balls between the Floor and
Ceiling with Changing Rhythms. 1968
Film, 16 mm, black and white, sound,
9 min.

*Dance or Exercise on the Perimeter of a
Square. 1968
Film, 16 mm, black and white, sound,
8–10 min., ca. 400'

Pinch Neck. 1968
Film, 16 mm, color, ca. 75'

*Playing a Note on the Violin While I
Walk around the Studio. 1968
Film, 16 mm, black and white, sound,
8–10 min., ca. 400'

*Walking in an Exaggerated Manner around
the Perimeter of a Square. 1968
Film, 16 mm, black and white, silent, 8–10
min., ca. 400'

*Slow Angle Walk. November 6, 1968
Videotape, black and white, sound,
60 min.

*Stamping in the Studio. November 16,
1968
Videotape, black and white, sound,
60 min.

*Flesh to Black to White to Flesh.
November 17, 1968
Videotape, black and white, sound,
60 min.

*Bouncing in the Corner, No. 1. November
27, 1968
Videotape, black and white, sound,
60 min.

*Wall-Floor Positions. 1968
Videotape, black and white, sound,
60 min.

*Bouncing in the Corner, No. 2: Upside
Down. 1969
Videotape, black and white, sound,
60 min.

*Lip Sync. 1969
Videotape, black and white, sound, 60 min.

*Pacing Upside Down. February 17, 1969
Videotape, black and white, sound,
60 min.

*Walk with Contrapposto. February 25,
1969
Videotape, black and white, sound, 60 min.

*Revolving Upside Down. March 2, 1969
Videotape, black and white, sound,
60 min.

*Violin Tuned D E A D. April 15, 1969
Videotape, black and white, sound,
60 min.

*Manipulating a Fluorescent Tube.
November 25, 1969
Videotape, black and white, sound,
60 min.

*Black Balls. 1969
Film (slow motion), 16 mm, black and
white, silent, 8 min.

*Bouncing Balls. 1969
Film (slow motion), 16 mm, black and
white, silent, 9 min.

*Gauze. 1969
Film (slow motion), 16 mm, black and
white, silent, 8 min.

*Pulling Mouth. 1969
Film (slow motion), 16 mm, black and
white, silent, 9 min.

Studio Problems, No. 1. 1971
Videotape, black and white

Studio Problems, No. 2. 1971
Videotape, black and white

*Elke Allowing the Floor to Rise Up over
Her, Face Up. 1973
Videotape, color, sound, 40 min.

*Tony Sinking into the Floor, Face Up and
Face Down. 1973
Videotape, color, sound, 60 min.

WITH FRANK OWEN
Pursuit. 1975
Film, 16 mm, color, sound, 28 min.
Camera and editing: Bryan Heath
Assistant cameraman: John Quinn
Sound: Michael Pretainger
Production assistant: Susan Heller

Good Boy Bad Boy. 1986
Two videotapes for installation with two
monitors
Color, sound, 60 min. (male) and 52 min.
(female)
Leo Castelli Gallery, New York

Violent Incident: Man-Woman Segment.
1986
Videotape, color, sound, 30 min.
Edition of 200, numbered and signed
Parkett Deluxe Edition No. 10

Clown Torture: I'm Sorry and No, No, No.
1987
Two videotapes for installation with two
monitors
Color, sound
Leo Castelli Gallery, New York

Clown Torture: Clown Taking a Shit;
Clown with Goldfish, Clown with Water
Bucket; Pete and Repeat; and No, No, No,
No (Walter). 1987
Four videotapes for installation with four
monitors and two projectors
Color, sound
Leo Castelli Gallery, New York

No, No, No, No. 1987
Videotape for installation with two
monitors, color, sound

Exhibitions

An asterisk indicates that a publication accompanied the exhibition.

One-man

1966

Nicholas Wilder Gallery, Los Angeles. May 10–June 2.

1968

"Bruce Nauman."* Leo Castelli Gallery, 4 East 77 Street, New York. January 27–February 17.

Nicholas Wilder Gallery, Los Angeles. March 17–April 7.

Sacramento State College Art Gallery, Sacramento, California. April.

"6 Day Week: 6 Sound Problems." Galerie Konrad Fischer, Düsseldorf, West Germany. July 10–August 8.

1969

Nicholas Wilder Gallery, Los Angeles. January 28–February 15.

"Holograms, Videotapes, and Other Works." Leo Castelli Gallery, 4 East 77 Street, New York. May 24–June 14.

Galerie Ileana Sonnabend, Paris. Opened December 2.

"Bruce Nauman: Photographs." School of Visual Arts, New York. December 9–19.

"Audio/Video Projects." The Palley Cellar, San Francisco. December 9, 1969–January 10, 1970.

1970

Nicholas Wilder Gallery, Los Angeles. January 28–February 15.

Galerie Konrad Fischer, Düsseldorf, West Germany. February 5–March 3.

2020 Gallery, London, Ontario. February 17–March 8.

Galleria Sperone, Turin. February 25–March 10.

San Jose State College, San Jose, California. First week of May.

"Studies for Holograms." Galerie Ricke, Cologne, West Germany. September 11–October 31.

1971

Leo Castelli Gallery, 4 East 77 Street, New York. February 13–March 6.

Galerie Ileana Sonnabend, Paris. Opened March 2.

Galerie Konrad Fischer, Düsseldorf, West Germany. March 5–April 1.

"Studies on Holograms, Five Silkscreens, and New Lithographs." Betty Gold Fine Modern Prints, Los Angeles. November 2–December 4.

"Left or Standing, Standing or Left Standing." Leo Castelli Gallery, 420 West Broadway, New York. November 20–December 11.

Galerie Bruno Bischofberger, Zürich.

Ace Gallery, Vancouver, British Columbia. December 1–15.

Joseph Helman Gallery, St. Louis. December.

Galleria Françoise Lambert, Milan. December 6, 1971–January 5, 1972.

1972

"Bruce Nauman: 16mm Filme 1967–1970." Projection Gallery Ursula Wevers, Cologne, West Germany. October 18–November 2.

"Bruce Nauman: Work from 1965 to 1972."* Los Angeles County Museum of Art, December 19, 1972–February 18, 1973, in conjunction with the Whitney Museum of American Art, New York, March 29–May 13, 1973; traveled to Kunsthalle, Bern, Switzerland, June 16–August 12, 1973; Städtische Kunsthalle, Düsseldorf, West Germany, August 24–September 23, 1973; Stedelijk van Abbemuseum, Eindhoven, the Netherlands, October 12–November 25, 1973; Palazzo Reale, Milan; Contemporary Arts Museum, Houston; San Francisco Museum of Art, May 31–July 14, 1974.

1973

"Bruce Nauman: Floating Room." Fine Arts Gallery, University of California at Irvine. January 12–February 18.

"Floating Room." Leo Castelli Gallery, 4 East 77 Street, New York. March 17–31.

"Flayed Earth/Flayed Self (Skin/Sink)."*

Nicholas Wilder Gallery, Los Angeles. December 17, 1973–January 11, 1974.

1974

"Installation." Ace Gallery, Vancouver, British Columbia. January.

"Yellow Body." Galerie Konrad Fischer, Düsseldorf, West Germany. February 4–March 6.

"Yellow Triangular Room." Santa Ana College Art Gallery, Santa Ana, California. February 10–March 6.

"Wall with Two Fans." Wide White Space, Antwerp, Belgium. March 8–April 10.

1975

"Cones Cojones." Leo Castelli Gallery, 420 West Broadway, New York. January 4–18.

"Sundry Obras Nuevas." Gemini G.E.L., Los Angeles. Opened April 24.

"The Consummate Mask of Rock."* Albright-Knox Art Gallery, Buffalo, New York. September 26–November 9.

"Forced Perspective: Open Mind, Closed Mind, Equal Mind, Parallel Mind." Galerie Konrad Fischer, Düsseldorf, West Germany. December 16, 1975–January 24, 1976.

1976

"Enforced Perspective: Allegory and Symbolism." Ace Gallery, Vancouver, British Columbia. February–March.

"White Breathing." UNLV Art Gallery, University of Nevada, Las Vegas. April 7–16.

"Enforced Perspective: Allegory and Symbolism." Ace Gallery, Venice, California. October 9–November 13.

"The Consummate Mask of Rock." Sperone Westwater Fischer, New York. October 30–November 27.

"The Consummate Mask of Rock." Leo Castelli Gallery, New York. November 2–27.

"The Consummate Mask of Rock." Ileana Sonnabend Gallery, New York. November 2–20.

1977

"The Consummate Mask of Rock." Nicholas Wilder Gallery, Los Angeles. May 31–July 1.

1978

Minneapolis College of Art and Design. January 16–February 17.

Leo Castelli Gallery, 4 East 77 Street, New York. February 4–25.

"Large studies in combinations of olive, mustard, and pink fiberglass and polyester resin in 4 groups and one study in cast iron all at 1:50 scale of combinations of shafts, trenches, and tunnels." Galerie Konrad Fischer, Düsseldorf, West Germany. June 3–30.

"Dokumentation 1."* Ink, Halle für Internationale neue Kunst, Zürich; two untitled fiberglass sculptures exhibited successively, July 2–August 30, and August 30–September 25; three films, *Bouncing Balls, Thighing, Walk Dance* (*sic*), August 23; *Floating Room* (1973), September 26–October 23.

"1/12 Scale Study in Fiberglass and Plaster for Cast Iron of a Trench and Four Tunnels in Concrete at Full Scale." Art Gallery, California State University at San Diego. September 18–October 14.

"Recent Sculpture." Ace Gallery, Vancouver, British Columbia. October 10–31.

1979

Galerie Schmela, Düsseldorf, West Germany. January 15–February 9.

Marianne Deson Gallery, Chicago. March 24–April 18.

"Bruce Nauman: An Installation." Portland Center for the Visual Arts, Portland, Oregon. September 6–October 14.

"Bruce Nauman: Prints." Hester van Royen Gallery, London. November.

1980

Leo Castelli Gallery, 420 West Broadway, New York. April 26–May 17.

"Bruce Nauman: New Sculpture." Hill's Gallery of Contemporary Art, Santa Fe, New Mexico. May–June.

"North, East, South, South East." Galerie Konrad Fischer, Düsseldorf, West Germany. September 6–27.

Carol Taylor Art, Dallas. December 6, 1980–January 10, 1981.

"Forced Perspective or False Perspective: Drawings by Bruce Nauman." Nigel Greenwood, London. December 16, 1980–January 31, 1981.

1981

"Arbeiten von Bruce Nauman." Ink, Halle für Internationale neue Kunst, Zürich. January–February.

Maud Boreel Print Art, The Hague, the Netherlands. January.

"Bruce Nauman: 1/12 Scale Models for Underground Pieces."* The Albuquerque Museum, Albuquerque, New Mexico. January 25–March 29.

"Stone Sculpture: Enforced Perspective, Allegory and Symbolism." Ace Gallery, Venice, California. February 24–March 14.

"Bruce Nauman, 1972–81."* Rijksmuseum Kröller-Müller, Otterlo, the Netherlands, April 5–May 25; traveled to the Staatliche Kunsthalle, Baden-Baden, West Germany, July 3–August 2.

"Lessons." Texas Gallery, Houston. May 23–June 20.

"New Iron Casting, Plaster, and Drawings." Young Hoffman Gallery, Chicago. May 29–June 27.

"Bruce Nauman: Photo Piece, Window Screen, Hologram, Neon Sculptures, Cast-Iron Sculpture, Drawings 1967–81." Galerie Konrad Fischer, Düsseldorf, West Germany. August 22–September 19.

1982

"Violins, Violence, Silence." Leo Castelli Gallery, 142 Greene Street, New York, and Sperone Westwater Fischer, New York. January 9–30.

"Bruce Nauman: Neons."* The Baltimore Museum of Art. December 19, 1982–February 13, 1983.

1983

Carol Taylor Art, Dallas. April.

"Hoffnung/Neid." Galerie Konrad Fischer, Düsseldorf, West Germany. November 5–December 6.

"Bruce Nauman."* Museum Haus Esters, Krefelder Kunstmuseen, Krefeld, West Germany. November 6–December 23.

1984

"Recent Neons and Drawings." Daniel Weinberg Gallery, Los Angeles. February 8–March 3.

"Bruce Nauman: New Sculptures and Drawings." Carol Taylor Art, Dallas. March 8–April 1.

"Room with My Soul Left Out." Leo Castelli Gallery, 142 Greene Street, New York. October 6–November 3.

"Seven Virtues and Seven Vices; White Anger, Red Danger, Yellow Peril, Black Death." Sperone Westwater, New York. October 6–November 3.

1985

"New Work: Neons and Drawings." Donald Young Gallery, Chicago. April 4–May 4.

"New Neons." Galerie Konrad Fischer, Düsseldorf, West Germany. September 14–October 17.

Leo Castelli Gallery, 420 West Broadway, New York. October 26–November 16.

1986

Texas Gallery, Houston. February 11–27.

Jean Bernier, Athens. February 24–March 20.

"Oeuvres sur Papier." Galerie Yvon Lambert, Paris. April 12–May 10.

"Bruce Nauman: Drawings/Zeichnungen 1965–1986."* Museum für Gegenwartskunst, Basel, May 17–July 13; traveled to Kunsthalle, Tübingen, West Germany, July 26–September 7, 1986; Städtisches Kunstmuseum, Bonn, September 30–November 16, 1986; Museum Boymans-van Beuningen, Rotterdam, November 29, 1986–January 18, 1987; Kunstraum, Munich, February

4–March 22, 1987; Badischer Kunstverein, Karlsruhe, West Germany, March 29–May 24, 1987; Kunsthalle, Hamburg, June 12–July 19, 1987; The New Museum of Contemporary Art, New York, September 18–November 8, 1987; Contemporary Arts Museum, Houston, December 5, 1987–January 17, 1988; The Museum of Contemporary Art, Los Angeles, February 9–April 11, 1988; University Art Museum, University of California at Berkeley, May 4–July 10, 1988.

"Bruce Nauman."* Organized by the Whitechapel Art Gallery, London; traveled to the Kunsthalle, Basel, July 13–September 7, 1986; ARC, Musée d'Art Moderne de la Ville de Paris, October 8–December 7; Whitechapel Art Gallery, London, January 23–March 8, 1987.

1987

Donald Young Gallery, Chicago. March 6–28.

Daniel Weinberg Gallery, Los Angeles. March 14–April 11.

Group

1966

"The Slant Step Show." Berkeley Gallery, San Francisco. September 9–17.

"New Directions: The Tenth SECA Show." San Francisco Museum of Art. September 9–October 9.

"Eccentric Abstraction."* Fischbach Gallery, New York. September 20–October 8.

"William Geis and Bruce Nauman."* San Francisco Art Institute. September 26–October 22.

1967

"American Sculpture of the Sixties."* Los Angeles County Museum of Art. April 28–June 25.

1968

"West Coast Now."* Portland Art Museum, Portland, Oregon. February 9–March 26.

"Three Young Americans."* Allen Memorial Art Museum, Oberlin College, Oberlin, Ohio. Early Spring.

"Documenta 4."* Museum Fridericianum, Kassel, West Germany. June 27–October 6.

"Prospekt 68."* Städtische Kunsthalle, Düsseldorf, West Germany. September 20–29.

"Anti-Form." John Gibson Gallery, New York. October 5–November 7.

"Soft and Apparently Soft Sculpture." The American Federation of Arts traveling exhibition. October 6, 1968–August 1969.

"Nine at Castelli." Castelli Warehouse, New York. December 4–28.

1969

"Here and Now."* Washington University Gallery of Art, St. Louis. January 10–February 21.

"31st Biennial of American Painting."* The Corcoran Gallery of Art, Washington, D.C. February 1–March 20.

"Drawings." Wide White Space, Antwerp, Belgium. March.

"Op Losse Schroeven: Situaties en Cryptostructuren."* Stedelijk Museum, Amsterdam, March 15–April 27; traveled to the Museum Folkwang, Essen, West Germany, May 9–June 22.

"When Attitudes Become Form."* Kunsthalle, Bern, Switzerland, March 22–April 27; traveled to Museum Haus Lange, Krefeld, West Germany, May 9–June 15; Institute of Contemporary Art, London, September 28–October 27.

"Anti-Illusion: Procedures/Materials."* Whitney Museum of American Art, New York. May 19–July 6.

"Nine Young Artists: Theodoron Foundation Awards."* The Solomon R. Guggenheim Museum, New York. May 23–July 27.

"7 Objekte/69."* Galerie Ricke, Cologne, West Germany.

"Konzeption/Conception."* Städtisches Museum, Schloss Morsbroich, Leverkusen, West Germany. October–November.

"Art by Telephone."* Museum of Contemporary Art, Chicago. November 1–December 14.

"Kompas 4: West Coast U.S.A."* Stedelijk van Abbemuseum, Eindhoven, the Netherlands. November 21, 1969–January 4, 1970.

"West Coast 1945–1969."* Pasadena Art Museum, Pasadena, California, November 24, 1969–January 18, 1970; traveled to the City Art Museum, St. Louis; Art Gallery of Ontario, Toronto; Fort Worth Art Center, Texas.

"Querschnitt II." Galerie Ricke, Cologne, West Germany. December.

"Time Photography."* School of Visual Arts, New York. December 3–19.

"Art in Process."* Finch College Museum of Art, New York. December 11, 1969–January 26, 1970.

1970

"String and Rope."* Sidney Janis Gallery, New York. January 7–31.

"Conceptual Art and Conceptual Aspects."* New York Cultural Center. April 10–August 25.

"Art in the Mind."* Allen Memorial Art Museum, Oberlin College, Oberlin, Ohio. April 17–May 12.

"N Dimensional Space."* Finch College Museum of Art, New York. April 22–June 15.

"Zeichnungen amerikanischer Künstler/ Drawings of American Artists." Galerie Ricke, Cologne, West Germany.

"American Art since 1960."* Princeton University Art Museum. May 8–27.

"Tokyo Biennale '70: Between Man and Matter, 10th International Art Exhibition of Japan."* Tokyo Metropolitan Art Gallery, May 10–30; traveled to the Kyoto Municipal Art Museum, June 6–28; Aichi Prefectural Art Gallery, Nagoya, July 15–26; Fukuoka Prefectural Culture House, August 11–16.

"Conceptual Art, Arte Povera, Land Art."* Galleria Civica d'Arte Moderna, Turin. June–July.

"Information."* The Museum of Modern Art, New York. July 2–September 20.

"Drawings of American Artists." Galerie Yvon Lambert, Paris. September.

"Holograms and Lasers."* Museum of Contemporary Art, Chicago. September 11–October 25.

"Grafiek van de West Coast." Seriaal, Amsterdam. September 24–October 8.

"Body Works." Breen's Bar, San Francisco. October 18.

"Looking West."* Joslyn Art Museum, Omaha, Nebraska. October 18–November 29.

"Young Bay Area Sculptors."* San Francisco Art Institute. November 3–December 5.

"3∞: New Multiple Art." Whitechapel Art Gallery, London. November 19, 1970–January 3, 1971.

"Against Order: Chance and Art."* Institute of Contemporary Art, University of Pennsylvania, Philadelphia. November 14–December 22.

"1970 Annual Exhibition. Contemporary American Sculpture."* Whitney Museum of American Art, New York. December 12, 1970–February 7, 1971.

1971

"Sixth Guggenheim International Exhibition."* The Solomon R. Guggenheim Museum, New York. February 11–April 11.

John Gibson Gallery, New York. February 20–March 19.

"Body." Loeb Student Center, New York University, New York. February 22–23.

"Lucht-kunst (Air Art)."* Stedelijk Museum, Amsterdam. April 30–June 6.

"11. Biennale Nürnberg: Was die Schönheit sei, das weiss ich nicht."* Kunsthalle, Nuremberg, West Germany. April 30–August 1.

"Sonsbeek 71."* Park Sonsbeek, Arnhem, the Netherlands. June 19–August 15.

"Kid Stuff."* Albright-Knox Art Gallery, Buffalo, New York. July 25–September 6.

"Septième Biennale de Paris."* September 24–November 1.

"Works on Film: Morris, Nauman, Serra, Sonnier." Leo Castelli Gallery, New York. September 25–October 9.

"11 Los Angeles Artists."* Hayward Gallery, London, September 30–November 7; traveled to Palais des Beaux-Arts/Paleis van Schone Kunsten, Brussels, and Akademie der Kunst, Berlin.

"The Artist as Filmmaker." Hansen-Fuller Gallery, San Francisco. September 30 and October 1.

"Prospect '71."* Städtische Kunsthalle, Düsseldorf, West Germany. October 8–17.

"Modern Painting, Drawing and Sculpture Collected by Louise and Joseph Pulitzer, Jr."* Fogg Art Museum, Cambridge, Massachusetts, November 15, 1971–January 3, 1972; traveled to the Wadsworth Atheneum, Hartford, Connecticut, February 2–March 19, 1972.

1972

"Films by American Artists." Whitney Museum of American Art, New York. March–April.

"Spoleto Arts Festival." Spoleto, Italy. June 23–July 9.

"Documenta 5."* Museum Fridericianum, Kassel, West Germany. June 30–October 8.

"Diagrams and Drawings."* Rijksmuseum Kröller-Müller, Otterlo, the Netherlands, August 13–September 24, 1972; traveled to Kunstverein, Stuttgart, West Germany; Kunstmuseum, Basel, Switzerland, January 20–March 4, 1973; Kunstmuseum, Düsseldorf, West Germany.

1973

"3D into 2D: Drawing for Sculpture."* New York Cultural Center. January 19–March 11.

"Amerikanische und englische Graphik der Gegenwart."* Staatsgalerie, Graphische Sammlung, Stuttgart, West Germany. February 17–March 18.

"Bilder, Objekte, Filme, Konzepte: Herbig Collection."* Städtische Galerie im Lenbachhaus, Munich, West Germany. April–May.

"American Drawings 1963–1973."* Whitney Museum of American Art, New York. May 25–July 22.

"American Art: Third Quarter Century."* Seattle Art Museum. August 22–October 14.

"Contemporanea."* Parcheggio di Villa Borghese, Rome. November 1973–February 1974.

1974

"Artisti della West Coast." Galleria Françoise Lambert, Milan. Opened February 24.

"Videotapes: Six from Castelli." De Saisset Art Gallery, University of Santa Clara, Santa Clara, California. March 12–April 28.

"Idea and Image in Recent Art."* The Art Institute of Chicago. March 23–May 5.

"Painting and Sculpture Today."* The Indianapolis Museum of Art, Indianapolis, Indiana, May 22–July 14; traveled to the Contemporary Arts Center and the Taft Museum, Cincinnati, Ohio, September 12–October 26.

"Art Now 74."* The John F. Kennedy Center for the Performing Arts, Washington, D.C. May 30–June 16.

"Kunst Bleibt Kunst: Project 74, Aspekte internationaler Kunst am Anfang der 70er Jahre."* Kölnischer Kunstverein und Kunsthalle, Cologne, West Germany. July–September.

"Johns, Kelly, Lichtenstein, Motherwell, Nauman, Rauschenberg, Serra, Stella: Prints from Gemini G.E.L."* Walker Art Center, Minneapolis, August 17–September 29, 1974; traveled to Akron Art Institute, Akron, Ohio, December 15, 1974–January 26, 1975; Ackland Art Center, University of North Carolina, Chapel Hill, February 23–April 6, 1975; The Winnipeg Art Gallery, Winnipeg, Manitoba, May 4–June 15, 1975; Denver Art Museum, July 13–August 24, 1975.

"4 x Minimal Art." Galerie Ricke, Cologne, West Germany. August 19–September 1.

1975

"Body Works."* Museum of Contemporary Art, Chicago. March 8–April 27.

"Spiralen und Progressionen."* Kunstmuseum, Lucerne, Switzerland. March 16–April 20.

"Menace."* Museum of Contemporary Art, Chicago. May 2–June 22.

"U.S.A.: Zeichnungen 3."* Städtisches Museum, Schloss Morsbroich, Leverkusen, West Germany. May 15–June 29.

"Functies van Tekenen/Functions of Drawing."* Rijksmuseum Kröller-Müller, Otterlo, the Netherlands, May 25–August 4; traveled to Kunstmuseum, Basel, February 7–April 4, 1976.

"Sculpture: American Directions 1945–1975."* National Collection of Fine Arts, Smithsonian Institution, Washington, D.C., October 3–November 30, 1975; traveled to Dallas Museum of Fine Arts, January 7–February 29, 1976; New Orleans Museum of Art, March 31–May 16, 1976.

"Language and Structure in North America."* Kensington Art Association, Toronto, Ontario. November 4–30.

1976

"Drawing Now: 1955–1975."* The Museum of Modern Art, New York, January 23–March 9; traveled to Kunsthaus, Zürich, October 10–November 14, 1976; Staatliche Kunsthalle, Baden-Baden, West Germany, November 25, 1976–January 16, 1977; Graphische Sammlung, Albertina, Vienna, January 28–March 6, 1977; Sonja Henie-Niels Onstad Foundations, Oslo, March 17–April 24, 1977; The Tel Aviv Museum, May 12–July 2, 1977.

"The Seventy-second American Exhibition."* The Art Institute of Chicago. March 13–May 9.

"200 Years of American Sculpture."* Whitney Museum of American Art, New York. March 16–September 26.

"Ideas on Paper 1970–76."* The Renaissance Society of the University of Chicago. May 2–June 6.

"Rooms."* P.S. 1, Institute for Art and Urban Resources, Long Island City, New York. June 9–26.

"Painting and Sculpture in California: The Modern Era."* San Francisco Museum of Art, September 3, 1976–January 2, 1977; traveled to the National Collection of Fine Arts, Smithsonian Institution, Washington D.C., May 20–September 11, 1977.

1977

"1977 Biennial Exhibition, Contemporary American Art."* Whitney Museum of American Art, New York. February 19–April 3.

"Ideas in Sculpture 1965–1977." The Renaissance Society of the University of Chicago. May 1–June 11.

"The Dada/Surrealist Heritage."* Sterling and Francine Clark Art Institute, Williamstown, Massachusetts. May 3–June 12.

"Words at Liberty."* Museum of Contemporary Art, Chicago. May 7–July 3.

"Documenta 6."* Museum Fridericianum, Kassel, West Germany. June 24–October 2.

"Skulptur-Ausstellung in Münster."* Westfälisches Landesmuseum für Kunst und Kulturgeschichte, Münster, West Germany. July 3–November 13.

"A View of a Decade."* Museum of Contemporary Art, Chicago. September 10–November 10.

"Drawings for Outdoor Sculpture: 1946–1977."* John Weber Gallery, New York, October 29–November 23, 1977; traveled to Amherst College, Amherst, Massachusetts, February 3–March 4, 1978; University of California at Santa Barbara, June 27–September 4, 1978; Laguna Gloria Art Museum, Austin, Texas, September 15–October 27, 1978; M.I.T., Cambridge, Massachusetts, November 17–December 22, 1978.

"Works from the Collection of Dorothy and Herbert Vogel."* The University of

Michigan Museum of Art, Ann Arbor. November 11, 1977–January 1, 1978.

"Works on Paper by Contemporary American Artists." Madison Art Center, University of Wisconsin at Madison. December 4, 1977–January 15, 1978.

1978

"Three Generations: Studies in Collage." Margo Leavin Gallery, Los Angeles. January 26–March 4.

"Salute to Merce Cunningham, John Cage, and Collaborators." Thomas Segal Gallery, Boston. February 8–March 4.

"Nauman, Serra, Shapiro, Jenney." Blum Helman Gallery, New York. February.

"Drawings and Other Work on Paper." Sperone Westwater Fischer, New York. February 18–28.

"XXXVIII Biennale di Venezia."* Venice. July–October.

"20th Century American Drawings: Five Years of Acquisitions."* Whitney Museum of American Art, New York. July 28–October 1.

"Made by Sculptors."* Stedelijk Museum, Amsterdam. September 14–November 5.

"Werke aus der Sammlung Crex."* Halle für Internationale neue Kunst, Zürich; traveled to Louisiana Museum, Humlebaek, Denmark; Städtische Galerie im Lenbachhaus, Munich, September 12–October 7, 1979; Stedelijk van Abbemuseum, Eindhoven, the Netherlands.

1979

"Related Figurative Drawings." Hansen-Fuller Gallery, San Francisco. January 9–February 3.

"The Sense of the Self: From Self-Portrait to Autobiography."* The New Gallery of Contemporary Art, Cleveland, Ohio. January 13–February 3.

"The Broadening of the Concept of Reality in the Art of the '60's & '70's." Museum Haus Lange, Krefeld, West Germany. January 21–March 18.

"Words, Words." Museum Bochum, Bochum, West Germany. January 27–

March 11; traveled to the Palazzo Ducale, Genoa, Italy. March 28–May 4.

"Images of the Self." Hampshire College Gallery, Amherst, Massachusetts. February 19–March 14.

"Great Big Drawing Show." P.S. 1, Institute for Art & Urban Resources, Long Island City, New York. March 25–April 1.

"73rd American Exhibition."* The Art Institute of Chicago. June 9–August 5.

"New Spaces: The Holographer's Vision." The Franklin Institute, Philadelphia. September 26, 1979–March 21, 1980.

"Thirty Years of Box Construction." Sunne Savage Gallery, Boston. November 2–30.

"Artists and Books: The Literal Use of Time." Ulrich Museum of Art, Wichita State University, Wichita, Kansas. November 28, 1979–January 6, 1980.

"Space, Time, Sound: Conceptual Art in the San Francisco Bay Area: The 1970s."* San Francisco Museum of Art. December 21, 1979–February 10, 1980.

1980

"Leo Castelli: A New Space." Leo Castelli Gallery, 142 Greene Street, New York. Opened February 19.

"From Reinhardt to Christo." Allen Memorial Art Museum, Oberlin College, Oberlin, Ohio. February 20–March 19.

"The New American Filmmakers Series." Whitney Museum of American Art, New York. March 25–June 22.

"Contemporary Art in Southern California." High Museum of Art, Atlanta. April 26–June 8.

"Pier + Ocean."* Hayward Gallery, London, May 8–June 22; traveled to Rijksmuseum Kröller-Müller, Otterlo, the Netherlands, July 13–September 8.

"Skulptur im 20. Jahrhundert."* Wenkenpark, Riehen-Basel, Switzerland. May 10–September 14.

"Contemporary Sculpture: Selections from the Collection of The Museum of Modern Art."* The Museum of Modern Art, New York. May 13–August 7.

"Sculpture in California, 1975–80."* San Diego Museum of Art. May 18–July 6.

"XXXIX Biennale di Venezia."* Venice. June–September.

"Donald Judd, Bruce Nauman, Richard Serra: Sculpture." Richard Hines Gallery, Seattle. July–August.

"Zeichnungen der 60er und 70er Jahre, aus dem Kaiser Wilhelm Museum." Museum Haus Lange, Krefeld, West Germany. August 17–October 12.

"Architectural Sculpture."* Los Angeles Institute of Contemporary Art. September 30–November 21.

"Bruce Nauman, Barry Le Va." Nigel Greenwood, London. November 20–December 31.

"American Drawing in Black and White."* The Brooklyn Museum. November 22, 1980–January 18, 1981.

"Drawings to Benefit the Foundation for the Contemporary Performance Arts, Inc." Leo Castelli Gallery, New York. November 29–December 20.

1981

"Kounellis, Merz, Nauman, Serra."* Museum Haus Lange, Krefeld, West Germany. March 15–April 26.

"Neon Fronts: Luminous Art for the Urban Landscape." Washington Project for the Arts, Washington, D.C. June 6–November 1.

"Art in Los Angeles: Seventeen Artists in the Sixties."* Los Angeles County Museum of Art. July 21–October 4.

"Cast, Carved, Constructed." Margo Leavin Gallery, Los Angeles. August 1–September 19.

"Drawing Distinctions: American Drawings of the Seventies."* Louisiana Museum, Humlebaek, Denmark, August 15–September 20; traveled to Kunsthalle, Basel, September 8–November 15; Städtische Galerie im Lenbachhaus, Munich, February 17–April 11, 1982; Wilhelm Hack Museum, Ludwigshafen, West Germany, September–October 1982.

"Soundings."* The Neuberger Museum, State University of New York at

Purchase. September 20–December 23.

1982

"A Century of Modern Drawing from The Museum of Modern Art, New York."* The Museum of Modern Art, New York, March 1–16; traveled to the British Museum, London, June 9–September 12; The Cleveland Museum of Art, October 20–December 5; The Museum of Fine Arts, Boston, January 26–April 3, 1983.

"Arte Povera, Antiform, Sculptures 1966–1969."* Centre d'Arts Plastiques Contemporains de Bordeaux, France. March 12–April 30.

"'60–'80: Attitudes/Concepts/Images."* Stedelijk Museum, Amsterdam. April 9–June 11.

"Castelli and His Artists: Twenty-five Years."* Organized by the Aspen Center for the Visual Arts, Aspen, Colorado; traveled to the La Jolla Museum of Contemporary Art, La Jolla, California, April 23–June 6; Aspen Center for the Visual Arts, June 17–August 7; Leo Castelli Gallery, New York, September 11–October 9; Portland Center for the Visual Arts, Portland, Oregon, October 22–December 3; Laguna Gloria Art Museum, Austin, Texas, December 17, 1982–February 13, 1983.

"Halle 6." Kampnagelfabrik, Hamburg, West Germany. May–June.

"74th American Exhibition."* The Art Institute of Chicago. June 12–August 1.

"Documenta 7."* Museum Fridericianum, Kassel, West Germany. June 19–September 28.

"Werke aus der Sammlung Crex."* Kunsthalle, Basel, Switzerland. July 18–September 1982.

"20 American Artists. Sculpture 1982."* San Francisco Museum of Art. July 22–September 19.

"The Written Word." Downey Museum of Art, Downey, California. September 9–October 17.

"Postminimalism."* The Aldrich Museum of Contemporary Art, Ridgefield, Connecticut. September 19–December 19.

"Sculptors at UC Davis: Past and Present." University of California at Davis. September 20–October 29.

1983

"The Slant Step Revisited."* Richard L. Nelson Gallery, University of California at Davis. January 13–February 13.

"Drawing Conclusions: A Survey of American Drawings, 1958–1983." Daniel Weinberg Gallery, Los Angeles. January 29–February 26.

"Neue Zeichnungen aus dem Kunstmuseum Basel."* Kunstmuseum Basel, Switzerland, January 29–April 24; traveled to Kunsthalle Tübingen, West Germany, May 21–July 10; Neue Galerie, Staatliche und Städtische Kunstsammlungen Kassel, West Germany, August 13–September 25.

"Objects, Structures, Artifice: American Sculpture 1970–1982." SVC/Fine Arts Gallery, University of South Florida, Tampa, April 9–May 30; Center Gallery, Bucknell University, Lewisburg, Pennsylvania, September 2–October 10.

"Recent Acquisitions." The Museum of Modern Art, New York. April 27–May 24.

"Kunst mit Photographie: die Sammlung Dr. Rolf H. Krauss."* Nationalgalerie, Berlin, West Germany. May–June.

"John Duff, Robert Mangold, Bruce Nauman." Blum Helman Gallery, New York. May 4–28.

"De Statua: An Exhibition on Sculpture." Stedelijk van Abbemuseum, Eindhoven, the Netherlands. May 8–June 19.

"Minimalism to Expressionism: Painting and Sculpture since 1965 from the Permanent Collection."* Whitney Museum of American Art, New York. June 2–December 4.

"Word Works." Minneapolis College of Art and Design and the Walker Art Center, Minneapolis, Minnesota. September 30–October 31.

"Bruce Nauman and Martin Puryear: Recent Outdoor Projects." Donald Young Gallery, Chicago. Opened September 24.

"Twentieth Century Sculptures: A Selection from the Permanent Collection." The Solomon R. Guggenheim Museum, New York. September 30–December 11.

"Sammlung Helga und Walther Lauffs im Kaiser Wilhelm Museum Krefeld."* Krefelder Kunstmuseen, Krefeld, West Germany. November 13, 1983–April 8, 1984.

1984

"Bruce Nauman–Dennis Oppenheim: Drawings and Models for Albuquerque Commissions." University Art Museum, University of New Mexico, Albuquerque. February 18–March 25.

"Drawings by Sculptors: Two Decades of Non-Objective Art in the Seagram Collection."* The Montreal Museum of Fine Arts, Montreal, May 3–June 10; Vancouver Art Gallery, Vancouver, August 10–September 23; The Nickle Arts Museum, Calgary, October 5–November 18; Seagram Building, New York, December 12, 1984–April 19, 1985; London Regional Art Gallery, London, Ontario, May 24–June 30.

"Skulptur im 20. Jahrhundert."* Wenkenpark, Merian-Basel. June 3–September 30.

"Projects: World's Fairs, Waterfronts, Parks and Plazas." Rhona Hoffman Gallery, Chicago. June 20–July 31.

"Selections from the Collection: A Focus on California." Los Angeles County Museum of Art. Opened July 7.

"Praxis Collection."* Vancouver Art Gallery, Vancouver, British Columbia. August 10–September 16.

"Rosc '84: The Poetry of Vision."* The Guinness Hop Stop, Dublin, Ireland. August 24–November 17.

"Sculptors' Drawings: 1910–1980, Selections from the Permanent Collection."* Organized by the Whitney Museum of American Art, New York; traveled to the Visual Arts Gallery, Florida International University, Miami, September 21–October 17, 1984; Aspen Center for the Visual Arts, Aspen, Colorado, November 8–December 30, 1984; Art Museum of South Texas, Corpus Christi, January 1–March 3,

1985; Philbrook Art Center, Tulsa, Oklahoma, March 31–May 26, 1985.

"Content: A Contemporary Focus, 1974–1984."* Hirshhorn Museum and Sculpture Garden, Smithsonian Institution, Washington D.C. October 4, 1984–January 6, 1985.

"1964–1984." Donald Young Gallery, Chicago. Opened October 4.

"Little Arena: Drawings and Sculptures from the Collection Adri, Martin, and Geertjan Visser."* Rijksmuseum Kröller-Müller, Otterlo, the Netherlands. October 13–November 25.

"Quartetto: Joseph Beuys, Enzo Cucchi, Luciano Fabro, Bruce Nauman."* L'Academia Foundation, Venice.

"L'Architecte est absent: Works from the Collection of Annick and Anton Herbert."* Stedelijk van Abbemuseum, Eindhoven, the Netherlands. November 24, 1984–January 6, 1985.

1985

"Large Drawings."* Bass Museum of Art, Miami Beach, Florida, January 15–February 17; traveled to the Madison Art Center, Madison, Wisconsin, August 18–September 29, 1985; Santa Barbara Museum, Santa Barbara, California, April 20–May 25, 1986.

"Large Scale Drawings by Sculptors." The Renaissance Society of the University of Chicago. January 27–February 23.

"Whitney 1985 Biennial Exhibition."* Whitney Museum of American Art, New York. March 12–June 2.

"The Maximal Implications of the Minimal Line."* Edith C. Blum Art Institute, Bard College, Annandale-on-Hudson, New York. March 24–April 28.

"Exhibition-Dialogue/Exposicao-Diálogo."* Centro de Arte Moderna, Fundação Calouste Gulbenkian, Lisbon, Portugal. March 28–June 16.

"Selections from the William J. Hokin Collection."* Museum of Contemporary Art, Chicago. April 20–June 16.

"Artschwager, Judd, Nauman 1965–85." Donald Young Gallery, Chicago. May.

"Mile 4: Chicago Sculpture International."
Illinois Not-for-Profit Organization,
State Street Mall, Chicago. May 9–June 9.

"New Work on Paper 3."* The Museum
of Modern Art, New York. June 27–
September 3.

"Dreissig Jahre durch die Kunst: Museum
Haus Lange 1955–85."* Museum Haus
Lange, Krefeld, West Germany.
September 15–December 1.

"Doch Doch." Arenberg Institute,
Louvain, Belgium. October.

"Werke aus dem Basler Kupferstich-
kabinett."* Staatliche Kunsthalle, Baden-
Baden, West Germany, October 12–
December 1; Tel Aviv Museum, Tel Aviv,
Israel, January 2–March 8, 1986.

"AIDS Benefit Exhibition: A Selection of
Works on Paper." Daniel Weinberg
Gallery, Los Angeles. November 9–30.

"The Carnegie International."* Museum of
Art, Carnegie Institute, Pittsburgh.
November 9, 1985–January 5, 1986.

"American Eccentric Abstraction." Blum
Helman Gallery, New York. November
16, 1985–January 18, 1986.

"Vom Zeichnen: Aspekte der Zeichnung
1960–1985."* Kunstverein, Frankfurt,
West Germany, November 19, 1985–
January 1, 1986; Kunstverein, Kassel,
West Germany, January 15–February 23,
1986; Museum moderner Kunst, Vienna,
March 13–April 27, 1986.

"Transformations in Sculpture: Four
Decades of American and European
Art."* The Solomon R. Guggenheim
Museum, New York. November 22,
1985–February 16, 1986.

"Amerikanische Zeichnungen 1930–
1980."* Städtische Galerie im
Städelschen Kunstinstitut, Frankfurt,
West Germany. November 28, 1985–
January 26, 1986.

"Benefit for the Kitchen." Brooke
Alexander Gallery, New York.
December 13–21.

1986

"Sculpture." Waddington Galleries,
London. January 7–February 1.

"The Real Big Picture." The Queens
Museum, New York. January 17–March 19.

"Sculpture and Drawings by Sculptors."
L.A. Louver Gallery, Venice, California.
April 4–26.

"Ironies of Freedom: Violent America."
Emily Lowe Gallery, Hofstra University,
Hempstead, New York. April 10–June 20.

"De Sculptura." Wiener Festwochen,
Messepalast, Vienna. May–June.

"Leo Castelli." Chicago International Art
Expo, Chicago. May 7–12.

"Preview Exhibition, M.O.C.A. Benefit
Auction." Margo Leavin Gallery and
Gemini G.E.L., Los Angeles. May 10–13.

"Between Geometry and Gesture:
American Sculpture, 1965–75."* Palacio
de Velasquez, Madrid. May 13–July 20.

"Deconstruct." John Gibson Gallery, New
York. June 4–July 31.

"Sonsbeek '86: International Sculpture."*
Arnhem, the Netherlands. June 18–
September 14.

"Chambres d'Amis."* Museum van
Hedendaagse Kunst, Ghent, Belgium.
June 23–September 16.

"Lost/Found Language: The Use of
Language as Visual or Conceptual
Component, Deriving Directly or
Indirectly from Popular Culture."
Lawrence Gallery, Rosemont College,
Rosemont, Pennsylvania. November 5–
December 2.

"Individuals: A Selected History of Contemporary Art, 1945–1986."* The Museum
of Contemporary Art, Los Angeles.
December 10, 1986–January 10, 1988.

1987

"1987 Biennial Exhibition." Whitney
Museum of American Art, New York.
April 11–July 5.

"Avant-Garde in the Eighties."* Los
Angeles County Museum of Art. April
23–July 12.

"Works on Paper." Anthony d'Offay
Gallery, London. May 2–29.

"L'Epoque, La Mode, La Morale, La
Passion." Centre Georges Pompidou,
Paris. May 21–August 17.

"Leo Castelli and His Artists: Thirty Years
of Promotion of Contemporary Art."
Centro Culturale, Arte Contemporaneo,
Mexico City. June–October.

"Skulptur Projekte in Münster, 1987."
Westfälisches Landesmuseum für Kunst
und Kulturgeschichte, Münster, West
Germany. June 14–October 4.

"Big Drawings." Center for Contemporary
Arts of Santa Fe, New Mexico. June 19–
August 11.

"Sculpture of the Sixties." Margo Leavin
Gallery, Los Angeles. July 11–August 22.

"Fifty Years of Collecting: An Anniversary
Selection; Sculpture of the Modern
Era." The Solomon R. Guggenheim
Museum, New York. November 13,
1987–January 15, 1988.

"Lead." Hirschl and Adler Modern, New
York. December 3, 1987–January 15,
1988.

1988

"Welcome Back: Painting, Sculpture, and
Works on Paper by Contemporary
Artists from Indiana." Indianapolis
Center for Contemporary Art, Herron
Gallery, Indianapolis. January 15–
February 27.

"Planes of Memory." Long Beach Museum
of Art, Long Beach, California. January
24–February 28.

"Committed to Print." The Museum of
Modern Art, New York. January 31–
April 19.

Selected Bibliography

Artist's Books and Writings

Pictures of Sculptures in a Room. 1965–68.
Clear Sky. 1967–68.
Burning Small Fires. 1968.
LAAir. 1970. In *Artists and Photographs.* New York: Multiples, Inc., 1971.
"Notes and Projects," *Artforum* 9, no. 4 (December 1970):44.
"Body Works," *Interfunktionen* (September 6, 1971):2–8.
Left or Standing, Standing or Left Standing. New York: Leo Castelli Gallery, 1971.
Floating Room. New York: Leo Castelli Gallery, 1973.
Flayed Earth, Flayed Self: Skin Sink. Los Angeles: Nicholas Wilder Gallery, 1974.
Cones Cojones. New York: Leo Castelli Gallery, 1975.
The Consummate Mask of Rock. Buffalo, New York: Albright-Knox Art Gallery, 1975.

Articles and Reviews

Antin, David. "Another Category: Eccentric Abstraction," *Artforum* 5, no. 3 (November 1966):56–57.
Armstrong, Richard. Review, *Artforum* 22, no. 1 (September 1983):68.
"The Avant-Garde: Subtle, Cerebral, Elusive," *Time* 92, no. 21 (November 22, 1968):70, 77 (illus.: 72, 74).
Baker, Elizabeth. "Los Angeles 1971," *Artnews* 70, no. 5 (September 1971):27–39.
Baker, Kenneth. "New York," *Artforum* 9, no. 8 (April 1971):77–78.
———. "Bruce Nauman at Castelli, Sonnabend, and Sperone Westwater Fischer," *Art in America* 65, no. 2 (March–April 1977):111–12.
Barnitz, Jacqueline. "In the Galleries: Bruce Nauman," *Arts Magazine* 42, no. 5 (March 1968):62.
Beatty, Frances. "Nauman's Art Downtown," *Art World* (November 20, 1976):9.
Bell, Jane. "Bruce Nauman," *Artnews* 81, no. 5 (May 1982):168, 170.
Bruggen, Coosje van. "Bruce Nauman: Entrance, Entrapment, Exit," *Artforum* 24, no. 10 (Summer 1986):88–98.
Burton, Scott. "Time on Their Hands," *Artnews* 68, no. 4 (Summer 1969):40–43.
Butterfield, Jan. "Bruce Nauman: The Center of Yourself," *Arts Magazine* 49, no. 6 (February 1975):53–55.
Calas, Nicolas. "Bodyworks and Porpoises," *Artforum* 16, no. 5 (January 1978):33.
Caldwell, John. "Creating Taste," *Dialogue* 9, no. 2 (March–April 1986):14–16.
Cameron, Dan. "A Whitney Wonderland," *Arts Magazine* 59, no. 10 (Summer 1985):66–69.
Carluccio, Luigi. "Un Tempo per l'Arte Americana d'Oggi," *Bolaffi Arte* 3, no. 17 (February 1972):42–44.
Catoir, Barbara. "Über den Subjectivismus bei Bruce Nauman," *Das Kunstwerk* 26 (November 1973):6.
Celant, Germano. "Bruce Nauman," *Casabella* 345, vol. 34 (February 1970):38–41.
"Collaboration Bruce Nauman," *Parkett* 10 (1986). Contributions by Jeanne Silverthorne, "To Live and to Die": 18–25; Patrick Frey, "The Sense of the Whole": 38–41; Rein Wolfs, "Bruce Nauman: Director of Violent Incidents": 46–49; Chris Dercon, "Keep Taking It Apart: A Conversation with Bruce Nauman": 54–61; Robert Storr, "Nowhere Man": 70–79.
Danieli, Fidel A. "The Art of Bruce Nauman," *Artforum* 6, no. 4 (December 1967):15–19.
Da Vinci, Mona. Review, *Artnews* 76, no. 3 (March 1977):142–44.
Davis, Douglas. "Veni, Vidi, Video," *Newsweek* 74, no. 15 (April 13, 1970):98–99.
———. "Man of Parts," *Newsweek* 77, no. 9 (March 1, 1971):70.
Domingo, Willis. "New York Galleries," *Arts Magazine* 45, no. 5 (March 1971):55–56.
———. "New York Galleries," *Arts Magazine* 45, no. 6 (April 1971):83–84.
Fargier, Jean Paul. "Bruce Nauman à l'Arc: No Man," *Les Cahiers du Cinéma* (November 1986).
Frackman, Noel, and Ruth Kaufmann. "Documenta 7: The Dialogue and a Few Asides," *Arts Magazine* 57, no. 2 (October 1982):91–97.
Galloway, David. "Report from Italy," *Art in America* 72, no. 11 (December 1984):9–19.
Gilardi, Piero. "Da New York," *Flash Art* 5 (1967):1–2.
———. "Microemotive Art," *Museum-journaal* 13, no. 4 (1968):198–203.
———. "Primary Energy and the Microemotive Artists," *Arts Magazine* 43, no. 1 (September–October 1968):48–50.
Glueck, Grace. "Bruce Nauman: No Body but His," *The New York Times* (April 1, 1973).
Gold, Barbara. "New Sensibility in Washington," *Arts Magazine* 42, no. 6 (April 1968):28–31.
Greenspun, Roger. "Screen: Palette of Art," *The New York Times* (April 14, 1972).
Hagen, Charles, and Lisa Liebman. "At the Whitney Biennial," *Artforum* 23, no. 10 (Summer 1985):56–57.
Handy, Ellen. Reviews, *Arts Magazine* 60, no. 5 (January 1986):134.
Harten, Jürgen. "T for Technics, B for Body," *Art and Artists* 92 (November 1973):29–33.
Johnson, Ellen H., and Athena T. Spear. *Bulletin of the Allen Memorial Art Museum* (Oberlin, Ohio) 25, no. 3 (Spring 1968):92–103.
Jones, Ronald. "Bruce Nauman," *Arts Magazine* 59, no. 6 (February 1985):4.
Kass, Ray. "Current Milestones," *Dialogue* 9, no. 2 (March–April 1986):17–19.
Kingsley, April. "New York Letter," *Art International* 17, no. 8 (October 1973):54.
Kirshner, Judith Rossi. Review, *Artforum* 21, no. 2 (October 1982):74–76.
Koepplin, Dieter. "Drei Zeichnungen von Bruce Nauman," *Kunst-Bulletin des Schweizerisches Kunstvereins* 7–8 (July 1986):8–11.
Kozloff, Max. "9 in a Warehouse," *Artforum* 7, no. 6 (February 14, 1969):38–42.
Kramer, Hilton. "At Whitney: In Duchamp's Footstep," *The New York Times* (March 30, 1973).
Kurtz, Bruce. "Interview with Giuseppe Panza di Biumo," *Arts Magazine* 46, no. 5 (March 1972):40–43.
Kurtz, Stephen. "Reviews and Previews," *Artnews* 68, no. 5 (September 1969):20.
Larson, Kay. "Privileged Access," *New York Magazine* 18, no. 28 (July 22, 1985):61–62.
Leider, Philip. "The Properties of Materials: In the Shadow of Robert Morris," *The New York Times*

(December 22, 1968):D31.

———. "New York," *Artforum* 8, no. 6 (February 1970):70.

Lichtenstein, Theresa. Review, *Arts Magazine* 59, no. 5 (January 1985):36.

Linker, Kate. Review, *Artforum* 23, no. 5 (January 1985):87.

Lippard, Lucy R. "Eccentric Abstraction," *Art International* 10, no. 9 (November 1966):28, 34–40, ill. p. 36. Reprinted from exhibition catalogue, Fischbach Gallery, New York, 1966.

McCann, Cecile N. "Bruce Nauman," *Artweek* (January 6, 1973):1,12.

McCormick, Carlo. Review, *Flash Art* 120, (January 1985):42.

Madura, Jalaine. "An Unusually Effective Installation," *Oregonian* (September 7, 1979).

Moore, Alan. Review, *Artforum* 13, no. 4 (April 1975):79–80.

Muchnic, Suzanne. "Nauman's Self-Involved Clinical, Examining Eye," *Los Angeles Times* (April 5, 1988):1–2.

Müller, Hans von. "Bilder wie Unfälle," *Basler Magazin* (Basel) 24 (June 19, 1982):6–7.

Nadelman, Cynthia. Review, *Artnews* 85, no. 3 (March 1986):115–18.

Nemser, Cindy. "Subject-Object Body Art," *Arts Magazine* 46, no. 1 (September–October 1971):38–42.

Nisselson, Jane E. "Contemporary Sculpture at MOMA," *Skyline* 2, no. 3 (Summer 1979):10.

Nittve, Lars. "Quartetto," *Artforum* 23, no. 1 (September 1984):107–08.

Parent, Béatrice. "Le Néon dans l'Art Contemporain," *Chroniques de l'Art Vivant* 20 (May 1971):4–6.

Perreault, John. "Art," *The Village Voice* (February 8, 1968).

———. "Bruce Nauman," *Artnews* 67, no. 1 (March 1968):22.

———. "Art," *The Village Voice* (December 2, 1971).

Perrone, Jeff. Review, *Artforum* 15, no. 5 (January 1977):58–60.

———. "The Salon of 1985," *Arts Magazine* 59, no. 10 (Summer 1985):70–73.

Perucchi-Petri, Ursula. "Hinweis auf einige Neuerwebungen: Bruce Nauman und Robert Ryman," *Jahresbericht, Kunsthaus Zürich* (1985):96–99.

Pincus-Witten, Robert. "New York," *Artforum* 6, no. 8 (April 1968): 63–65.

———. "Bruce Nauman: Another Kind of Reasoning," *Artforum* 10, no. 6 (February 1972):30–37. Reprinted in Robert Pincus-Witten, *Postminimalism,* pp. 70–78. New York: Out of London Press, 1977.

Plagens, Peter. "Roughly Ordered Thoughts on the Occasion of the Bruce Nauman Retrospective in Los Angeles," *Artforum* 11, no. 7 (March 1973):57–59.

———. Review, *Artforum* 12, no. 7 (March 1974):85–86.

———. "Nine Biennial Notes," *Art in America* 73, no. 7 (July 1985):115–18.

Pohlen, Annelie. Review, *Artforum* 22, no. 9 (May 1984):95–96.

Price, Jonathan. "Video Art: A Medium Discovering Itself," *Artnews* 76, no. 1 (January 1977):41–47.

Princenthal, Nancy. Review, *Artnews* 84, no. 1 (January 1985):137.

Raffaele, Joe, and Elizabeth Baker. "The Way-Out West: Interviews with 4 San Francisco Artists," *Artnews* 66, no. 4 (Summer 1967):39–40, 75–76.

Ratcliff, Carter. "New York Letter (Spring: Part I)," *Art International* 15, no. 4 (April 20, 1971):25–26.

———. "New York Letter (Spring: Part II)," *Art International* 15, no. 5 (May 20, 1971):39.

———. "New York Letter," *Art International* 16, no. 2 (February 20, 1972):52–56.

Rauh, Emily S. "Among Recent Acquisitions," *The Saint Louis Museum Bulletin* 7, no. 6 (March–April 1972):4–6.

Richardson, Brenda. "Bay Area Survey: The Myth of Neo-Dada," *Arts Magazine* 44, no. 8 (Summer 1970):46–49.

Rickey, Carrie. "Studs and Polish: L.A. in the Sixties," *Art in America* 70, no. 1 (January 1982):80–89.

Russell, John. Review, *The New York Times* (November 12, 1976):C18.

———. "Art: Contemporary Sculpture at the Modern," *The New York Times* (June 15, 1979):C25.

———. "A Contemplative Chicago Show," *The New York Times* (July 29, 1979):D31.

———. "Bruce Nauman," *The New York Times* (October 12, 1984):C24.

Schjeldahl, Peter. "New York Letter," *Art International* 13, no. 7 (September 1969):70–71.

———. "Only Connect," *The Village Voice*

(January 20–26, 1982):72.

———. "Profoundly Practical Jokes: The Art of Bruce Nauman," *Vanity Fair* 46, no. 3 (May 1983):88–93.

Sharp, Willoughby. "Nauman Interview," *Arts Magazine* 44, no. 5 (March 1970):22–27.

———. "Body Works," *Avalanche* 1 (Fall 1970):14–17.

———. "Bruce Nauman," *Avalanche* 2 (Winter 1971):23–25.

Smith, Bob. "Interview with Bruce Nauman," *Journal, Los Angeles Institute of Contemporary Art,* no. 32 (Spring 1982):35–38.

Stavitsky, Gail. "The 1985 Carnegie International," *Arts Magazine* 60, no. 7 (March 1986):58–59.

Stiles, Knute. "William Geis and Bruce Nauman," *Artforum* 5, no. 3 (November 1966):65–66.

Tarshis, Jerome. "San Francisco," *Artforum* 9, no. 6 (February 1971):85–86.

Trebay, Guy. "An Opinionated Survey of the Week's Events," *The Village Voice* (January 20–26, 1982):56.

Tucker, Marcia. "PheNAUMANology," *Artforum* 9, no. 4 (December 1970):38–44.

Warren, Lynne. Review, *New Art Examiner* (May 1979):13.

Warren, Ron. Review, *Arts Magazine* 59, no. 4 (December 1984):39–40.

Wilson, William. "A Critical Guide to the Galleries," *Los Angeles Times* (February 14, 1969):IV4.

———. "Bruce Nauman's Unsettling Art Given a Masterful Touch," *Los Angeles Times* (March 23, 1970):IV6.

Winer, Helene. "How Los Angeles Looks Today," *Studio International* 183, no. 937 (October 1971):127–31.

Wortz, Melinda. "Los Angeles," *Artweek* (December 1976):82–83.

———. "Bruce Nauman," *Artnews* 81, no. 4 (April 1982):108.

Yau, John. In *Flash Art* 126 (February–March 1986):48.

Young, Joseph E. "Los Angeles," *Art International* 14, no. 6 (Summer 1970):113.

General References

Albright, Thomas. *Art in the San Francisco Bay Area, 1945–1980.* Berkeley:

University of California Press, 1985.
Alloway, Lawrence. *Topics in American Art since 1945*, pp. 204, 208. New York: W. W. Norton and Company, 1975.
Amsterdam, The Stedelijk Museum. *The Stedelijk Museum Collection*, pp. 48, 75. Edited by Edy de Wilde.
Arnason, H. H. *History of Modern Art*, 3d ed., rev. New York: Abrams, 1986.
Billeter, Erika. *Leben mit Zeitgenossen: Die Sammlung der Emanuel Hoffmann Stiftung*, pp. 284–89, 335, 336, 337. Basel: Emanuel Hoffmann Stiftung, 1980.
Castelli/Sonnabend Tapes and Films, vol. 1. New York: Leo Castelli and Ileana Sonnabend, 1974. Notes on Nauman by Nina Sundell.
Celant, Germano. *Ars Povera*. Milan: Gabriele Mazzotta, 1969. In English, New York: Praeger Publishers, 1969. In German, Tübingen: Verlag Ernst Wasmuth, 1969.
———. *Preconista 1966–69*, pp. 11, 37, 48, 51, 58, 88, 89, 104, 113, 114, 122, 151, 152. Florence: Centro Di, 1975.
———. *Das Bild einer Geschichte 1956–1976: Die Sammlung Panza di Biumo*, pp. 295, 297–308, 347. Milan: Electa, 1980.
Glozer, Laszlo. *Westkunst: Zeitgenossische Kunst seit 1939*, pp. 313, 471. Cologne: DuMont Buchverlag, 1981.
Johnson, Ellen H. *Modern Art and the Object*, pp. 40, 44–45, 47, 201–04. New York: Thames and Hudson, 1976.
———. *American Artists on Art from 1940 to 1980*, pp. 184, 225–32. New York: Harper and Row, 1982.
Knight, Christopher. *Art of the Sixties and Seventies: The Panza Collection*. New York: Rizzoli, 1988.
Krauss, Rosalind E. *Passages in Modern Sculpture*, pp. 240, 241, 242, 282. New York: Viking Press, 1977.
Lippard, Lucy R. *Six Years: The Dematerialization of the Art Object from 1966 to 1972*, pp. 10, 11, 23, 34, 39, 69, 71, 162–63, 206–07. New York: Praeger Publishers, 1973.
Meyer, Ursula. *Conceptual Art*, pp. 186–91. New York: E. P. Dutton, 1972.
Müller, Grégoire, and Gianfranco Gorgoni. *The New Avant-Garde: Issues for the Art of the Seventies*, pp. 18, 21–22, 116–28. New York: Praeger Publishers, 1972.
Otterlo, the Netherlands, Rijksmuseum

Kröller-Müller. *Sculptuur: Beeldhouwwerken van het Rijksmuseum Kröller-Müller*, pp. 172–75. 1981.
Pincus-Witten, Robert. *Postminimalism*, pp. 70–78. New York: Out of London Press, 1977.
Plagens, Peter. *Sunshine Muse: Contemporary Art on the West Coast*, pp. 136, 168, 170. New York and Washington, D.C.: Praeger Publishers, 1974.
Rauh, Emily S. *Modern Painting, Drawing, and Sculpture Collected by Louise and Joseph Pulitzer, Jr.*, vol. 3. Cambridge, Massachussets: Fogg Art Museum, 1971.
Rosenberg, Harold. *The De-Definition of Art*, pp. 32, 59. Chicago: University of Chicago Press, 1972.
Schjeldahl, Peter. In *Art of Our Time: The Saatchi Collection*, pp. 23–25. New York: Rizzoli, 1984.

Exhibition Catalogues

One-man

Albuquerque, New Mexico, Albuquerque Museum. *Bruce Nauman: 1/12 Scale Models for Underground Pieces*. 1981.
Baltimore Museum of Art. *Bruce Nauman: Neons*. 1983. Text by Brenda Richardson.
Basel, Museum für Gegenwartskunst. *Bruce Nauman, Drawings/Zeichnungen, 1965–1986*. 1986. Texts by Coosje van Bruggen, Dieter Koepplin, Franz Meyer.
Buffalo, New York, Albright-Knox Art Gallery. *The Consummate Mask of Rock*. 1975. Text by Linda L. Cathcart.
Krefeld, West Germany, Krefelder Kunstmuseen, Museum Haus Esters. *Bruce Nauman*. 1983. Text by Julian Heynen.
London, Whitechapel Art Gallery. *Bruce Nauman*. 1986. Introduction by Nicholas Serota. Texts by Jean-Christophe Ammann and Joan Simon.
Los Angeles County Museum of Art. *Bruce Nauman: Work from 1965 to 1972*. 1972. Texts by Jane Livingston and Marcia Tucker. Also published in German and Dutch.
New York, Leo Castelli Gallery. *Bruce Nauman*. 1968. Text by David Whitney.
Otterlo, the Netherlands, Rijksmuseum Kröller-Müller. *Bruce Nauman 1972–1981*. 1981. Introduction by Rudolf

Oxenaar, texts by Katharina Schmidt, Ellen Joosten, and Siegmar Holsten.

Group

Amsterdam, Stedelijk Museum. *Op Losse Schroeven: Situaties en Cryptostructuren*. 1969. Texts by Wim Beeren and Piero Gilardi.
Amsterdam, Stedelijk Museum. *Made by Sculptors*, 1978. Texts by Rini Dippel and Geert van Beijeren.
Baden-Baden, West Germany, Staatliche Kunsthalle. *Räume heutiger Zeichnung: Werke aus dem Basler Kupferstichkabinett*. 1985. Introduction by Siegmar Holsten, texts by Dieter Koepplin, Marie Therese Hurni, and Paul Tanner.
Basel, Kunsthalle. *Werke aus der Sammlung Crex*. 1982. Text by Jean-Christophe Ammann.
Basel, Kunstmuseum. *Neue Zeichnungen aus dem Kunstmuseum Basel*. 1982. Text by Dieter Koepplin.
Basel, Museum für Gegenwartskunst. *Minimal + Conceptual Art aus der Sammlung Panza*. 1980. Text by Franz Meyer.
Basel, Skulpturenausstellung Merian-Park. *Skulptor im 20. Jahrhundert*. 1984. Text by Antje von Graevenitz.
Bern, Kunsthalle. *When Attitudes Become Form*. 1969. Text by Harald Szeeman.
Bloomfield Hills, Michigan, Cranbrook Academy of Art Museum. *Instruction Drawings*. 1981. The Gilbert & Lila Silverman Collection.
Bonn, West Germany, Kunstverein. *Concetto-Imago: Generationswechsel in Italien*. 1983. Text by Zdenek Felix.
Bonn, West Germany, Städtische Museum. *Zeichnungen der 50er bis 70er Jahre aus dem Kaiser Wilhelm Museum, Krefeld*. 1980. Text by Gerhard Storck.
Bordeaux, France, Centre d'Arts Plastiques Contemporains de Bordeaux. *Arte Povera, Antiform*. 1982. Text by Germano Celant.
Cologne, West Germany, Museum Ludwig. *Handbuch Museum Ludwig*. 1979. Text by Karl Ruhrberg.
Cologne, West Germany, Galerie Max Hetzler. *Carl Andre, Günther Forg, Hubert Kiecol, Richard Long, Reinhard Mucha, Bruce Nauman, Ulrich Rückriem*. 1985.

Davis, California, Richard L. Nelson Gallery, University of California at Davis. *The Slant Step Revisited.* 1983. Texts by Cynthia Charters and L. Price Amerson.

Eindhoven, the Netherlands, Stedelijk van Abbemuseum. *Kompas 4: West Coast U.S.A.* 1969. Text by Jean Leering.

Eindhoven, the Netherlands, Stedelijk van Abbemuseum. *L'Architecte est absent: Works from the Collection of Annick and Anton Herbert.* 1984. Texts by Rudi H. Fuchs et al.

Fort Worth, Texas, Fort Worth Art Museum. *Drawings.* Text by Peter Plagens.

Frankfurt, West Germany, Kunstverein. *Vom Zeichnen: Aspekte der Zeichnung 1960–1985.* 1985. Text by Peter Weiermair.

Frankfurt, West Germany, Städtische Galerie im Städelschen Kunstinstitut. *Amerikanische Zeichnungen 1930–1980: A Guide by Walter Hopps and Dominique de Menil.* 1985.

Ghent, Belgium, Museum van Hedendaagse Kunst. *Chambres d'Amis.* 1986. Text by Jan Hoet.

Groningen, the Netherlands, Groninger Museum. *Kunst nu/ Kunst unserer Zeit.* 1982. Text by Antje von Graevenitz.

Hamburg, West Germany, Kunstverein. *U.S.A. West Coast.* 1972. Text by Helmut Heissenbuttel and Helene Winer.

Humlebaek, Denmark, Louisiana Museum. *Drawing Distinctions: American Drawings of the Seventies.* 1981. Edited by Alfred Kren.

Kassel, West Germany, Museum Fridericianum. *Documenta 6: Handzeichnungen, utopisches Design, Bücher.* 1977. Text by Wieland Schmied.

Kassel, West Germany, Museum Fridericianum. *Documenta 7.* 1982. Introduction by Rudi H. Fuchs. Texts by Coosje van Bruggen, Germano Celant, Johannes Gachnang, and Gerhard Storck.

Krefeld, West Germany, Museum Haus Lange. *Kournellis, Merz, Nauman, Serra: Arbeiten um 1968.* 1981. Texts by Gerhard Storck and Marianne Stockebrand.

Krefeld, West Germany, Museum Haus Lange. *Dreissig Jahre durch die Kunst.*

Museum Haus Lange 1955–85. 1985. Introduction by Gerhard Storck. Texts by Paul Wember and Julian Heynen.

Krefeld, West Germany, Museum Haus Lange and Museum Haus Esters. *Dreissig Jahre durch die Kunst: Katalog zur Ausstellung.* 1986.

Leverkusen, West Germany, Städtisches Museum, Schloss Morsbroich. *Konzeption-conception.* 1969. Texts by Rolf Wedewer and Konrad Fischer.

London, British Museum Publications Ltd. *A Century of Modern Drawing from The Museum of Modern Art New York.* 1982. Preface by John Elderfield, text by Bernice Rose.

London, The Tate Gallery. *The Tate Gallery 1972–4: Biennial Report and Illustrated Catalogue of Acquisitions.* 1975.

Los Angeles County Museum of Art. *American Sculpture of the Sixties.* 1967. Text by Maurice Tuchman.

Münster, West Germany. Westfälisches Landesmuseum für Kunst und Kulturgeschichte. *Skulptur-Ausstellung in Münster.* 1977. Text by Laszlo Glozer.

New York, Finch College Museum of Art. *N Dimensional Space.* 1970. Text by Elaine H. Varian.

New York, Joseph E. Seagram and Sons, Inc. *Drawings by Sculptors: Two Decades of Non-Objective Art in the Seagram Collection.* 1984. Edited by David Bellman.

New York, The Museum of Modern Art. *Information.* 1970. Text by Kynaston L. McShine.

New York, The Museum of Modern Art. *Drawing Now.* 1976. Text by Bernice Rose.

New York, School of Visual Arts. *Time Photography.* 1969. Text by Robert Fiore.

New York, The Solomon R. Guggenheim Museum. *9 Young Artists: Theodoron Awards.* 1969. Foreword by Thomas M. Messer. Text by Diane Waldman.

New York, The Solomon R. Guggenheim Museum. *Guggenheim International Exhibition 1971.* 1971. Texts by Diane Waldman and Edward F. Fry.

New York, The Solomon R. Guggenheim Museum. *Transformations in Sculpture.* 1985. Text by Diane Waldman.

New York, Whitney Museum of American

Art. *Anti-Illusion: Procedures/Materials.* 1969. Texts by James Monte and Marcia Tucker.

Oberlin, Ohio, Allen Memorial Art Museum. *Art in the Mind.* 1970. Text by Athena Tacha Spear.

Otterlo, the Netherlands, Rijksmuseum Kröller-Müller. *Diagrams and Drawings.* 1972. Introduction by Rudolf Oxenaar. Text by Carter Ratcliff. German edition, Kunstmuseum Basel, 1973.

Otterlo, the Netherlands, Rijksmuseum Kröller-Müller. *Functies van Tekenen/ Functions of Drawing.* 1975. Text by Rudolf Oxenaar.

Otterlo, the Netherlands, Rijksmuseum Kröller-Müller. *Little Arena: Drawings and Sculptures from the Collection of Adri, Martin, and Geertjan Visser.* 1984. Introduction by Rudolf Oxenaar.

Pasadena, California, Pasadena Art Museum. *West Coast 1945–1969.* 1969. Text by John Coplans.

Purchase, New York, The Neuberger Museum, State University of New York at Purchase. *Soundings.* 1981. Texts by Suzanne Delehanty, Dore Ashton, Germano Celant, and Lucy Fischer.

San Francisco, Museum of Modern Art. *Space, Time, Sound: Conceptual Art in the San Francisco Bay Area, the 1970s.* 1981. Text by Suzanne Foley, Chronology by Constance Lewallen.

Seattle Art Museum Pavilion. *American Art: Third Quarter Century.* 1973. Text by Jan van der Marck.

Stuttgart, Staatsgalerie, Graphische Sammlung. *Amerikanische und englische Graphik der Gegenwart.* 1972. Text by Gunther Thiem.

Turin. *Conceptual Art, Arte Povera, Land Art.* 1970. Texts by Germano Celant, Lucy R. Lippard, et al.

Venice, L'Academia Foundation. *Quartetto.* 1984. Texts by Achille Bonito Oliva and Julian Heynen; interview with Alanna Heiss by Donald Kuspit.

Zürich, Ink, Halle für Internationale neue Kunst. *Werke aus der Sammlung Crex, Zürich.* 1978. Introduction by Urs Raussmüller. Text by Christel Sauer.

Illustrations

Photographs have been supplied in many instances by the owners named in the captions. Those for which an additional credit is due are listed below.

David Allison, Courtesy Sperone Westwater, New York, 84. Courtesy the artist, 49 top, 63 center, 65, 72–73, 81, 85 top right, 88, 149 right, 166, 171 top right, 173 top, 185, 190, 221, 243, 255 right. Katja Becker, Zürich, 80 top. Roger van den Bempt, Antwerp, Belgium, 59. Galerie Bruno Bischofberger, Zürich, 244 right. Rudolph Burckhardt, Courtesy Leo Castelli Gallery, New York, 39, 41 bottom left, 50, 133, 171 bottom right, 248 top, 249 top, 265, 275. Balthasar Burkhard, Bern, Switzerland, 61, 64, 184. Courtesy Eduardo Caldéron, Seattle, 51 bottom left. Courtesy Leo Castelli Gallery, New York, 30, 31, 32, 33, 34, 35 top left and right, 38, 40, 43 right, 44 left, 51 top left and right, 53 top, 54, 56, 62 center and bottom, 135, 136 left, 137, 138, 139 left, 143, 145 top left and right, 146, 148 left, 149 left, 154–55, 156, 162 top, 199, 219 bottom, 245, 248 bottom, 276, 280, 281. Courtesy William Copley, 140 right. Crex Collection, Zürich, 206 top right, 213. Bevan Davies, Courtesy Leo Castelli Gallery, New York, 62, 66, 68, 71, 219 top, 220 bottom; Courtesy Sperone Westwater, New York, 224. Dorothee Fischer, Düsseldorf, West Germany, 52 bottom, 63 top, 85 top left, 124, 127 bottom, 171 top left, 176 right, 177, 182, 183, 187, 218 bottom, 220 top, 223, 254, 256, 257. Rick Gardner, Courtesy Texas Gallery, Houston, 20, 72. Gianfranco Gorgoni, New York, 179, 241, 250 top, 251 bottom, 252, 253, 259, 260, 261, 267 bottom. Courtesy Sidney Janis Gallery, New York, 43 bottom left. Bruce C. Jones, Courtesy Leo Castelli Gallery, New York, 207 right, 212, 218 top. Al Jung, Courtesy Joseph A. Helman, New York, 132. Courtesy Krefelder Kunstmuseen, 78, 85 bottom right, 282 top, 283. Pam Maddock, Courtesy the Archives, Richard L. Nelson Gallery and the Fine Arts Collection, University of California at Davis, 129 bottom, 130 top left. Babette Mangolte, Courtesy Leo Castelli Gallery, New York, 258. Andrew Moore, Courtesy Joseph A. Helman, New York, 134 left, 139 right. Ann Munchow, Aachen, Courtesy Museum Ludwig, Cologne, West Germany, 144. Courtesy Museum of Contemporary Art, Los Angeles, 180. Otto E. Nelson, Courtesy Sidney Janis Gallery, New York, 48 bottom. Marco de Nood, Dordrecht, the Netherlands, 164. The Nova Scotia College of Art and Design, Halifax, 152, 163, 244 left. Courtesy Oeffentliche Kunstsammlung, Basel, 123 bottom, 129 top left, 142 left, 186, 191 bottom. Douglas M. Parker, Courtesy Daniel Weinberg Gallery, Los Angeles, 89, 103. Eric Pollitzer, Courtesy Leo Castelli Gallery, New York, 46, 47, 48 top, 62 top, 101, 134 top right, 147 right, 151 bottom, 153, 165, 176 left, 202, 203, 272, 278; Courtesy Sonnabend Gallery, New York, 246, 247. Renate Ponsold, New York, 136 center and right. Andreas Rosasco, Zürich, Courtesy Ink, 201. Friedrich Rosenstiel, Greven, West Germany, Courtesy the artist, 52 top. Paolo Mussat Sartor, Turin, Courtesy Leo Castelli Gallery, New York, 148 right. Shunk-Kender, Courtesy Leo Castelli Gallery, New York, 53 bottom, 270, 271. Gian Sinigaglia, Milan, 277, 279. Glenn Steigelman, Inc., New York, Courtesy Leo Castelli Gallery, New York, 67, 74, 83, 127 top, 142 right. Duane Suter, Baltimore Museum of Art, 158. Frank J. Thomas, Los Angeles, Courtesy Leo Castelli Gallery, New York, 28, 29, 57, 58, 60, 63 bottom, 147 left, 170 bottom left and right, 174 top, 206 bottom right, 264, 269; Courtesy Katherine Bishop Crum, 131. Gwenn Thomas, Courtesy Leo Castelli Gallery, New York, 36, 266 top right, 268 top, 273 bottom, 274 bottom. Michael Tropea, Courtesy Donald Young Gallery, Chicago, 284. Thomas P. Vinetz, Santa Monica, California, Courtesy Leo Castelli Gallery, New York, 80 center and bottom. Phil Weidman, Courtesy the Archives, Richard L. Nelson Gallery and the Fine Arts Collection, University of California at Davis, 129 top and bottom right. Courtesy Donald Young Gallery, Chicago, 69, 70, 128, 161, 181. Dorothy Zeidman, Courtesy Leo Castelli Gallery, New York, 37, 75, 76, 77, 79, 87, 91, 92, 93, 94, 95, 96, 97, 98, 99, 100, 102, 167, 172, 173 bottom, 174 bottom, 175, 178, 188, 189, 192, 197, 206 left, 222, 250 center and bottom, 251 top and center, 263, 266 bottom left and right, 267 top right and bottom, 268 bottom, 269, 273 top, 274 top, 282 bottom; Courtesy Sperone Westwater, 86–87, 104, 160 top, 162 bottom, 168, 169, 207 left. Alan Zindman, Courtesy Sperone Westwater, New York, 8, 20, 82, 126. Zindman/Fremont, New York, Courtesy Sonnabend Gallery, New York, 45 bottom, 55, 121, 123 top, 151 top.

I wish to thank Ingrid Sischy, former Editor of *Artforum,* for her support and editorial advice on the first chapter, which previously appeared in that magazine, and Charles Hagen, for his editorial assistance on the other chapters. The resourceful and inspired design of Pierluigi Cerri has given the book visual clarity. The tenacity of Kaatje Cusse in pursuing data for the captions, chronology, exhibition history, and bibliography has helped to make this book an extremely useful source for future research. Paula Jean Hoffman typed the manuscript with unremitting enthusiasm. I am grateful to Leo Castelli and his staff and to Angela Westwater, Nicholas Wilder, Konrad Fischer, Dorothee Fischer, Donald Young, Daniel Weinberg, and Juliet Myers for their help in locating works, verifying data, and placing photographic materials at my disposal. I also thank the many museum curators and collectors who have so generously replied to my never-ending inquiries. Finally I thank Bruce Nauman for patiently answering my questions, for provoking me through his multiple disguises to take on the role of Dr. Watson, and for arranging over and over again his escape along another unpredictable exit, leaving it up to the author to find the next "connecting riddle."

C.B.

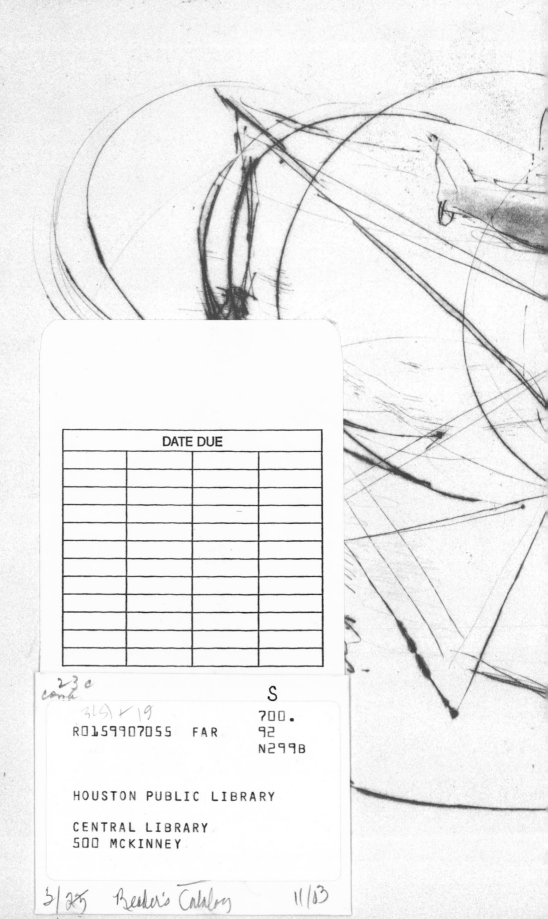

DATE DUE

5/25   Reader's Catalog   11/03